TRANSNATIONAL CIVIL SOCIETY

AN INTRODUCTION

TRANSNATIONAL CIVIL SOCIETY

AN INTRODUCTION

Edited by

Srilatha Batliwala

and

L. David Brown

Kumarian
Press, Inc.

Transnational Civil Society: An Introduction
Published in 2006 in the United States of America by Kumarian Press, Inc.
1294 Blue Hills Avenue, Bloomfield, CT 06002 USA

The text of this book is set in 10/12.5 New Baskerville

Proofread by Beth Richards
Index by Barbara DeGennaro

Production and design by Victoria Hughes Waters,
Hughes Publishing Services, Worcester, MA

Printed in the United States of America by Thomson-Shore, Inc. Text printed with vegetable oil-based ink.

♾ The paper used in this publication meets the minimum requirements of the American National Standard for Information Sciences-Permanence of Paper for printed Library Materials, ANSI Z39.48-1984

Library of Congress Cataloging-in-Publication Data

Transnational civil society : an introduction /edited by Srilatha Batliwala and L. David Brown.
    p.   cm.

Summary: "Contains an introduction to the history, achievements, and challenges of transnational civil society initiatives on several critical issues and the forces that catalyzed and shaped those initiatives" — Provided by publisher.

Includes bibliographical references and index.
    ISBN-13: 978-1-56549-211-0 (hardcover : alk. paper)
    ISBN-10: 1-56549-211-0 (hardcover : alk. paper)
    ISBN-13: 978-1-56549-210-3 (pbk. : alk. paper)
    ISBN-10: 1-56549-210-2 (pbk. : alk. paper)
    1. Civil society. 2. International organization. 3. Non-governmental organizations. 4. Globalization- — Social aspects.
I. Batliwala, Srilatha. II. Brown, L. David (Lloyd David), 1941–
    JC337.T73 2006
    300–dc22

                                    2005023904

14 13 12 11 10 09 08 07 06 05   10 9 8 7 6 5 4 3 2 1   First Printing 2006

To our granddaughters,
Zara Shireen Batliwala
and Devon Lloyd Bump,
and all the future generations
who will hopefully take the
transnational civil society
project to new levels.

Contents

List of Boxes

List of Tables and Figures

Acknowledgments

The preparation of this volume would not have been possible without our contributors: Sarah Alvord, Peggy Antrobus, Alison Brysk, John Clark, Marsha Darling, Dan Gallin, Peter Dobkin Hall, Céline Jacquemin, Sanjeev Khagram, Motoko Mekata, Kumi Naidoo, Gita Sen, and Wendy and Andrew Torrance. Each of them undertook to write for us amid a host of more pressing commitments, out of a desire to share their knowledge and insight with people wanting to learn about the exciting terrain of progressive transnational activism.

Pulling together this volume was possible thanks to the thoughtful and tireless support of Erin Belitskus, Sarah Alvord, and Laura Ax at the Hauser Center, and our skilled text editor, Afried Raman. We have benefited from countless ideas and comments from our colleagues involved in transnational civil society at the Hauser Center, particularly Marty Chen, Tiziana Dearing, Peter Dobkin Hall, Sanjeev Khagram, Peggy Levitt, and Mark Moore.

We are grateful to the Hauser Center's Transnational Studies program (IF4) for the financial and practical support provided to the project, as well as to the Ford Foundation for the grant that supported Srilatha's work on this volume. We must also thank the colleagues at Kumarian Press who encouraged and supported us in undertaking this project: Krishna Sondhi, Guy Bentham, and Jim Lance in particular. Their patience and understanding with the inevitable delays of an ambitious transnational volume like this one were exceptional.

Dave Brown has been the beneficiary of ongoing support, challenge, and humor from the Brookline Circle: Lee Bolman, Tim Hall, Adam Kahane, Bill Kahn, Todd Jick, Phil Mirvis, and Barry Oshry; and from a wide range of colleagues and partners in the transnational civil society community — especially Rajesh Tandon, Kumi Naidoo, Jeremy Hobbs, Peter Eigen, Joel Lamstein, and Ray Offenheiser. In writing this volume, as in the rest of his life, Jane Covey has been a continuous source of new ideas, practical implications, and strategic perspective.

Srilatha Batliwala was egged on, contradicted, and challenged by a worldwide circle: Sheela Patel, Alan Fowler, Aruna Rao, Sanjeev Khagram, Kumi Naidoo, Gabriele Bammer, Frances Kunreuther, David Bonbright, Peggy Levitt, Martha Chen, Ralph Taylor, Michael Edwards, her New York support group sisters, and the amazing people in the grassroots transnational movements she studies. Living on two continents for different parts of the year while this book was coming together was not easy; her sanity was preserved through the loving support of husband Zarir in India and the Blooms (sister Lakshmi, and David, Sonali, and Sahil) of Weston, Massachusetts, as well as her parents, children, and their spouses.

We also want to acknowledge our debt to each other. We brought very different perspectives and resources to this project — Indian and American, female and male, flowery Indo-English and terse Americanese, scholarly practitioner and practical scholar. Although we have often differed in how we understood the issues of transnational civil society, those differences have almost always been complementary and stimulating rather than polarizing and problematic.

And finally, thank you, World Wide Web. This particular transnational effort would have been impossible without you!

Srilatha Batliwala and L. David Brown
Cambridge, Massachusetts
June 2005

FOREWORD

This book is enormously important for all those who wish to understand the world of globalization and to change it for the better. The contributors share a broad sense that the new possibilities, connections, and aspirations enabled by recent technological and economic advances should be both accessible for and accountable to the largest possible number of people. Thus, equity, access, and empowerment are the prime values of the movements described in this book, varied as they are in their interests, histories, and constituencies.

The term "transnational civil society" suggests something already formed, fixed, and institutionalized, a sociological noun of some kind. But in fact, it is several other things: it is a project, a process, and a space, all in search of an unresolved sociological form. Finding such a form is the central challenge of all those actors who want to make this vision real.

The *project* of transnational civil society movements and organizations takes strength from its often single and local aims. But the potential of such movements to take on transnational scope and power rests on something subtle and valuable: their capacity to recognize and identify each other, across numerous boundaries of language, history, strategy, and location. What is the source of this recognition? It is the sense that many of these actors are struggling to make democratic claims that can no longer be made within an older model, in which civil society was — roughly speaking — the social space between the family and the State. Since nation-states have in many instances ceded remarkable amounts of ground to transnational strategic, economic, legal, and political forces, civil society can no longer have real effects without confronting the new global order. Thus, a different way to look at the relationship between the words "transnational" and "global" is that transnational civil society is a strategy to make global processes visible and accountable to ordinary citizens who might otherwise be confined to national political arenas.

The *process* that is captured in the term "transnational civil society" is, by extension, a process of network building, alliance formation, and advocacy (all richly documented in this book) which seeks to take advantage of the resources of nonofficial communications strategies (Web sites, email, etc.) to enhance exchange across a range of sites, movements, and organizations, with the common aim of affecting transnational governance decisions and organizations, some permanent and visible (like the World Trade Organization) and some exactly the opposite (such as the global trade in organs, arms, or sex workers). There is a built-in paradox in this process, which has no easy resolution. Since the strength of many actors and movements that wish to join their efforts across national boundaries is often their ad hoc, unstructured, and evanescent material shape, they always face the danger of becoming hierarchical, bureaucratized, slow, and conservative as they become better networked, supported, and institutionalized. This is not a simple matter of cooptation, corruption, or elite capture, as is sometimes argued by the voices of the backlash against transnational civil society. It is a deeper strategic challenge to generate permanent and large-scale organizational forms that can nevertheless stay fluid, responsive, and flexible. In this regard, transnational civil society would be better off using global corporations as its model rather than multilateral governmental organizations. This idea may run against the ethical grain of many readers of this volume, but it should be carefully examined since global corporations are constantly incubating new ways of combining high-order coordination with granular localization and rapid readiness to change strategies and methods.

Finally, the *space* within which the transnational society project is located runs counter to the commonsense geographies of nation, region, and world that we commonly carry in our heads. These spaces are often interstitial, overlapping, and uneven, as emerges (for example) in Sanjeev Khagram's careful classification of different sorts of advocacy movements. The spaces are interstitial in the sense that they often inhabit the spaces between traditional spaces and institutions, as with movements that take place in the sites available to both men and women in rural societies; or in spaces that are at the edge of major official organizations such as the United Nations, in the bodies now mandated to represent NGOs in the UN; or in zones where municipal and state governance meet in a no man's land, in areas such as the area of disability rights.

These spaces are also overlapping insofar as the terrains and regions of interest to human rights movements might overlap with those movements committed to environmental issues, or to intellectual property issues or to gender violence issues. These overlapping zones are often the crucibles of higher-level actions and organizations, such as the World Social Forum. Finally, these spaces are uneven, in that certain movements, such as the movement for human rights, now virtually cover the planet and may fairly be described as global in aspiration and in fact. At the other extreme, you could have a movement for literacy among female weavers in Lucknow that is exceedingly small in scale and scope.

These three features of transnational civil society as a space — its interstitial, overlapping, and uneven qualities — are all assets from the point of view of range, inclusiveness, and closeness to the ground, but are not necessarily advantages in the battle to shape the future of globalization.

Those engaged with the project of building a transnational civil society — and a "civil global society" as editors Batliwala and Brown stress — whose variety and range are richly described in this book, stand in a complex relationship to the project of globalization. So it is important to warn against two equally common mistakes. The first is the tendency of some observers to see transnational civil society as a simple and benign democratic counterpart of globalization, doing the same across national boundaries what it historically (even if only theoretically) did within national boundaries. In this image, transnational civil society is simply the unofficial extension of international politics and economics, a sort of democratic lubricant for primarily official negotiations between states and corporations about the rules and norms of globalization.

The opposite mistake is the image of transnational civil society as wholly driven by its opposition to market-driven globalization, as a primarily oppositional project, committed to slowing down the global flow of ideas, goods, people, and products. Antiglobalization movements have many interesting claims and objectives, but transnational civil society is not the same as the network of movements described collectively as standing for antiglobalization.

If these twin mistakes are avoided, a third challenge faces those who see themselves as engaged in building transnational civil society. This is the challenge of shaping globalizing so that it is more inclusive, more responsive, more equitable, and more ethical, all words used by many contributors to this volume. The question is how to understand the dimensions of this challenge.

As a short form to identify some choices about how to shape the relationship between transnational civil society and the emergent legal, political, and economic regimes of globalization, let us borrow from Albert Hirschmann's famous categorization of political and economic attachments as falling into three types, which he called loyalty, exit, and voice.[1] "Loyalty" represents followers, customers, or adherents to a product, party, or movement who are fully committed to its virtues. "Exit" refers to those who have walked away — in this analogy, those who have moved consciously into the antiglobalization camp. Voice, which is Hirschmann's most interesting type, is the position of those who have stayed committed to a party, a product, a nation, or a cause, but are vociferous in their criticisms of it. I propose that transnational civil society has its main purpose to strengthen the "voice" approach to the current shape of globalization. That is, transnational civil society is best served by making its central project the building of a critical voice in the face of what look like the inevitable demands of economic globalization.

On the face of it, this suggestion may look both weak and obvious. After all, who does not recognize that transnational civil society seeks to move globalization in more progressive directions? What news does this suggestion bring to the authors and readers of this book? The answer lies in looking harder at exactly what it means to bring critical debate into the official spaces of globalization. What are the larger points to bring into the light of critical debate? I suggest a few, which transcend the agendas of specific movements and apply equally to many of them.

The first concerns the market and its changing forms and functions. Can we accept the principle that exchange through markets of some sort is an ancient principle that long precedes the arrival of industrial capitalism? Keith Hart has demonstrated the logic of this distinction brilliantly in a recent book on money, markets, and democracy.[2] If we accept it, as I am strongly inclined to do, this distinction forces us to ask how the capacity of markets to heighten efficiency (the very basis of modern economics) can be reconciled with their indifference to equity. Can we go beyond our current arsenal of weapons, which is largely ameliorative in this regard (welfare, social security, insurance, and charity are our main current solutions), to others which actually bend market principles deliberately to produce desirable social equilibria, even if at some cost to efficiency? Ideas now afloat in regard to microcredit, or to making property protocols available to the poor in the De Soto model,[3] do not address the possibility of changing market structures in some fundamental way, going beyond drawing more people into the efficiencies and incentives of the market. In this area, progressive economists, activists, and policymakers have a major challenge.

A second fundamental challenge involves the global spread of violence, especially violence against civilians. Many societies, notably in the African subcontinent but also elsewhere, now have violence as the working condition of everyday life, rather than its opposite. Civil war now is the order of things in many societies, and is fed by many global forces, not least the international trade in arms. In many societies, drawing a sharp line between civilians and combatants is difficult, especially in those cases where ethnic principles have joined other causes of endemic warfare and brutal physical violence. In these cases, whose number is growing, we are faced with the stark question: can there be civil society without civilians?

The challenge this poses to transnational civil society advocates and groups is what they can do to stem the global increase in everyday violence, even beyond the terrain of "official" wars. Taking up this challenge poses some fundamental dilemmas. One of them is whether everyday peace is the prerequisite to the building of peace, prosperity, and productivity or vice versa? The answer is not straightforward, and transnational civil society and its advocates will need to make some informed bets on this question. Another dilemma is whether highly local bonds of trust and cooperation are the best guarantees against intranational violence or whether the growth of transnational identities, networks, and solidarities is an even more secure asset in this regard. There is no absolute zero-sum choice here, but it is a matter of priorities.

The third and perhaps the most crucial question that is raised by "voice" as the key to transnational civil society is how it can position itself in relation to the nation-states in which local civil society movements are still embedded. Put in stark terms, the first option is to recognize that globalization is increasingly putting national sovereignty at risk and that the role of transnational civil society is to oppose and contest this trend. The second option is the opposite and would lead us to say that transnational civil society has no more to gain from the architecture of national sovereignty than many other interests and that its best interests are served by hastening the erosion of national sovereignty. Anyone who has tried to pass a serious convention through UNESCO, for example, knows how hard it is to pass any progressive global conventions against the interests of the member-states, which is one reason that the United Nations, as a whole, has been unable to serve its highest humanitarian ideals more forcefully. Many local civil society organizations and community-based organizations have found it useful to work in partnership with local, regional, and national agencies to advance their agendas. This may be a good strategy in the short run, but is its long-run future really progressive? This debate should be openly fostered in the effort to build a durable transnational civil society.

Wherever such debates may lead, the contributors to this volume share some important intuitions, values, and aims, as do the movements they describe. I conclude this brief foreword with a reference to my own work on what I have called "the capacity to aspire,"[4] by which I mean the unevenly distributed social capacity to form concrete horizons of desire, hope, and optimism that is one of the harshest costs and dimensions of poverty. In that argument, I proposed that it is the task of those concerned with shrinking poverty by empowering the poor themselves to focus specifically on the capacity to aspire, as a capacity without whose systematic strengthening many other capacities and resources will remain out of the reach of the world's poor and marginal populations. From this point of view, hope is not just a mood or a disposition; it is a socially and culturally sustained capacity, which can be systematically nurtured and redistributed. Transnational civil society, and the many movements that constitute it, faces many challenges, some of which I have outlined here. But if it has one credible common aim across all its diversities, it is to build the capacity to aspire among groups who are now poorly positioned in this respect. If this project is a success, then those large populations who make up transnational civil society will themselves gain "voice" and take up the struggle to shape globalization to their own ends. At that point, the project of transnational civil society will have become both global and fully democratic.

Arjun Appadurai
Bethany, Connecticut
August 2005

Notes

1. Albert Hirschmann, *Exit, Voice, and Loyalty* (Cambridge, MA: Harvard University Press, 1970).

2. Keith Hart, *The Memory Bank: Money in an Unequal World* (London: Profile Books, 2000).

3. Hernando De Soto, *Mystery of Capital* (New York: Basic Books, 2000).

4. Arjun Appadurai, "The Capacity to Aspire: Culture and the Terms of Recognition," in *Culture and Public Action*, ed. V. Rao and M. Walton (Stanford, CA: Stanford University Press, 2004): 59–84.

Introduction:
Why Transnational Civil Society Matters

Srilatha Batliwala and L. David Brown

In the early 1970s, news began to leak out that the multinational corporation Nestle was using some questionable marketing practices to promote sales of its baby-food formula in developing countries. A study by European civil society organizations found that Nestle had come up with a very effective marketing strategy: they recruited hospital personnel to recommend to new mothers that they feed their infants with Nestle's tinned formula. But when mixed with unsafe water the formula was a recipe for infant dysentery — a major scourge among African children in villages and urban slums without potable water. When the study was published under the title of "Nestle Kills Babies," outraged Nestle executives instituted a libel suit. The resulting trial initiated a widespread public debate on corporate responsibilities and formed the basis for campaigns to regulate the marketing practices of transnational corporations.[1]

Over a ten-year period, the International Babyfood Campaign, comprising such diverse elements as churches, unions, nongovernmental development organizations, and various other citizen initiatives, organized a worldwide boycott of Nestle products. Their aim was to highlight the necessity for transnational corporations to adopt ethical marketing practices. Not surprisingly, they faced determined resistance from their corporate targets. The Babyfood Campaign eventually produced a Code of Conduct for transnational corporations operating in the developing countries, which was adopted by the United Nations. It also created a continuing network to monitor the compliance of Nestle and other corporations with the Code's provisions.

The Babyfood Campaign is an example of transnational civil society at work. It mobilized an alliance of diverse associations and individuals to challenge Nestle's practices and to build a social consensus on appropriate marketing practices across national boundaries. Such initiatives are increasingly important as the world of the twenty-first century becomes more connected and interdependent across national boundaries. They are important actors in defining, assessing, and innovating ideas and

1

actions to solve social and institutional problems with transnational rami-
fications — problems that have frequently outpaced the capacities of
existing institutions for governance and problem solving.

This book provides some concepts for understanding transnational
civil society (TCS), describes TCS initiatives on a variety of important
issues, and explores the characteristics of effective TCS initiatives in a
world where they have growing roles to play.

What Is Transnational Civil Society?

The concept of civil society has a long and complicated history that has produced both diverse and contentious definitions. Some analysts organize
these differing conceptual perceptions into different "optics" or views of
civil society and its role in societies.[2] Sifting through these, we found that
for the purpose of this volume it is helpful to think of TCS as a concept that
has three interrelated aspects: the sector of civil society associations; the values, norms, and aspirations of a society governed by civil processes; and the
provision of spheres for public discourse on issues and ideas.[3]

The most commonly recognized aspect of civil society emphasizes that
it is a sector of associations. It is composed of nonprofit and nongovernmental organizations, churches, unions, social movements, and many
other agencies, and is formed independently by citizens in pursuit of
their interests (in contrast to organizations in the government or business
sectors). This aspect of the definition focuses attention on the *nature* of
civil society organizations (CSO) and their purpose and activities as self-
governed, value-based actors.

A second aspect of civil society emphasizes values, aspirations, and
norms for governance and problem solving that enable civil engagements
to solve social problems. Civil norms and values — such as tolerance,
trust, cooperation, nonviolence, inclusion, and democratic participation
— foster very different patterns of decision making from the reliance on
"might makes right" or "the divine right of kings." This aspect of the definition focuses attention on the *quality* of the society as a whole. It also suggests that analysts must pay attention to other sectors, since the activities
of government agencies and business firms help to shape the quality of
societal governance and decision making as well.

A third aspect of civil society focuses on its creation of a sphere for public discourse, in which citizens discuss and debate issues, examine their
underlying causes, explore options, and build social consensus about
appropriate action. Such discourses can create or reinforce civil society
values and norms. This aspect of the definition focuses attention on *communication processes and structures* that enable widespread sharing and dissemination of discourses on critical issues.

These three aspects of civil society — organizations and associations; societal values, aspirations, and norms; and spheres for public discourses — are of course interrelated. Discussions about critical social issues, such as civil rights in the United States or communal relations among caste and religious groups in India, depend on the existence of public spheres that enable such debates on widely held values and norms, and on organizations and associations that can raise and defend positions for assessment in these debates. So while this three-part definition of civil society focuses attention on quite different aspects, all of them contribute to civil society's role in exploring and acting on critical social issues.

How does this definition of civil society help us understand the nature of transnational civil society? In the first place, TCS associations and organizations are organized, controlled, and operated across more than one country. The International Babyfood Campaign, for example, had branches in many countries and was supported by many different kinds of organizations from within these countries. It drew on this international and national diversity to influence a wide range of delegates at the UN to vote for the Code of Conduct. In the second place, a civil society at the transnational level would accept norms of civic engagement — tolerance, inclusion, cooperation, and so on — as important factors in global decision making. It is important to note that this kind of civil global society would promote an international rule of law rather than the principle of might makes right. Whether such an international society can exist will turn greatly on the behavior and perspectives of powerful governments, intergovernmental organizations, and transnational corporations. The UN adoption of the Babyfood Campaign's Code of Conduct involved engagement with transnational corporations and governments as well as CSOs, and that adoption suggested that civil engagement is possible under some circumstances. Finally, the possibilities of transnational discourse have been greatly expanded by technological developments (such as computers and the Internet) and by the recent rise of global discourses on many issues. In the case of the Babyfood Campaign, the expanding debate over corporate responsibilities produced the consensus embodied in the UN Code, but it also created in many countries sensitivity to corporate misbehavior that has been the basis for considerable subsequent transnational discussion and action. The Babyfood Campaign illustrates the interplay between associations and organizations, norms and regulations for a better global society, and public discourses over emerging global issues.

Finally, our definition of civil society also sets up one of the important boundaries of this book: it does not deal with all transnational civic formations, but with a particular set that we call *progressive* TCS — namely, initiatives and movements that promote the values and goals of tolerance, equity, nonviolence, and democratic participation. However, for stylistic ease, we refer to these progressive entities throughout the book simply as "transnational civil society," and hope the reader will remember that we are not including in our analysis those formations that foster other kinds of goals or values.

Transnational Civil Society and Global Problem Solving

Transnational civil society has become increasingly important in global governance and problem solving over the last two decades. But transnational civil society organizations (TCSO) have existed for many years: the international antislavery or abolition movement was established more than 150 years ago, and transnational campaigns for women's suffrage, ending, among other practices, foot binding in China and female genital mutilation in Africa, were all launched over a century ago.[4] But in the closing decades of the twentieth century, TCS has emerged in a much more active and powerful form. The rise of civil society in national and international contexts has been characterized as "a global associational revolution" that is comparable to the earlier rise of the nation-state.[5]

Changes in the international context have played a catalytic role in creating new spaces and opportunities for TCS. The end of the Cold War has diminished the need for framing all international decisions in accordance with the demands of bipolar global tensions, and so opened up space for civil society influence. The declining role of the State in many arenas has been countered by dramatic increases in the roles played by business and civil society in many international issues. Information and communication technologies have made transnational initiatives much easier and less expensive to launch and coordinate, enabling and accelerating civil society initiatives as well as those from other sectors. The economic effects of globalization have often increased the already huge gaps between the rich and the poor, and so created a demand for a transnational voice and action by marginalized and impoverished groups. Existing institutional arrangements are now more responsive to national and international elites, resulting in democracy deficits that make it likely that the poor will bear many of the burdens and gain few of the benefits of global policies, creating another demand for a grassroots voice in global and national decision making. Globalization has also produced or accentuated a number of problems that cross national boundaries — such as environmental degradation, HIV/AIDS, collapsing States, wars and civil conflicts, and cross-border migrations — whose solutions require international discussion, analysis, negotiation, and action. These challenges have often overloaded the capacity of existing transnational mechanisms, such as the United

Nations, for problem identification and solution, and so created the context for the rapid rise of TCS.

It is possible to identify a variety of roles played by TCSOs in response to these critical transnational issues. These roles reflect their special capacities and positions in the transnational arena:

- TCSOs have been a vehicle for *identifying issues and articulating their value implications*. Thus, the Babyfood Campaign identified the problem of marketing infant formula in ways that harmed infants in the developing world.

- TCSOs have acted to *mobilize concerned citizens* to speak out to key stakeholders about their values and their concerns, which may involve training people for effective influence with those stakeholders. The Babyfood Campaign framed the issue in terms that mobilized large constituencies against formula-marketing practices.

- TCSOs can contribute to *balancing power differences* so that otherwise marginalized populations have a voice and a hearing. The ability of the Babyfood Campaign to mobilize customers in industrialized countries through churches, unions, and NGOs to boycott Nestle was critical to gaining wider attention to the fates of African infants and mothers.

- TCSOs can use information and expertise to catalyze the *setting of new standards and norms* for powerful actors. The Babyfood Campaign helped to create a new code of conduct for businesses operating in the developing world.

- TCSOs can *create transnational social capital* in the form of bonds of trust and collaboration among members that can be used for subsequent initiatives. The Babyfood Campaign, for example, created connections among activists that have influenced many subsequent campaigns.

- TCSOs can sometimes *exert direct influence on decision makers and policies*, articulating policy alternatives, providing research and arguments for preferred options, creating demonstration projects, or mobilizing support for adopting policies. The Babyfood Campaign helped the UN adopt the new Code in spite of strong corporate resistance.

- TCSOs can also help with *monitoring and enforcing compliance* with new standards. After the adoption of the Code, the Babyfood Campaign recomposed itself as a monitoring network to ensure compliance by the relevant corporations.

This list of potential roles includes elements related to all three aspects of TCS that we defined at the outset, namely, voluntary organizations as major actors in transnational problem solving, civil values and norms as shapers of peaceful transnational policymaking, and global public discourse as a means of identifying a problem, assessing options, and choosing policies on a critical issue. The Babyfood Campaign is one illustration of these roles. In this book the reader will find several others. TCSOs are regularly inventing and reinventing new ways to grapple with the challenges of an ever-shrinking world.

Transnational Civil Society: Emerging Questions

Transnational civil society faces challenges for which national experience may provide little preparation. The scale of the problems can be intimidating even to civil society actors from large countries. Initiatives to reduce global poverty, for example, must grapple with the problems of billions of people, not just thousands or even millions. Another challenge is the diversity of actors that must be engaged in TCS initiatives. Spanning the differences in resources, power, culture, language, and expectations to reach agreements on values and strategies across many countries is in itself an intimidating task. A third important difference is dealing with differences across levels. Constructing goals and strategies that integrate the interests of grassroots groups with those of national and transnational actors may be quite challenging. Another transnational challenge is selecting appropriate targets for influence. Civil society organizations at the national level often focus on government activities; there is usually no comparable authority in the transnational arena, so TCSOs may have to focus on intergovernmental institutions like the World Bank or the World Trade Organization. In some cases, the absence of a global regulatory institution, such as courts for prosecuting war crimes, itself becomes the target of advocacy and action by TCSOs.

The chapters in this book offer opportunities to explore some important questions about TCS and its evolution. These questions can be clustered within the different aspects of civil society outlined above.

Organization and Structure

The first aspect of TCS is the nature of its associations and organizations. Many transnational organizations are set up as bureaucratic hierarchies, coordinating through centralized authorities supervising national branches. Intergovernmental organizations, like the World Bank and the UN Development Program, use central headquarters to supervise branch offices in many different countries. Many transnational corporations also have international headquarters that supervise national and regional sub-units. Some TCSOs are also organized as international bureaucracies with varying degrees of formality and centralized control, as in the case of large-scale relief and development NGOs like CARE or Médecins sans Frontières.[6]

But many TCSs operate from more loosely structured forms of organization, and use more collegial and consensual methods of decision making to coordinate the activities of multiple organizations.[7] Some are organized, for example, as transnational *networks*. Networks are loosely linked collectives of organizations and individuals that hold common values, exchange information about shared interests, and engage in a common discourse about critical issues. The collection of local NGO monitors that succeeded the Babyfood Campaign after the UN adopted the Code of Conduct is an example of this network form.

Others organize as transnational *coalitions or campaigns*. Such coalitions have shared values, information, and discourses, and they are also committed to shared strategies and tactics. The Babyfood Campaign operated as a coalition of diverse organizations — churches, unions, NGOs, concerned citizen groups — with shared strategies and tactics as it campaigned for adoption of the Code. But coalitions require more close coordination than networks, and so are also more expensive in time and energy to hold together.

A third form of interorganizational cooperation, less common than the other two, is transnational *movements*. Such movements have all the features of networks and coalitions/campaigns — common values, shared information and discourse, common strategies and tactics — but, in addition, they also engage in sustained mobilization around an issue to challenge the status quo in multiple countries. Movements can be short-term or long-term. The anti–Iraq War movement, for example, organized simultaneous peace demonstrations of millions of people in scores of countries over a span of a few months. The labor movement has mobilized workers around the world for nearly a century. Movements are a demanding form of transnational organization precisely because they require such high levels of mobilization, coherence, and unified strategies.

This aspect of TCS's organizational forms raises several important questions, and the chapters that follow suggest many different approaches and responses to them. Some key questions include: Given their limited resources and lack of formal power, how do TCSOs manage to mobilize people and support? How do TCSOs span huge differences in wealth, power, culture, interests, and expectations to organize people across multiple countries and regions? How do TCSOs deal with the differences in interests, capacities, and expectations to organize across local, national, and transnational levels?

Values and Norms

The second aspect of transnational civil society is that of a *civil global society* that is characterized by norms of civic engagement and respect for values like tolerance, trust, cooperation, nonviolence, inclusion, and democratic participation. Creating such a society requires negotiating aspirations and tradeoffs with intergovernmental organizations and transnational corporations as well as TCSOs. Negotiating such agreements requires active engagement with many stakeholders, such as the long struggle among governments, businesses, and CSOs over the acceptability of marketing practices in the Babyfood Campaign.

On many of the issues in this book, civil society initiatives to catalyze a better transnational society have demonstrated more capacity to block action than to create a new consensus on appropriate norms and standards. In part this stems from the fact that campaigns often depend on mobilizing outrage at unacceptable behavior ("Nestle Kills Babies"), but it is difficult to transform that indignation into negotiating agreements that would support more civil relations in the future. So the key questions about civil global society might include: How can the TCS challenge to governments and corporations be converted into agreements that mobilize resources *across* sectors for sustainable problem solving? How can such cross-sectoral engagement be sustained and leveraged *across issues?*

Transnational Public Discourse

The third aspect of TCS is its shaping of a transnational public discourse about problems and issues. We focus in this book particularly on discourses and public deliberations that contribute to the development of a civil global society. Some of these issues have long histories — the Universal Declaration of Human Rights, for example, is more than fifty years old — but getting agreement in principle is often quite different from ensuring compliance in practice. The evolution of issues through public debate and deliberation in the transnational context may take years before formal normative and legal agreements are enacted, and years more before those frameworks become part of the way things are done.

But considerable evidence suggests that some transnational discourses — such as those about environmental conservation and women's rights, for example[8] — have reshaped transnational agreements on values, norms, and assumptions, which have in turn shaped the behavior of inter-governmental institutions, national governments, and even ordinary citizens and their communities. Emerging questions about the transnational public discourse aspect of transnational civil society include: How do TCSOs actually frame and place issues on the public agenda as topics of concern? When and how do such public discourses reshape institutional values, norms, standards, and/or expectations?

The Creation of This Book

As the growth and influence of civil society in general has become more widely recognized, exciting interest among students, practitioners, social scientists, and the general public, a great deal is being written and published about it. Given the rapid rise in the number and influence of TCSOs in particular, the last decade has witnessed the publication of a large number of books and articles on the subject.[9] As more and more universities around the world are offering undergraduate and postgraduate programs and courses on civil society, often including the study of TCS, the need has increased for an introductory textbook that would help first-time students make sense of this complex yet exciting terrain.

We have conceived and edited this book because our own experience has convinced us that TCS — in all its varied forms and hues — has become an increasingly critical force in global politics. The media's images of the protesters at the Battle of Seattle and at World Trade Organization meetings around the world have reached people in every corner of the globe. We are all aware that people are joining hands across all sorts of formerly insurmountable geographic and political boundaries to speak out and act on issues that were once the exclusive domain of powerful leaders. Through the essays in this book, we show how progressive TCS initiatives have gained the capacity to influence, shape, and sometimes discipline governments, business, and public opinion.

We have tried in creating this book to follow several core principles. First and foremost, we wished to create a volume that would be as transnational as its subject. The dominance of Northern universities and academics in today's world often means that texts are suffused with perspectives of the industrialized world. We have tried to include developing as well as industrialized perspectives rather than emphasize the view of just one country or region. Second, to strengthen a truly transnational perspective, we worked hard to find chapter authors from the geographic and global South, and to recruit authors from the industrialized world who have the capacity to represent critical and Southern viewpoints as well as Northern perspectives.

We also wanted this volume to present the analyses of people who could bring to their chapters the authenticity of their own experiences as participants in the initiatives they write about. The passion of experience and participation is very evident in these chapters. We have not attempted to hide the diverse stances and politics of our contributors — indeed, we believe these in themselves reflect the diversity of TCS actors and movements. In this book, readers will learn about transnational causes from experts who have been in the midst of the processes they now stand back to analyze. We believe this gives the chapters a unique voice that many students will find inspiring.

We have also ensured that the book focuses on the broad sets of actors who joined hands to create these initiatives, rather than on particular individuals, no matter how outstanding. Readers who are accustomed to thinking in terms of social initiatives as powered by great men and women may find the lack of attention to individuals an important omission. We do not deny the vital role played by some individuals, but we want to emphasize that movements are more significant than leaders, even when stories about movements often emphasize the roles played by individuals.

Finally, we have tried to ensure that the complex and challenging ideas and histories in this volume are articulated in an accessible, direct style, avoiding intimidating academic jargon as much as possible. The style is straightforward, but the content and analysis is often far from simple. We hope this style finds approval among our student readers in particular.

Chapter Overview

Following this introduction, our volume is organized in two parts. Part One focuses on transnationalism and global power, and contains four chapters that help explain some of the global economic, social, and political forces that set the context for the evolution of TCS. In chapter 1, "The New Globalism," Peter Dobkin Hall demonstrates that several events and forces — the electronic media's capacity to beam images of events around the world into our homes, and growing cross-border migration, for instance — have shrunk the world in our imaginations, and that the internationalization of higher education has created a new breed of global citizens with a more global identity.

Marsha Darling's hard-hitting chapter "Who Really Rules the World?" (chapter 2) examines the architecture of global power and inequality that has given rise to much of the progressive transnational activism described in this volume. Through her examination of colonialism and slavery, she demonstrates that economic and political globalizations are not new phenomena, and helps us understand their different components. She also intends for the reader to grasp the daunting challenges of creating a civil global society given current levels of inequality and exclusion.

In "Claiming Global Power: Transnational Civil Society and Global Governance" (chapter 3), Kumi Naidoo describes the growing role of TCS in global policymaking. He emphasizes that TCS is not a result of globalization but a response to it, and goes on to trace the fascinating history of progressive transnational action, including the global events and mechanisms that spurred its growth. Naidoo also discusses the backlash to the growing influence and power of TCS and its organizations — increased scrutiny and criticism of its activities, including challenges to its accountability and legitimacy — and how these will have to be faced.

To counter our tendency to think about TCS as only progressive networks and coalitions working for "good" causes, Sanjeev Khagram and Sarah Alvord's chapter on "The Rise of Civic Transnationalism" (chapter 4) demonstrates that these are but one slice of a broad range of transnational formations. The authors place progressive TCS within a comparative perspective, and startle us with the similarities of structure, strategy, and forms of power that these formations bear to "uncivil" entities like transnational terror and fundamentalist networks. They also examine different streams within TCS.

Part 2 of this volume, "Movements That Changed the World," contains chapters on six of the most influential and important TCS initiatives. These initiatives have shaped the world in terms of norms and values as well as discourses and debates. We give pride of place to the oldest surviving transnational movement, that of labor, with Dan Gallin's chapter, "Transnational Pioneers: The International Labor Movement" (chapter 5). He traces the tumultuous history of cross-border labor organizing from before World War I to the present day, and takes a critical look at the challenges confronting the movement in a globalized world, where it is forced to contend with new kinds of work and forms of production that demand new organizing strategies.

In "Spinning the Green Web: Transnational Environmentalism" (chapter 6), Wendy and Andrew Torrance introduce us to the history and development of another seasoned transnational movement, focused on protecting and preserving the Earth's natural resources and environment. Through a series of fascinating case examples, the Torrances demonstrate how groups with diverse backgrounds and concerns — scientific experts and animal-rights activists from different corners of the world — can coalesce around issues like the environment and shape the way we think about it. They also show how TCS can work with other sectors, like governments and business, to create sustainable solutions and common agendas.

John Clark's chapter, "Dot-Causes and Protest: Transnational Economic Justice Movements" (chapter 7), deals with the rise of probably the most well-recognized TCS groupings, often called antiglobalization groups by the media. Clark offers a compelling analysis of five democracy deficits that have reduced confidence in traditional institutions of democracy and so stimulated citizens to engage in independent advocacy and action at the transnational level. Clark offers a critical view of the structure and politics of these networks, and discusses the crisis of legitimacy and accountability that they face. He also demonstrates the powerful facilitating role played by the Internet in the formation, growth, and coordination of these networks, which gave rise to their being called "Dot-Causes."

In "The Personal Is Global: The Project and Politics of the Transnational Women's Movement" (chapter 8), Gita Sen and Peggy Antrobus portray the evolution of the women's movement — another movement with more than a century of transnational history — and its engagement with both transnational allies and opponents. They offer a compelling history of the movement's engagement with and impact on our understanding of the gendered nature of economic policies, environmental dynamics, human rights, and sexual and reproductive rights. They conclude with a set of insightful challenges that have implications for several other movements as well: how to balance identity politics with a broader social project, address intergenerational leadership challenges, and make strategic alliances with other groups.

In "Bridging Borders for Human Rights" (chapter 9), Alison Brysk and Céline Jacquemin define human rights and place them within the context of current trends in globalization and transnationalism. Through a series of powerful cases, they demonstrate how the rights discourse has been reshaped by TCS actors, and how they have influenced the expansion of existing human rights norms. They also help us understand some of the important current debates in human rights, such as cultural relativism versus universal rights; where the line between common cultural practice and violation of human rights becomes blurred; and whether human rights is a Western invention, as some contend that human rights standards developed in the West are not relevant or appropriate in other areas of the world.

Motoko Mekata's "Waging Peace: Transnational Peace Activism" (chapter 10) brings this part of the volume to a close. Mekata offers a comprehensive history of the transnational peace movement since World War II and its different phases. She demonstrates how important new multilateral mechanisms like the International Court for Criminal Justice and the celebrated International Campaign to Ban Landmines emerged out of antiwar and peace initiatives. She gives much food for thought through her analysis of how the post–September 11, 2001, war on terror and the war in Iraq have created new challenges for peace activists around the world.

Finally, the book concludes with the editors' review of the preceding chapters and their implications for our understanding of TCS. "Shaping the Global Human Project: The Nature and Impact of Transnational Civil Activism" begins by taking us back to the larger global context in which TCS operates, and suggests different ways of understanding the information in this book. It suggests some key learning from the chapters; highlights emerging patterns in structure, strategy, and challenges; and attempts to answer some of the questions raised earlier in this chapter.

Readers who seek a basic grounding in TCS and its implications will probably want to read straight through the book. Those who want a quick overview may find it helpful to read the first and last chapters and then sample others that are of particular interest. We recommend reading more than one of the chapters on issue-based transnational initiatives (labor, human rights, environment, etc.), since comparison across several examples is a good way to get a sense of more general patterns. In the end, we hope that readers will see why understanding TCS — its characteristics, strategies, achievements, and challenges — is critical to understanding what is happening in our world today.

Notes

1. For a description of the Babyfood Campaign see Douglas A. Johnson, "Confronting Corporate Power: Strategies and Phases of the Nestle Boycott," in *Research in Corporate Social Performance and Policy,* ed. Lee Preston and James Post: 323–44 (Greenwich, CT: JAI Press, 1986).

2. See, for example, Mary Kaldor, *Global Civil Society: An Answer to War* (Cambridge: Polity, 2003); John Keane, *Transnational Civil Society* (Cambridge: Cambridge University Press, 2003); Michael Edwards, *Civil Society* (Cambridge: Polity, 2004); and Alan Fowler, "Social Economy in the South: A Civil Society Perspective" (unpublished monograph, May 2001). Obtainable from ALANFOWLER@compuserve.com.

3. This definition is based on the work of Edwards, *Civil Society.* For an analysis that produces a similar multiaspect definition of civil society, focusing on the structures of associational life, the norms of civic community, and the networks of public communication structures, see also Michael Bratton, "Civil Society and Political Transition in Africa," *Institute for Development Research Reports* 11, no. 6 (1994): 1–21.

4. For a discussion of the emergence of transnational advocacy networks, see Margaret E. Keck and Kathryn Sikkink, *Activists Beyond Borders* (Ithaca, NY: Cornell University Press, 1998); for a discussion of the emergence of civil society as a concept, see Kaldor, *Global Civil Society*.

5. Lester M. Salamon, "The Rise of the Non-Profit Sector," *Foreign Affairs* 73, no. 4 (1994): 109–22.

6. For descriptions of the organizational arrangements of the largest relief and development NGOs, see Marc Lindenberg and Coralie Bryant, *Going Global: Transforming Relief and Development NGOs* (Bloomfield, CT: Kumarian Press, 2001).

7. This discussion is based on the definitions developed in Sanjeev Khagram, James V. Riker, and Kathryn Sikkink, eds., *Restructuring World Politics: Transnational Social Movements, Networks, and Norms* (Minneapolis: University of Minnesota Press, 2002).

8. See Gita Sen and Peggy Antrobus, this volume; and Andrew Hoffman, *From Heresy to Dogma: An Institutional History of Corporate Environmentalism* (San Francisco: New Lexington Press, 1997).

9. On the nature of transnational civil society, see Keane, *Transnational Civil Society*, and Kaldor, *Global Civil Society*. For more information on the rise of transnational civil society organizations, networks, and movements, see Lindenberg and Bryant, *Going Global*; Keck and Sikkink, *Activists Beyond Borders*; Khagram, Riker, and Sikkink, *Restructuring World Politics*; and Ann Florini, ed., *The Third Force: The Rise of Transnational Civil Society* (New York: Carnegie Endowment for International Peace; Tokyo: Japan Center for International Exchange, 2000).

PART ONE

Transnationalism
and Global Power

CHAPTER ONE

The New Globalism

Peter Dobkin Hall

Introduction

Twenty years ago, the terms "globalism," "globalization," and "transnationality" were rarely used; today they are ubiquitous. Hardly a day passes now when they are not used in newspapers, magazines, and book titles. However, there is as yet no single, universal standard for the meanings of these terms. To some, they connote global Westernization, the expanding influence and power of the large, developed nations of Europe and North America; the replacement of local and regional markets by a consolidated world market; and the concomitant homogenization of cultures that have the capacity to challenge and counteract the influence of these Western power centers.

In important ways, the difficulty in defining the architecture of the emerging global order is more than just the fundamental issue of acceptable positions between the powerful and the powerless; it is also a struggle to define the language, terms, and concepts describing supranational institutions and relationships. The global Westernizers have tended to see globalization as a process in which major nation-states and the international institutions created and controlled by them are the dominant partners in any matter of global importance. The proponents of multicentered globalization look to institutions that transcend States, directly linking together people with common concerns and problems through a variety of new, usually nongovernmental, movements and organizations. This chapter seeks to provide an overview of the origins and development of these perspectives.

Creating Global Communities

A community is an act of imagination through which we define who we are, to which larger collectivities we belong, to whom we are accountable, and what our obligations are to one another. Mere locational proximity does not automatically entitle a person to fellowship, nor does geographical distance preclude membership, citizenship, mutual obligations, and shared goals and values. At the same time, the community is an institution that routinizes practices, interactions, and exchanges among individuals, which in turn depend on the technologies that make relationships and transactions possible; communities become institutions to the extent that technology and resources facilitate these patterns of association and exchange.

The connections between an imagined global community and its realization are tenuous and contingent on a variety of factors. For centuries, humanity has dreamed of creating political and religious global unities. From Alexander the Great and the founders of the world's major religious traditions to the despots of our own time, leaders have endeavored to impose their *imperia* on the world's peoples. Inevitably, these efforts have failed, in part because of technological and organizational shortcomings, in part because leaders have underestimated the extent to which the success of political, social, and economic orders, especially geographically extensive ones, must be based on compliance, not coercion. A despot's dreams of a world order instituted from above are therefore bound to be fundamentally different in aspirations, methods, and goals from the masses' vision of a global community.

Since the end of World War II, we have come closer to establishing a compliance-based world order than at any time in the past, in large part as an effort to counter the imperial ambitions of authoritarian States. This order has been predicated on the idea of the global polity as a system of nation-states linked by treaties, mutual security and trade arrangements (the North Atlantic Treaty Organization, the Warsaw Pact, the British Commonwealth, etc.), and a system of international institutions (the United Nations, the World Bank, the International Monetary Fund, among others). A variety of nongovernmental institutions and relationships, paralleling these intergovernmental arrangements, also emerged during this period, including multinational businesses, international social movements, transnational epistemic and religious communities, and flows of migrant labor from one nation to another. Because their growth was often facilitated by nation-states seeking to expand their influence by nonpolitical means, they were not regarded as significant challenges to the nation-state system.

The growth of these international arrangements has not gone unchallenged. While governments and their leaders have established formal institutions, global economic integration and a revolution in communication have helped to inspire the world's peoples to develop their own visions of the possibility of a global community. When, why, and how did people begin thinking of alternatives to global community as the sum of its nation-state components? More specifically, how did these visions of a transnational community become a part of the popular imagination throughout the world?

Democratizing the Global Community

It is widely believed that images of Earth from the 1968 Apollo 8 space flight wrought a fundamental change in people's understanding of the world: for the first time, we had a "God's eye" view of what our planet looked like. Since the beginning of modern cartography (which, not surprisingly, had coincided with the formation of nation-states), the world had been represented as demarcated by national boundaries, like a classroom globe. Suddenly, Earth could be seen as it actually is: a blue-green sphere orbiting through the vast reaches of space, its only divisions those between water and land. The complete absence of the artificial political constructs of humans, so cherished and aggressively defended, was brought home with stunning force.

The power of these images of Earth was also due to their universal dissemination. Only a year earlier, in June 1967, the first global television program had been broadcast by Telstar, initiating world-spanning satellite transmission technology with a live performance of the Beatles singing "All You Need Is Love." An estimated 350 million viewers watched the broadcast in every nation that had an adequate telecommunications infrastructure and permitted the free circulation of ideas. This infrastructure also permitted the dissemination of the powerful images of the Earth when the Apollo 8 astronauts brought them back from their moon voyage.

Ironically, the whole-Earth images from space and the global telecast by Telstar also served to express the ambiguous character of the emerging global order. On the one hand, they evoked the transcendent unity of humankind. On the other, their dependence on American technology and use of the English language and musical forms implied a new world order dominated by the West. That the West under US leadership should presume to speak and act for humanity echoed — in new, less obviously oppressive forms — the ethos of discredited nineteenth-century European imperialism.

But symbols and images, once produced, take on lives of their own, independent of their creators' intentions. If the Beatles' "All You Need Is Love" was intended to serve as an emblem of the benevolence of expanding Western influence, it also became an anthem of countercultures that were resisting the power of authoritarian States throughout the world.

The technology intended to expand the market for Western products and ideas also disseminated images of the civil rights movement, American race riots, protests against the Vietnam War, Czech resistance to Soviet domination, the struggle against apartheid in South Africa, and the dismantling of colonial empires in the Third World. Instantaneous global communication meant that popular movements throughout the world could draw inspiration from each another. It also meant that oppressive regimes could not — with the whole world watching — crush these movements with impunity. This unprecedented exposure helped local activists understand their efforts as part of a universal struggle for human rights. At the same time, they forced governments to take these rights seriously.

The telecommunications revolution called attention to the disparities in development between the West and the rest of the world. The rights movements that sought to empower racial and ethnic minorities, women, and the disabled in the United States during the 1960s and 1970s were widely publicized. Although the latter were generally framed in terms of national legal and constitutional claims, their global dimension was acknowledged as Native Americans recognized their kinship with the oppression of indigenous peoples in the Third World, black Americans identified with the aspirations of emerging African nations, and the peace movement questioned on humanitarian grounds the moral claims of American foreign policy.

Globalizing Economies

These shifts in world political culture were paralleled by changes in the global economy. While American and European multinational corporations continued to extend their influence, former colonies that controlled vital resources, like petroleum, began to sense their power. By the late 1960s, the Organization of Petroleum Exporting Countries (OPEC) began to control oil prices and then tilt them in favor of oil-producing countries. In 1973, OPEC shut off the world's oil supply to enforce its demands.

At the same time, the world labor market began to respond to the growing disparities in wealth and opportunities between the First and Third worlds. This took several forms. One involved the increasing outsourcing of unskilled manufacturing from the First to the Third World. In 1945, South America, Africa, and Asia accounted for only 6 percent of nonfuel exports to the developed countries; in 1980, they constituted 45 percent, and by 1989, 71 percent. Another aspect of the globalization of labor markets involved the migration of people from the Third World to the First, to perform the unskilled jobs that workers in advanced nations were no longer willing to do.[1] Unlike earlier migrations, in which people permanently left their native lands, the migrant labor force of the late twentieth century, using the possibilities of global economic and communications infrastructures, largely retained ties to their native lands. Remittances by migrant workers dramatically affected their native economies, reducing poverty, raising per capita incomes, and fueling the growth of the middle class.

The impact of these transnational labor forces on advanced nations was no less dramatic. The ethnically homogeneous nations of Western Europe were transformed by large populations of "guest workers" from North Africa and the Middle East; Canada and the United States attracted large numbers of migrants from South and Central America, India, China, Japan, and the Middle East. This intermingling exposed more people to the sights, sounds, and cuisines of one another's cultures than any other event in history, but these benefits were not without their attendant problems. Many Western European nations, whose social and political institutions had never been required to accommodate religious and ethnic diversity, now experienced new kinds of strain and discord in their polities. Then, as now, they generally resisted efforts by migrant communities to assimilate and naturalize, while also placing obstacles in the way of migrants who wanted to maintain their own distinct identities.

Technology and the Transformation of Ethnicity

On the other side of the Atlantic, ethnic and religious pluralism have compelled the United States and Canada, albeit reluctantly, not only to adapt to the growth of nonnative communities but also to acknowledge, in the face of historical myths that portrayed them as primarily Anglo-American, the true extent of their diversity. As recently as fifty years ago, it was not uncommon for upwardly mobile immigrants to abandon their languages, customs, and birth names in order to aspire to a homogenized American or Canadian identity. Today, diversity in origin is accepted as common, and "hyphenated Americans" proudly state their origins and ethnicity as a base for making claims on social and governmental institutions. The melting pot has, in effect, been replaced by the rainbow.

Technology is a key factor in the transformation of ethnic communities. While many nineteenth-century migrants came to North America in the expectation of returning home, the financial and technological obstacles to maintaining ties to their communities of origin were formidable. Today, with the low cost of communication via telephone and the Internet and the ease of remitting funds back to their native lands, it is possible — and increasingly common — not only for migrants to maintain continuous contact with their communities of origin but also to maintain dual citizenship. No longer living in isolated ghettos far from their native lands, the migrants are able to create and sustain their ethnicity and sense of community far more effectively than in the past.

Higher Education — The Great Unifier

The development of civil society in the United States in the eighteenth and nineteenth centuries provides a valuable paradigm for understanding the emergence of transnational civil society today. Like the world itself, the country in its early days covered a huge geographical expanse and, unlike many nations, contained a multitude of peoples, each with their own traditions and languages. Even among the Americans who spoke English, there were differences in religion, modes of production, and lifestyles sufficient to bring about a destructive civil war less than a century after its independence from Britain.

If American nationality did not spring from a common language, religion, race, or political allegiance, where did it come from? What made it possible for Americans to form large collectivities that operated across vast geographical expanses? The answer appears to lie in the efforts of a handful of educators to systematically create national elites and a national culture.

One part of the effort was rooted at Yale in the 1820s. The largest college in America at the time, Yale was already looking beyond its New England confines and recruiting students from across the nation. Fearing the rise of "infidelity" — the abandonment of religion — and the corruption of the democratic process, Yale made a conscious effort to educate leaders and imbue them with common values so that they could disseminate these throughout the country.

Yale sought, as its faculty wrote in the famous Yale Report of 1828, to provide its students with a peculiarly democratic and egalitarian conception of leadership,

> where offices are accessible to all who are qualified for the superior intellectual attainments ought not to be confined to any description of persons. *Merchants, manufacturers,* and *farmers,* as well as professional gentlemen, take their places in our public councils. A thorough education ought therefore to be extended to all these classes. It is not sufficient that they be men of sound judgment, who can decide correctly, and give a silent vote, on great national questions. Their influence upon the minds of others is needed; an influence to be produced by extent of knowledge, and the force of eloquence.[2]

Though geographically dispersed, Yale's alumni formed nationally extensive social networks. Many were recruited into national economic, educational, and religious enterprises anchored at Yale and/or directed by Yale alumni. They became particularly active in propagating the use of voluntary associations and corporations as mechanisms for collective action.

The other great educational institution, Harvard, had remained a parochially Bostonian institution until the Civil War, when its graduates distinguished themselves through their military service and civilian leadership. Its insularity, however, concerned Boston's economic leaders, whose business activities were increasingly involving them in enterprises outside New England. Their concerns were shared by a young chemistry instructor, Charles W. Eliot, who, during a tour of Europe, conducted an extensive study of the relationship between education and economic and political development in England, France, and Germany.

On his return, Eliot wrote "The New Education" for the *Atlantic Monthly*, in which he set forth the ideas that would become the standard for all modern research universities.[3] In 1869, the businessmen who controlled Harvard made him its youngest president (he was only thirty-five!) and gave him a free hand and generous financial support for the running of the institution. Within a decade, Harvard had become the preeminent American university, attracting an internationally renowned faculty and placing its graduates in the nation's most important public and private enterprises.

Where Yale had directed its efforts to creating a nationally dispersed elite network, Harvard concentrated on building leadership cadres in emerging economic centers like Boston, Philadelphia, New York, and Chicago. The increasing importance throughout the country of university graduates intentionally educated for national leadership provided the vision that inspired the organizational consolidations of the late nineteenth century in government and business, while the consolidation of large-scale organizations helped to provide the resources needed to establish and support national cultural institutions.[4]

The creation of national economic and cultural institutions and the growth of government in the late nineteenth and early twentieth centuries were similarly linked. Nationwide enterprises required human and intellectual capital produced by universities, and both required the social capital enabling people operating in large, geographically extensive enterprises to work productively together. The progressive movement of the early twentieth century was less a social movement concerned with economic justice than a mobilization of the masses by educated elites determined, as one leading intellectual put it, to "fulfill the American national promise."[5] The success of this national elite enabled the United

States to become a world leader in the years following World War I.

The changing demographics and goals of contemporary higher educational institutions suggest that a process very similar in manner to the one that led to the comprehensive nation building of America a century ago may be unfolding. Higher education appears to be a critically important element, training leaders who gravitate to the global centers of commerce, culture, and international organizations as well as those who work in and with indigenous organizations, transnational coalitions, and network organizations.

The globalization of higher education has been a key factor facilitating transnational communities. As Table 1 suggests, the percentage of doctorates awarded by US universities to individuals who were Asian, Hispanic, or nonresident aliens (foreign students) doubled between 1980 and 2000 — with the largest increase in the nonresident alien category, which tripled in size during this twenty-year period. The percentage of non-US citizens receiving master's and doctoral degrees from US universities between the late 1970s and mid 1990s increased from 27 percent to 38.7 percent of all degrees awarded.[6]

Table 1.1: Number of Doctorates Awarded, 1980–2000 (by Ethnicity and Citizenship)

YEAR	NO. TOTAL PhDs	NO. ASIAN	NO. HISPANIC	NON-RESIDENT ALIEN	% ETHNIC
1980–81	32,839	877	456	4,203	17
1984–85	32,307	1,106	677	5,317	22
1990–91	38,547	1,459	732	9,715	31
1995–96	44,645	2,646	984	11,450	34
1999–2000	44,808	2,380	1,291	11,238	33

(This table was prepared in August 2001)

Source: Higher Education General Information Survey (HEGIS), "Degrees and Other Formal Awards Conferred" surveys, and Integrated Postsecondary Education Data System (IPEDS), "Completions" surveys, National Center for Education Statistics, US Department of Education.

While there has been an increase in the percentage of non-US students committed to remaining in the United States after receiving their degrees (from 46 percent in 1985 to 54 percent in 1995), the fact that nearly half the non-US graduates intended to return to their countries of origin suggests that higher education may not be viewed by all students as a means of gaining permanent entry into the United States. While some are staying on, at least as many are returning home to become scholars, officials of national governments or international bodies, and executives in transnational business firms, agencies, or NGOs. They serve as cultural ambassadors for their countries while in the United States and as disseminators of American ideas and values in their homelands.

Significantly, the globalization of higher education has not been a one-way proposition. Over the past decade, the number of US students studying abroad has more than doubled, from 71,154 in 1991–92 to 160,920 in 2002–3.[7] While this in no way compares with the 586,323 non-US students enrolled in American universities, the number of American students studying abroad is impressive and rapidly growing.[8] Although the countries of choice for Americans studying abroad are, not unexpectedly, primarily Western European (63 percent), the number of students choosing to study in "nontraditional" countries — particularly in Asia, Latin America, and Africa — has increased dramatically, largely because of the relatively lower costs of study abroad coupled with the availability of quality, specialized education, increasing competition for places in American universities, and the growing interest among American students in overseas careers.

The United States is not the only site of globalization of higher education. According to a study by the Institute for International Education, a dramatically reduced rate of growth of foreign enrollment in US universities has occurred since September 11, 2001: the rate for the academic year 2002–3 was down to under 1 percent, the lowest in seven years — not only because of the actual tightening of immigration rules but also because of the perception in the minds of potential international students that the United States has made student visas harder to obtain.[9]

This trend has led to an increased enrollment in other countries, such as the United Kingdom, Australia, and New Zealand, where English is the language of higher education and the quality of their institutions is highly rated. For instance, enrollment by Chinese students in British universities increased by 36 percent in the academic year 2003–4; enrollment in Australian colleges by Indian students increased by 31 percent and by Chinese students 25 percent in the same year.[10]

Other statistics, on the number of dissertations on or relating to globalization, globalism, and transnationalism, reflect the shift in perception of these issues in American academia. No dissertations were written on these subjects before 1975. In 1980, 19 were written; in 1992, 37; in 1995, 121; and in 2000, 316.[11] The dissertations were written in virtually every field and profession, from arts and culture through theology and urban planning. (It is interesting to note from the abstracts that globalization and related terms are construed in widely divergent ways in different fields.)

Not only has the number of dissertations addressing globalization and related issues increased substantially but also, and more interestingly, as Table 2 suggests, the percentage written by non-US students — or US students of complex ethnicity — comprises nearly half the number of dissertations on topics of an international nature.

Table 1.2: Number of Dissertations on Globalization and/or Related Topics, and Dissertations Written or Advised by Individuals with Names Suggesting Complex Ethnicity

YEAR	NO. DISSERTATIONS	NO. ETHNIC AUTHORS OR ADVISORS	% ETHNIC
1970	31	3	10
1980	18	1	5
1985	16	7	43
1990	37	9	24
1995	121	48	39
2000	316	152	48

Source: Peter Dobkin Hall, "Globalization: A Chapter in the Sociology of Knowledge," paper presented to the panel on Discerning Globalization: Language, Identity, and Emergent Transnational Collectivities, Social Science History Association, St. Louis, MO, October 25, 2002.

The term "complex ethnicity" derives from the increasingly multiethnic/multicultural characteristics of the college-going student population in the United States. Half a century ago, graduate education was overwhelmingly the preserve of privileged, Anglo-Saxon, mainly Protestant, white males. Today, in addition to the considerable body of non-US students, a substantial proportion of the students is composed of children or grandchildren of immigrant families, or products of mixed-ethnicity marriages. As late as the 1950s, such people would have looked to graduate education as a way of camouflaging their foreign origin. Today, Japanese-American, Chinese-American, and Korean-American students, children or grandchildren of immigrants, are likely to be studying alongside and socializing with Japanese, Chinese, and Korean students in ways that make difficult clear demarcations of ethnic identity. Moreover, American students with ethnic origins are increasingly likely to seek careers in the nations from which their parents or grandparents emigrated.

In a chapter titled "The Invention of the Asian-American" in his study on standardized educational admissions testing in the United States, Nicholas Lemann offers a remarkably detailed account of the impact of interactions between Asian students, assimilated Asian-Americans, and children of recent immigrants from Asia at Yale in the 1960s and 1970s. The chapter describes the impact of Yale's decision in the late 1960s to recruit students meritoriously on a group of young people of varied Asian ethnicity, many of them of immigrant and/or working-class backgrounds, to an institution that had been overwhelmingly white, male, Protestant, and upper class.

> At a university where they were very much in the minority and constantly reminded of their marginality, the students began exploring their own history and identity, inspired in part by the rising discipline of African-American studies. "Having . . . become more self-consciously ethnic and more politically confrontational, and having been influenced by the rising note of protest on campus, . . . a small group . . . founded the Asian-American Student Association of Yale."[12]

"The notion of an 'Asian-American' was a bold and new one," Lemann writes.

> It was also a completely artificial construct, but Caucasians didn't have to know that. They seemed to be willing to accept the notion of a monolithic, on-the-march, slant-eyed juggernaut, so why not use it? At that point Asian-Americans at Yale were an amalgam mainly of two groups, Chinese-Americans and Japanese-Americans, which spoke different languages, lived back home in different ethnic enclaves, and had been taught by their war generation parents to think of each other as the enemy.[13]

While joining with other ethnic student groups in left-wing campus crusades, the Asian-Americans made admissions work their main activity. They worked relentlessly, both through pressuring the university to admit more Asian students and through personal recruiting excursions, to increase the Asian presence at Yale. The class admitted the year these students started at Yale had 9 students of Asian ancestry, and the number had risen to 35 the year they organized their association. By the late 1990s, Asian-Americans constituted nearly 15 percent of incoming Yale College freshmen and 12 percent of university students overall.[14] Combined with the 569 Asians from among Yale's international students, Asians and Asian-Americans made up 17 percent of the Yale student body.[15]

Judging from the number of Asian-American student associations throughout the United States, and the high representation of Asians among the rising numbers of international student enrollments at American colleges and universities in the 1980s and 1990s, American institutions of higher education, rather than serving as they traditionally had as melting pots intended to Americanize ethnic students, were becoming locations in which students were able to redefine themselves in terms of ethnicity rather than citizenship. It was not uncommon, as in one of Harvard's doctoral fellows programs, to have two students of Chinese ethnicity — one a second-generation Chinese-American, the other a Chinese student studying in America — both writing dissertations on indigenous Chinese voluntary associations and social movements.

The effects of these kinds of interactions on postgraduate professional careers and social networks merit further study. The Chinese students who studied at Yale and other American institutions before the 1960s almost invariably returned to China to pursue careers in government, education, or business. Today, Chinese students are as likely to pursue careers in the United States as Chinese-American students are to pursue careers in China. One way or another, ethnicity seems to trump nationality.

Conclusion

The demographics and self-representations of contemporary higher education suggest that the American nation-building process of a century ago offers a paradigm for contemporary globalization. Just as there were tensions between the urban, elite-centered model of nationality and the multicentered network model offered by Yale (the historic conflict between Wall Street and Main Street), today we see analogous tensions between nation-state-based global Westernization and more egalitarian and multicentered transnationality. In both, higher education appears to be a centrally important element, training both the leaders who gravitate to the global centers of commerce, culture, and international organizations and those who work in and with indigenous organizations and transnational coalitions and network organizations.

More significant than the expansion of career opportunities for students, whatever their ethnicity or nationality, is the extent to which education and scholarship have become arenas for the exploration and negotiation of personal identity. In universities throughout the world, students are discovering new forms of community, collective action, identity, and solidarity. These not only shape careers but the values that animate them, and the networks through which they are pursued.

One thing is clear: the power to define globalization does not lie with nation-states. Nationalists' dreams of world domination have been definitively displaced by the yearning of men and women throughout the world for other forms of solidarity. More to the point, history suggests that the ways in which global leaders are educated, rather than politics and policy, determine the ultimate form and meaning of globalism.

Notes

1. World Bank, www.worldbank.org/data/quickreference/quickref. html (accessed June 6, 2004).

2. Jeremiah Day and James L. Kingsley, "Original Papers in Relation to a Course of Liberal Education," *American Journal of Science* 15 (January 1829): 297–351.

3. C. W. Eliot, "The New Education," pts. 1 and 2, *Atlantic Monthly* 23 (February 1869): 202–20; 23 (March 1869): 363–66.

4. L. Galambos, "The Emerging Organizational Synthesis in American History," in *Men and Organizations: The American Economy in the Twentieth Century,* ed. E. J. Perkins, 1–15 (New York: G. P. Putnam, 1977); L. Galambos, "Technology, Political Economy, and Professionalization: Central Themes of the Organizational Synthesis," *Business History Review* 57 (Winter 1983): 471–93; Peter Dobkin Hall, *The Organization of American Culture, 1700–1900: Institutions, Elites, and the Origins of American Nationality* (New York: New York University Press, 1982); M. J. Sklar, *The Corporate Reconstruction of American Capitalism, 1890–1916* (New York: Cambridge University Press, 1988).

5. H. Croly, *The Promise of American Life* (New York: Macmillan, 1909).

6. National Center for Education Statistics, 1997, http://nces.ed.gov/das/library/tables_listing/show_nedrc.asp?rt=p&tab leID=233 (accessed June 6, 2004).

7. Institute of International Education, "American Students Study Abroad in Growing Numbers," www.opendoors.iienetwork.org/?p=36524 (accessed November 17, 2003).

8. Institute of International Education, "International Student Enrolment," www.opendoors.iienetwork.org/?p=36523 (accessed November 17, 2003).

9. Institute of International Education, "Open Doors 2003: International Students in the United States," www.opendoors.iienetwork.org (accessed November 17, 2003).

10. CNN.com International, quoting the United Kingdom's Universities and Colleges Admissions Service, November 3, 2003.

11. Peter Dobkin Hall, "Globalization: A Chapter in the Sociology of Knowledge," paper presented to the panel on Discerning Globalization: Language, Identity, and Emergent Transnational Collectivities, Social Science History Association, St. Louis, MO, October 25, 2002.

12. Nicholas Lemann, *The Big Test: The Secret History of the American Meritocracy* (New York: Farrar, Straus, and Giroux, 2000), 174–84.

13. Ibid., 176–77.

14. B. Waters, *A Yale Book of Numbers, 1976–2000* (New Haven, CT: Yale University Office of Institutional Research, 2001), Figure B-3. Also available at www.yale.edu/oir/pierson_update.htm#D (accessed June 6, 2004).

15. Ibid., Table A-10 and Table B-1.

CHAPTER TWO

Who Really Rules the World?

Marsha J. Tyson Darling

Introduction

World capitalism and its vehicle for building a universal infrastructure, economic globalization, are dominant forces at the planetary level today. A world economic system — an increasingly interconnected and interactive exchange of goods and services, money, labor, ideas, and trade in commodities and markets — has been developing over the course of the past five centuries. At the same time, other dominant forces in pursuit of the exercise of human and political rights have also developed, such as the modern secular state, democratization, abolitionism, decolonization, collective bargaining, and civil society institutions, as have (more recently) class, gender/sexuality, and movements supporting ethnic identity and rights for those with disabilities. These social developments have not been a part of capitalism's plan, or an inevitable by-product, or indeed a natural outgrowth of its reach; rather, they represent the other side of emergent capital's interests — namely, the concerns, work, and achievements of everyday people who organized mass social change movements.

This chapter examines the architecture of global power: the evolution of key institutions, power blocs, values, and interests that shape the economic and political realities of today's world. In delineating who really rules the world, I provide a brief overview of the emergent dominance of world capitalism and corporations, and suggest that the process of pursuing an integrated global economic infrastructure is not a new phenomenon. Following from this I examine the elements of what has most recently been termed "globalization," including the power of transnational corporations (the engines of globalization); the reach of international finance capital and international financial institutions; the recently minted authority of international trade institutions; their tools, the structural adjustment policies; and the societal institutions (including institutions not elected by popular vote), technology, and the enclosure of knowledge that have come to define it.

The Beginnings of Emergent Capitalism

We begin our examination of forms of emergent capitalism by noting that the Ottoman, Safavid, Mughal, and Qing empires of the late Middle Ages dominated economic integration in Asia well before its conquest by European nations; in contrast, contemporary Europe's economic activity was largely restricted to the Atlantic economy[1] (although it came to dominate many other systems of production by the late nineteenth century). Although this Asian trade expansion and its consequent network of overland commerce is important in its own right (however much this aspect was subsequently subsumed after European military conquest and economic imperialism eventually brought much of Asia into its pursuit of industrial capitalism), it is Europe's expansionism that is summarized below.

By the start of the twentieth century, business and political interests in Europe and the United States used the military, economic, and political power of their respective nation-states for expansionist interventions and wars to further the goal of establishing capitalism through economic imperialism. World capitalism historically developed from the expansion of the Atlantic economy and the growth of mercantilism in the seventeenth century. In this period, the Atlantic slave trade expanded enormously, providing accumulating profits for those European countries engaged in it. As time passed, the profits from this trade fueled the creation of European, and later, American, economic and industrial systems.

Slavery and the crimes against humanity committed against the indigenous populations of the Americas, Asia, Australia, and Africa required justifications, and none more suited the age or the decades that followed than the creation of a knowledge system that constructed and institutionalized the invention of the idea of "race" as a justification for slavery, and for the belief that all brown-, ebony-, yellow-, and beige-skinned people were innately inferior to white-skinned people.[2]

Race was not the only pernicious social invention of the age. The degradation of the poor as a "class" accelerated in the seventeenth century. An example of this was the enclosure movement in England, which usurped the public commons, forcing millions of the English poor into towns and cities. Here they became landless laborers in search of employment, either as industrial laborers or on ships bound for the American colonies, or to Australia as indentured labor. Nearly everywhere also, though its forms differed in important ways across cultures, women lived under the yoke of patriarchy and its debilitating message of women's inherent inferiority.[3]

The wealth that accrued to Europe from the Atlantic economy reflected the deeply forged alliances among business, the church, and the military (on behalf of the crown).[4] As time passed and ideas about utilitarianism came to dominate Western thought, the quest for resources, which fueled ever-expanding economic growth aided by a predatory behavior toward indigenous peoples, prompted the rise of aggressive European national empires. The French, the British, and the Dutch, particularly, controlled Asia, while Portugal, France, Belgium, Britain, and Germany ensured their continent-wide imperial dominion over Africa at the Treaty of Berlin following the Congress of Berlin in 1885.[5] Imperialism and then colonialism secured the processes of escalating European and American economic growth and development, while retarding the economic growth and development of many indigenous peoples in North, Central, and South America; Asia; Africa; the Pacific Islands; and Australia. This conquest at gunpoint imparted a particular dimension to the emerging world trade system — that of military and economic domination of people of color in the global South as well as in the global North by white-skinned peoples from the global North.

The Growth of Corporations

The historical configuration of wealth and economic power described above — along with the acceleration of industrial development with its attendant growth in knowledge, particularly in the fields of technology (the cotton gin, telegraph, Gatling gun, steam engine, lightbulb, railways, telephone, etc.) and science — have prompted a number of ideas about rationality, utilitarianism, liberty, finance, trade and the marketplace, the role of labor, the scale of productivity, the environment (the relationship between resources in the natural world and industrial production), governance and its responsibility and obligation/reciprocity, and the behaviors, attitudes, and conduct that should influence or govern business culture.

In the 1700s, joint-stock trading companies, banks, and insurance companies, and increasingly militarized European nation-states (Portugal, Spain, England, France, and Holland) vied for currency, commodities, and what Karl Marx, in his classic *Das Kapital* described as the "chief momenta of primitive accumulation."

> The discovery of gold and silver in America, the extirpation, enslavement and entombment in mines of the aboriginal population, the beginning of the conquest and looting of the East Indies, the turning of Africa into a warren for the commercial hunting of black skins, signalized the rosy dawn of the era of capitalist production. These idyllic proceedings are the chief momenta of primitive accumulation. The treasures captured outside Europe by undisguised looting, enslavement, and murder, floated back to the mother-country and were turned into capital.[6]

It was the development of chartered companies and subsequently the development of small and then larger capitalist manufacturing companies that gave birth to the corporations that dramatically accelerated production and profits for Europeans and whites in the Americas.

Chartered companies operated through nation-state mandates that prescribed an impressive range of exclusive rights, options, and protections for the economic operations and business capital they engaged in abroad.[7] Invariably, the profits from economic exploitation benefited economic development at home. Thus, the Dutch financed the construction of State highways and reduced their national debt with profits from the Dutch East Indies (now Indonesia) between 1850 and 1872. These profits provided one-third of the total budget of Holland. Furthermore, European colonizers "organized their colonies so that each one grew just two or three different crops. India grew jute, cotton and tea. Ceylon grew tea. Malaya grew rubber."[8]

Many, including one of Europe's most erudite eighteenth-century philosophers, Adam Smith (1723–90), were positive about the emergence of capitalism's bourgeoisie. Indeed, given the popularity of Smith's writings in his day, both his *Theory of Moral Sentiments* (1759) and *The Wealth of Nations* (1776) celebrated the emerging European bourgeoisie and called for a "moral energy" that would infuse civil society with "mutual sympathy" and "self-interest." However, while Smith revered the idea of breaking with feudalism's hold on society, he and many others were immensely distrustful of corporations, suggesting that corporate business practices pursued self-interest while undermining a moral imperative towards fairness, justice, and accountability.[9]

In the early nineteenth century, many believed that corporations rivaled governments: they reduced every issue to one of money, failed to regulate themselves, and created abuses that reduced the quality of life for people and the environment, while destroying rather than embracing and promoting civil society's "sense of mutual self-interest." As a result, by the middle of the nineteenth century, many State corporate charters in the United States were so written as to safeguard the public from the excesses of private corporations. Severyn T. Bruyn argues persuasively that legislators, Supreme Court justices, and politicians favoring some measure of justice and fairness enacted laws and interpreted the US Constitution as supportive of their "inalienable right" to regulate and govern corporations so as to establish and maintain moral principles in the marketplace.[10]

By the closing decades of the nineteenth century, however, corporations wielded an enormous amount of power and influence, in large part because by then they enjoyed tremendous legal protection. For example, between 1865 and the turn of the twentieth century, corporations in the United States had attained an important status that has over time proven to be highly contentious. Supreme Court decisions such as *Santa Clara County v. Southern Pacific Railroad* (1886) gave individual rights to private corporations under the US Constitution. Equally important, the moral boundaries in State charters were softened, so that corporate freedom became more dominant than the interests of the people. Corporations received agency, or rights, but without accountability. Such liberties resulted in many corporations merging with one another between 1898 and 1903, in an attempt to impose their dominance over domestic markets and seek greater access to markets overseas.[11]

Historically, most corporations used their court-interpreted agency or rights to pursue the unrestrained pursuit of profits, and engaged in self-aggrandizing competition without any regard for the impact of corporate choices, decisions, or policies on the larger social communities in which they operated. This aspect of corporate history has over time served to define capitalist corporate culture, and has been integrated into the modus operandi of many twentieth-century multinationals, and now many of the twenty-first century's transnational corporations.

Of course, not all corporations in the United States avoided self-regulation; some corporations developed associations that worked to adhere to industry-created business standards that were substantively self-regulating in nature. But, in the main, the result of allowing corporations a level of agency not afforded to individuals was the emergence of rampant corporate self-interest, greed, and competitiveness. Dubbed "freedom in the market," corporate agency was left to its own devices, in many ways eventually proving often to be corrosive of labor and consumer interests. In the first few decades of the twentieth century, the US government was eventually required to establish regulations; antipoverty, labor, and consumer legislation; and antimonopolization laws and policies in order to bring some measure of fairness, compassion, and justice into the dealings of the corporations. An increasing number of government agencies were required to negotiate, mediate, legislate, and regulate the normative and distributive justice problems now created by the regressive distribution of assets and wealth under laissez-faire capitalism.

Given the history of economic recessions (between 1892 and 1899, and 1929 and 1937), the US government in the 1930s seemed aware of the need to negotiate between the competing interests of corporations and labor, and corporations and consumers. Economic restructuring required creating legislation and policies that regulated excessive competition as well as crafting a welfare State: in effect, laws that responded to the widespread popular discontent with the gross inequalities in earnings.[12]

As corporations agreed to political reforms like the Wagner Act (1935), which legalized unions and collective bargaining; New Deal laws like the Social Security Act (1935) that helped the needy and vulnerable in American society with an entitlement to state assistance; and later the Employment Act (1946), it might have appeared that some semblance of Adam Smith's "mutual sympathy" accompanied "self-interest" as an important ideological basis for the interface between corporate business interests and the interests of the people. Certainly, for a while, a rede-fined relationship between business management and labor unions devel-oped following the progressive legislation of the New Deal. In the following decade, however, the momentous events of World War II proved particularly decisive in strengthening US corporate power.

Rise of Postwar Corporate Dominance

Wartime production meant profits for corporations in the United States and abroad. In this period, the US corporations furnished one-half of all industrial output in the world, and the United States emerged from WWII as the world's economic superpower.[13] Many nations devastated by the war stood in need of financial assistance for infrastructure restoration and economic reconstruction, and the United States now took the lead in promoting world capitalist development. In 1944, it convened a meeting at Bretton Woods, New Hampshire, which brought together leaders rep-resenting forty-five governments. The goal of the conference was the cre-ation of the International Bank for Reconstruction and Development (the World Bank) and the International Monetary Fund (IMF). At about the same time, the United States set the dollar as the reserve currency standard in the world, thus ensuring that US-based businesses could exer-cise the natural advantages that accrued from having the world's central currency.

In its first year of operation in 1947, the World Bank lent France USD 250 million for reconstruction. The Bank provided monies for disasters, humanitarian emergencies, postwar rehabilitation, and the reduction of poverty. Initially one single financial institution, the bank over several decades became a consortium of financial development institutions. The IMF's mandate was similar to that of the World Bank, in that as a lending institution it saw its principal role as funding development on a global scale.

In 1945, the United Nations was established; in 1947, the Marshall Plan, also designed to assist Europe with economic recovery, was created; and in 1949, the North Atlantic Treaty Organization (NATO) was formed to protect the physical freedom of its members. During the same five-year period, people of color subjugated by colonialism began to demand lib-eration; Indian independence was attained; the Pan-African Congress met; and peasants in China launched a revolution.

Ironically, while funds from the World Bank, the IMF, and the Marshall Plan helped many European nations and their home-based corporations rebuild national infrastructures, including manufacturing production and trade and markets at home, they also helped European nations and many of their corporations hold onto their colonial empires in the global South. In many instances, neocolonial relationships between erstwhile colonies, European nation-states, and corporate business interests replaced what had been the explicit colonial expropriation and domination of resources, political affairs, and economic development.

In casting isolationism aside, US-based corporations, banks, and the State itself stood poised to increasingly intervene and dominate global economic development. American corporations invested millions of dollars in overseas markets and production opportunities, greatly advantaged by the accelerating rate of technological innovation, the removal of many trade barriers, corporate-friendly revisions to the US tax code, and the liberty to pursue global markets without restrictions. Spurred by the prospect of the world as its market, many in government and private industry sought to further capitalize on global trade by creating an international trade organization.

After much debate about liberalizing global trade, promoting greater levels of employment, and addressing the economic realities of poorer nations, and with the goal of expanding trade and capitalizing on markets abroad, the US Congress approved a rather narrow-sighted measure that was designed to reduce trade barriers for American corporations. The General Agreement on Tariffs and Trade (GATT), established by signatory countries in 1948, developed regulations for trade among member States. GATT's chief work consisted of advancing protocols to reduce trade barriers for mostly US exports, though it failed to stipulate any measures for full employment. In the following decades, as European and Japanese corporations grew in size and activity, GATT has increasingly been used to monitor and coordinate trade among members, and as a lever to open new markets for corporate exports and production outlets for expanding multinational corporations.[14]

In addition to seeking to create business-friendly opportunities for manufacturing and industrial or electronic production in the global South, the military, paramilitary, and covert intelligence operations of primarily the US government, but also those of Britain and some European Union countries, have subverted many grassroots, populist, nationalist, or progressive social movements in several global South countries. In tandem with physical force, many global South elites have been cajoled and pressured by the terms and agreements proposed by international financial institutions (IFI) like the World Bank, the IMF, or the many regional and global-level lending institutions. Also at work to maintain neocolonial control over global South choices and decisions are government-to-government bilateral trade agreements; some of the terms of international aid; measures proposed by corporate banks; and financial, military, and food assistance dictated by US and European foreign policy.

The consequence of the above set of arrangements is that while some elites and a very small capitalist class in most global South states have, by and large, prospered in the decades since WWII, there remain staggering levels of poverty for the majority of the global South's population. Unequal trade agreements, debt servicing, and the ever-present urgency for foreign capital have led to the intensification of mineral resource extraction and agricultural production of export crops; a reversion to the monoculture of the past; petroleum-products-based cash-crop farming;[15] and export-driven agricultural, industrial, and electronic production. The price competitiveness demanded by the global North has meant that sweatshops and practically nonexistent labor protection laws continue to be the norm in many countries of the global South. In addition, very low corporate taxes and severe, often toxic, environmental pollution and degradation by corporate production sites define the inability of most global South countries to embark on a course of action that actually benefits the majority of their people.

With pro-democracy movements destabilized by coercion or physical suppression, and attempts at collective bargaining and union formation consistently undermined, neocolonialism has persistently defined the narrow limits of what is possible relative to aspirations of self-determination in many global South countries. Global wealth inequality is captured in the correlation of population and Gross National Product (GNP) represented in the table below:

Table 2.1
Global Wealth Inequality[16]

CONTINENT	POPULATION IN MILLIONS	PERCENTAGE OF WORLD POPULATION	GNP IN BILLIONS OF DOLLARS	PERCENTAGE OF WORLD GNP
Africa	794	13.1%	495.4	1.8%
Asia	3,672	60.6%	7,172.6	25.5%
Europe	727	12.0%	9,606.3	34.2%
North America	314	5.2%	8,933.6	31.8%
South America	519	8.6%	1,430.7	5.1%
Oceania	31	0.5%	442.4	1.6%
TOTAL	6,057	100%	28,801	100%

Sources of data: UN Population Division, www.un.org/esa/pop; World Bank, www.worldbank.org.

Policing the Debt Crisis

From the perspective of rapidly expanding finance and capital-intensive world capitalism, the development crisis of the past three decades can be encapsulated in the following few words: global South (or Third World) debt crisis.

By the 1970s, the pace of industrialization and economic development in global South economies could not possibly keep pace with the stages of finance/capital's industrial development, the search for export markets by corporations in the global North, and the movement of corporations abroad as multinational business entities.

Increasingly, global South countries could not continue to engage in an export-driven economy in order to earn foreign currency to pay their debt obligations, while at the same time undertaking to finance industrial development and stymie or delay social advancement domestically. Such uneasy choices and decisions flowed from the continuing neocolonial core/periphery relationship shared by even newly independent global South countries and some global North States and powerful multinational corporations (the majority of which were still based in the United States).

The oil crisis of the 1970s vastly deepened global South debt as oil prices multiplied three- to fourfold in one decade. Only oil-producing nations, and those nations with banking infrastructures that received revenues from oil profits and then lent those petrodollars were best able to ride out the oil crisis. Governments of poor countries with little or no oil of their own had to now borrow, often heavily, from Western banks to continue their work, which the IMF supported. Western banks and the IFIs seeking to earn interest on loans to global South governments lent freely, assuming that their clients would not default on their payments.

The borrowed money paid for the costs of energy, Western-style large-scale industrial projects, graft and corruption, military spending, and interest repayments. When many global South governments could not repay even the interest payments, let alone the principal, the resulting debacle was massive global debt. Although the global South was repaying global North governments, banks, and IFIs millions of dollars each month, such massive debt was and continues to be wholly untenable. The human cost of global South debt has been staggering: quality-of-life indicators consistently portray the enormous poverty and suffering endured by millions of women, men, and children in the global South as their economies often marginalize basic social services in favor of developing foreign-exchange-earning capabilities.

Since the 1980s, many global South countries have struggled under the weight of their mounting debts. These were initially most pronounced during the oil pricing crisis of the 1970s, at which point most global South debt was owed to banks. But in recent decades, multilateral debt owed to loan servicing institutions like the IMF and World Bank has become a major source of concern: multilateral debt occurs when the IFIs lend monies pooled from many countries, and when both institutions seek to avoid canceling any outstanding global South debts. However, by the 1990s, even with structural adjustment policies (SAP) in place, the IFIs either postponed or canceled some debt under the terms of the 1996 Heavily Indebted Poor Countries Initiative (HIPC).

The IMF and the World Bank now became not just financiers but debt police as well. According to the World Bank, global South debt now exceeds USD 2 trillion.

In an effort to tighten the reins of control over poor countries with outstanding debt, the IMF has imposed adjustment policies on debtor governments. Structural adjustment policies *require* governments with outstanding debt to curtail spending for social services (including health care and education);[17] remove State-sponsored food and cooking oil subsidies; privatize public electric and water utilities; remove trade tariffs that protect their own countries' businesses; devalue their own currency; cut real wages; increase interest rates and limit credit; increase exports of commodities desired in Western countries; establish favorable conditions and incentives for multinational corporations and foreign investors; increase military and police powers; suppress social dissent, social justice, and labor movements; and abolish trade unions.

While the exact terms of these policies vary depending on a country's circumstances and relationship with the IMF and the World Bank, SAPs influence the direction of development by prioritizing the use of the best soil to grow not food for hungry citizens but exportable, non-edible cash crops (coffee, cotton, soybeans, tobacco, sugar cane) that invariably replicate the dominant pattern of the past, namely, the creation of wealth for large landowners, and in industrializing economies for an industrial elite that is most often educated in the West. SAPs reinforce a development paradigm that abandons and blames the poor for their poverty, while relegating the vast majority of global South citizens to economic marginalization as savage poverty, epidemic-level disease, and the near absence of a viable human rights framework perpetuate much of the oppression of the past.

Many global South governments have been compelled to operate under an austere regime of adjustments that have benefited the largest landowners, a relatively small minority of business owners, and nationally-based companies, while exposing their countries to debilitating relationships with multinational corporations that are only interested in cheap, exploitable laborers who have no or little collective bargaining strength. SAPs came into force at the same time as multinational corporations became transnational in their scope and reach; by removing tariffs and barriers to foreign investment in many global South countries, SAPs have helped the ascent of global-scale transnational corporations.

The consequence of World Bank and IMF intervention in the domestic policies of sovereign States is that SAPs have altered the economies of global South nations away from self-sufficiency and toward a reliance on export production and trade. As envisioned, GATT, and more recently the World Trade Organization (WTO) and regional trade treaties, have worked assiduously and effectively at enabling the movement of money and goods across national boundaries in the global North and South. Not surprisingly, the goals of increasing economic growth, international trade, and foreign investment in the decades since WWII have been met, as all three sectors have expanded exponentially.[18]

The conditionality of IFI-imposed SAPs, the bilateral agreements and regional and global trade, the record levels of corporate and financial mergers in the global North, and the flight of corporate production to countries where they are guaranteed low-wage workers, little if any taxation, no environmental regulations, no collective bargaining rights, and consumer or human rights legislation that is adverse to corporate interests, have enabled transnational corporations to extend their control over workers, consumers, and, above all, national governments in the global South.

Essentially, at the same time, and connected with the neoliberal policy imperatives of the major IFIs in charge of the lending and investment intended to promote international economic development and wealth generation for corporations, the chasm between the rich and the poor has grown wider globally; personal alienation, violence, and corporate corruption now tear at the fabric of societies in ways that would have been unimaginable two decades ago. A system that seems to promote the notion that might is right is resulting in civilian populations reexposed to genocide and terrorism, the Earth's ecosystem rapidly deteriorating, and its millennia-old biological diversity rooted in natural evolution being directly threatened by the enclosure of knowledge. The pursuit of unrestrained economic expansion and waning corporate accountability for, and responsibility to, mutual engagement in participatory democracy have over the past two decades challenged the existence of the state and given rise to the particular phenomenon of economic globalization.

The Dominance of Economic Globalization

Globalization is a set of processes that reorder the spatial organization and flow of economic, political, and social activities within and across regions and nation-states.

Globalization exerts political impacts that affect nation-states; economic impacts that affect the markets, profits, and wages of global Northern and Southern nations and peoples; and social/cultural impacts that affect the human rights and human security of the vast majority of the people on the planet. Economic globalization utilizes and reflects the philosophical/ideological beliefs that serve as its driving force, that is, it is propelled by economic liberalization and the utilization of technological innovation.

Because the rise of economic and political globalization is central to understanding who really rules the world today, this section discusses the dominant theories, policies, and institutions that since the 1970s have eradicated barriers to the global movement of capital, technology, and goods and services (imports, exports, investments, tourism, media, and migrating labor) across national boundaries in the service of capitalism. At its root, economic globalization has proceeded from certain ideas and beliefs about the role of capital in generating economic growth; emerging in the last third of the twentieth century, "monetarism" (which replaced Keynesian economic policy)[19] and "neoliberalism" have been embraced as the new mantras by many prominent Western leaders.

Monetarism, so named by the University of Chicago Nobel laureate Milton Friedman, is a capitalist economic theory that posits that economic growth can be controlled by money supply. In a return to capitalism's fundamentals, monetarists contend that if the economy swings into overdrive, governments, through their central banks (the Federal Reserve, the Bundesbank, the Bank of England), can increase interest rates, thereby lowering the supply of money, which slows the economic engines and thus reduces inflation. Monetarists have also argued that governmental intervention in the social sector in the post-WWII Keynesian era adversely affected successful economic management, thereby suggesting that social democracy is bad for business.

Furthermore, monetarists contend that private enterprise and the private sector must be protected from governmental intervention and regulations, and kept free of public interference. This latter includes unions (who, monetarists suggest, interfere with the liberties of employers and workers); trade unions, in their thinking, prevent the market from working properly by resisting falling wages, pressing upon governments to regulate industry standards and working conditions, and subsidizing health and social security benefits. Ever preoccupied with the laws governing individual exchange, monetarists see the existence and influence of trade and consumer unions as impediments to the liberty of employers. Hence, popular sovereignty and social democratic governance (popular sovereignty's political tool), both arising from worker and voter influence in the creation of laws and political and bureaucratic regulation of many aspects of business conduct, weaken the liberty of employers.[20]

Participatory political decision making strengthens democracy (i.e., the effectiveness of trade union, consumer, environmental, civil, and human rights movements), which in monetarist thinking impinges on the liberty and rights of corporations. In the last two decades, neoliberal theory has been the driving ideological force that serves as the foundation for macro-economic policy and corporate and governmental/political decision making. Implicit in theory two decades ago, globalization is now a reality.

Steering economic globalization, the advocates of neoliberalism have increasingly targeted the State, particularly its governance and regulatory regimes; trade unions; consumer and environmental organizations; development agencies; and civil society institutions (particularly in the global North), while pursuing neocolonial relationships with many global Southern nations. As a result, outside of the constitutional democracies in the West, neoliberalism has served as the impetus for the austerity policies (SAPs) and the practices of conditionality held steadfastly in place by global IFIs. The pursuit of neoliberal economic globalization, including some efforts such as the National Poverty Reduction Strategies of the World Bank, has been represented as promoting economic growth, which neoliberal theorists maintain will end poverty and economic decline in global Southern countries.

Neoliberalism has emerged out of the monetarist position that free markets are hindered by the influence of popular sovereignty on the creation of governments and governance. The argument that markets should be free of all trade barriers and impediments is an important aspect of neoliberal thinking that encourages the shrinking of government taxation and regulation of business, the privatization of public industries, draconian cuts in government spending on social programs, increased foreign investment, export-focused growth, strict monetary policies on deficits and balance of payments, and competitive market capitalism, even if it impinges on private property and individual liberty. While advocating the free operation of the markets and opposing State intervention in the economy, neoliberalism also proposes that business and industry will self-regulate.

A significant aspect of neoliberalism is that at exactly the same time that business opposition to State intervention has emerged, the creation and effectiveness of global trade institutions has collapsed barriers to corporate expansion and foreign investment; eliminated protective trade tariffs; restricted safety and environmental policies and laws; lowered the cost of corporate manufacturing and production; weakened, collapsed, or prevented the organization and growth of trade unions and collective bargaining; and expanded the number of people impoverished by low wages, many of whom are forced to survive in the informal sector or in a marginal economic limbo.

The adage "consumerism and expansion: more and more is better" promoted a wholly unsustainable concept and dominated much of Western thinking in the decades accompanying the expansion of corporate production and financial investments. The neoliberal globalization engine has fed itself on the idea of a continually expanding economic output as the barometer of economic growth, as "for twenty years world trade grew faster than world output, primarily expressed as the growing volume of trade in manufactured goods between advanced industrial countries which were one another's best customers."[21]

Regrettably, in the view of many, neoliberal economic restructuring has not prioritized human social development or the sustainability of an economic growth model that does not overstress environmental space and ecosystem biodiversity. Indeed, many are alarmed that as a tool of globalization, the technologies that are genetically altering seeds, plants, animals, and humans will portend grave consequences for natural evolution because very often the precautionary "take care to do no harm" principle is ignored. Further, many are alarmed at the efforts of biotechnology to privatize and patent the genetic knowledge of plants, animals, and humans. This amounts to enclosure of all life and all knowledge that belongs to the public domain. There is something threatening to all sentient life in such a posture, and it is resisted because it appears capable of potentially placing all life in the hands of a few, thereby extinguishing human security. Genetically modified foods remain contentious issues for millions of farmers and consumers concerned about the survival of grains and cereals that have stood the test of time for centuries. And, high on the list of intellectual property issues, biopiracy expropriates the human, plant, and animal DNA of global South countries. All these efforts, if successful, would result in the further impoverishment of global South countries, thereby deepening their marginalization, diminishing capacity building and thus reducing their chances of competing in an unequal world. Many civil and human rights advocates and civil society practitioners now insist that neoliberalism has transferred much of the burden of human social development, particularly human security, onto civil society institutions. It has been grassroots social justice movements and progressive civil society advocates, now increasingly transnational in scope, that are challenging the growing unresponsiveness of States to citizen needs and deepening manifestations of corporate oligarchy, while also responding to human security concerns.

Evidence of corporate oligarchy now appears everywhere around us: today, powerful transnational corporations operate in a borderless world. IFIs and binding trade agreements shape world capitalism by dominating nation-states, and economically, politically, and culturally defining the marketplace itself. Often, large corporations operate across national boundaries with financial assets that exceed the GNP of most of the member States of the United Nations. According to a recent report, "of the world's top one hundred economies, based on a comparison of annual corporate sales and nations' GDPs, 51 were companies, 49 were countries. By 1999, GE was bigger than Venezuela, Citigroup exceeded Chile, and Boeing topped Peru. Between 1983 and 1999 the profits of the top 200 corporations grew by 362.4% while the number of workers they employed rose only by 14.4%."[22]

The creation of supranational economic regions and trade agreements have been the chief vehicle for establishing trading blocs, pursuing tariff reduction or removal, and borderless manufacturing, investment, and trade. In recent decades, business and corporate leaderships have used lobbying and the creation of nonelected governing bodies within Western nation-states, in addition to the GATT, to further their interests in promoting and expanding interregional free trade in goods and services. The opening of Chinese markets, the establishment of the European Common Market, the creation of the Organization for Economic Cooperation and Development (OECD), the North American Free Trade Agreement (NAFTA), Central American Free Trade Agreement (CAFTA), Multilateral Agreement on Investment (MAI), the tremendously powerful World Trade Organization (WTO), the Association of Southeast Asian Nations (ASEAN), and the European Roundtable of Industrialists (ERT) have increasingly placed decision-making powers in economic and political matters under the authority of transnational corporations.

It is the WTO, developed through a series of trade talks convened at the Uruguay Round (1986–94) and created in 1995, that now issues its own binding agreements and regulations that are often in conflict with, or sometimes totally preempt, nation-state laws and regulations. The WTO pursues the same goals and directives as the GATT, though it is more powerful in its reach, often crafting agreements, regulations, and protocols that void or negate nation-state regulatory regimes and citizen/consumer/environmental protection governance in the global South, as well as in the much more powerful global North. It is unarguable that government leaders and the leaderships of transnational corporations, who have given the WTO its charge and mandate, are using it to eliminate all barriers to the movement of capital, goods, and services.

The WTO is the new power broker, as many of its contracts, which it issues as binding signatory agreements — Agreement on Trade Related Aspects of Intellectual Property Rights (TRIPS), Agreement on Agriculture (AOA), Agreement on Trade Related Investment Measures (TRIMS), Agreement on Textiles and Clothing (ATC), etc. — shackle the leadership of nation-states to actions that eclipse protective and social welfare, and local, state, and national laws and regulations.

The WTO now rivals all existing governance mechanisms anywhere in the world. People the world over are concerned that the gains of the twentieth century — hard-won laws and regulations governing labor and collective bargaining; consumer, environmental, racial/ethnic, gender, disability, age, and sexual orientation rights; global human rights; and the freedom achieved by independence — are being swept away by the decline of the modern State apparatus. It is this shift from State to corporate governance that bodes ill for universal citizen rights, civil and human; from past evidence, there is little to suggest that transnational corporate governance will further human security, other than for an elite minority.[23]

Conclusion

Over the course of just two centuries, the formation of the modern State and participatory democracy ushered in a period of broader representation and transformation of social relations that were previously based on inequality. At the same time, accelerating economic development inevitably led to the creation and growth of corporations.

In an attempt to make the case for who really rules the world, much of this chapter's focus has rested on examining the historical choices and motivations that spurred their growth, and of the need, even in the early nineteenth century, of the State as a regulatory apparatus.

The economic imperatives of newly emergent nations in the twentieth century led to an unprecedented growth in the size and power of corporations. Transforming into multinational and transnational behemoths, these corporations have been aided by financial institutions that have outgrown their creators. While a minority elite push for further regressive neoliberal and monetarist policies, now is the time to summon the collective will to restore global rules for transparency and accountability that promote human security for the many, protect biodiversity and the survival of natural evolution, and promote sustainable development and an environmentally sound economic growth.

The global community is today at a critical juncture. Many of the ideas that have compelled domination, utilitarianism, and exploitation toward people and the Earth's resources must now be seriously challenged and put aside. As stakeholders in planetary matters, we are all investors in the present and the future. Markets must not be allowed to function without a regulatory apparatus, and modern, representative systems, which have so far served to protect and advance global citizen rights and human security, must be shored up and reaffirmed. Civil society must ensure, in its own interests, that unrepresentative IFIs and unrepresentative transnationals do not usurp the power to decide its fate and that of the planet. It can be done, and civil society has the means to do it, if the United Nations, numerous intergovernmental agencies, and nongovernmental organizations are strengthened in their positions as mediating, empowering institutions.[24]

Notes

1. The Atlantic economy was the economic system that developed as trade in people and materials linked Africa with the Americas and Western Europe. Also called the "triangular trade," the slave trade in captive Africans generated profits that were reinvested in Spain, Portugal, England, and also in the "New World," the Americas-based colonies. The raw materials and commodities produced in North, Central, and South America and the Caribbean were shipped to Western Europe, where the finished goods were then shipped primarily to Europe and the Americas.

2. Once conceived, the ideological rationale and behavior (both personal and institutional) of modern racism took on a life of its own, constantly advancing the belief that skin color accounted for the proposition that all that was positive and good about humanity and progress was white-skinned, whether European or American in character and substance.

3. Significantly, the birth of the modern State, especially the secular State in the United States and the "natural rights" doctrine of the Enlightenment, empowered an antislavery, abolitionist movement, as a result of which white women, some black women, and later some women of color organized a human and political rights movement based on gender and racial/ethnic gender rights.

4. In Haiti, a revolution of the enslaved destroyed slavery in 1804. In Mexico, a revolution by the oppressed indigenous population expelled the Spanish by 1825. The influence of the Enlightenment and its

empowerment of popular representation, and the distrust of the power of the church, prompted revolution in the Atlantic economy's English colonies in North America in 1776, and revolution in France in 1789 (which led to the creation of the modern secular State).

5. Only Liberia and Ethiopia were not parceled out. "By mid-century the British controlled all of India, which was ruled by a British viceroy; the Dutch assumed similar control over Indonesia, then known as the Netherlands East Indies; and the French seized Indochina. The entire continent of Africa, except for Ethiopia and Liberia, was divided up among the European powers after the Congress of Berlin in 1885. The British had almost all of eastern and southern Africa as well as large portions in the west; the French took over the areas north and south of the Sahara Desert; Germany took territories on the Atlantic coast and on the Indian Ocean; Portugal extended its coastal enclaves of Angola and Mozambique toward the interior; and Belgium obtained the Congo." See Bob Peterson, "Burning Books and Destroying Peoples: How the World Became Divided between Rich and Poor Countries," in *Rethinking Globalization: Teaching for Justice in an Unjust World,* ed. Bill Bigelow and Bob Peterson, 38–43 (Milwaukee: Rethinking Schools, 2002), 41.

6. Karl Marx, *Das Kapital,* vol. I, pt. 8, Chapter 31. (Washington, DC: Regnery Gateway, 2000). Also see Samir Amin, *Accumulation on a World Scale: A Critique of the Theory of Underdevelopment,* 2 vols. (New York: Monthly Review Press, 1974), for a brilliant exploration of the stages of capital accumulation on a global scale.

7. Large profits from chartered companies, based on the slave trade and later exclusive economic dominion under colonialism, were invested in numerous other capital-producing ventures and economic activities. The financial vehicles that made this possible were, among others: the Dutch East Indies Company, the English East India Company, the French East Indies Company, the Royal African Company, the Royal French Guinea Company, the Swedish African Company, the Havana Company, the Virginia Company, the Hudson Bay Company, the Dutch West Indies Company, the Danish West Indies Company, the French West Indies Company, and the South Sea Company. The Atlantic economy also greatly benefited from the training of enslaved African laborers as carpenters, blacksmiths, brickmasons, wheelwrights, etc. By using a plantation's own artisans and skilled laborers, large plantation owners in the American South were able to ensure increased profits for themselves. This early form of vertical integration, a business practice that became a hallmark of corporate profit-making in the nineteenth and twentieth centuries, well predated Andrew Carnegie's and Henry

Ford's successful utilization of vertical integration to reduce the cost of production inputs, while capturing as profits the savings from such production decisions.

8. Bill Bigelow and Bob Peterson, "Colonialism: The Building Blocks," in *Rethinking Globalization: Teaching for Justice in an Unjust World,* ed. Bill Bigelow and Bob Peterson, 35–37 (Milwaukee: Rethinking Schools, 2002), 35.

9. Adam Smith observed that corporations seemed to reinforce feudalistic ideas about power. Smith, Karl Marx (1818–1883), and others observed that people served corporations instead of corporations serving the people, and they noted that corporations very often ignored moral principles to the detriment of the marketplace and society.

10. Severyn T. Bruyn, *A Civil Economy: Transforming the Market in the Twenty-first Century* (Ann Arbor: University of Michigan Press, 2000), 4.

11. Corporations became persons under the law because they were accorded "natural rights," but with what was clearly a politically influenced mind-set, corporations were largely excused from presenting themselves as moral beings, that is, responsible and accountable entities. This is instructive, because in constitutional terms, individual agency required the perception of a moral balance between rights and responsibilities. For mergers, see Ralph L. Nelson, *Merger Movements in American Industry, 1895–1956* (New Brunswick, NJ: Princeton University Press, 1959).

12. In supporting welfare-state concessions in the economically hard times of the 1930s, President Franklin D. Roosevelt is quoted as saying, "The true conservative seeks to protect the system of private property and free enterprise by correcting such injustices and inequalities as arise from it." See William A. William, *Americans in a Changing World* (New York: Harper and Row, 1978), 263.

13. William Ashworth, *A Short History of the International Economy since 1850* (London: Longmans, Green, 1962).

14. For instance, when US consumer rights groups won litigations against US-based tobacco companies, the latter imposed upon the US government to pressure Asian, Latin American, and African countries to open their cigarette markets to American tobacco companies or deal with US sanctions. Essentially, the US government became a tool of the tobacco industry. Again, in 2003, in the face of European reluctance to accept US-grown genetically modified agricultural products, the agriculture and seed/chemical/fertilizer corporations pressured the US government to force African leaders to accept genetically modified organisms both in bilateral trade negotiations as well as in international aid arrangements. The State Department, the Agency for International

Development, the Agriculture Department, and the Food and Drug Administration are all being used to promote the economic interests of US-based corporations.

15. Petroleum-based cash-crop farming refers to the full range of agricultural inputs that are produced or derived from petroleum processing: fertilizers, pesticides, and herbicides; petroleum for tractors, combines, and other farming equipment; and engine oil to lubricate the equipment.

16. Bob Peterson, "Introduction to Inequality Activities," in *Rethinking Globalization: Teaching for Justice in an Unjust World,* ed. Bill Bigelow and Bob Peterson (Milwaukee: Rethinking Schools, 2002), 68.

17. According to the United Nations Development Report for the year 2000, Mali and Nigeria spent USD 88 million and USD 1.5 billion, respectively, servicing debt, while health care and education lagged pitifully behind. United Nations Development Programme, www.undp.org (accessed January 15, 2004).

18. "Aggregate data show the same general picture of rapid growth of US foreign investment. . . . The value of all US direct investment abroad stood at roughly $11 billion in 1950; by 1960 the total had risen to over $30 billion; and in 1970 the figure was over $70 billion." See A. Mac-Ewan, "World Capitalism and the Current Economic Crisis," in *The Capitalist System,* ed. Richard C. Edwards, Michael Reich, and Thomas E. Weisskopf (Englewood Cliffs, NJ: Prentice-Hall, 1986), 390–96.

19. John Maynard Keynes (1883–1946) was educated at Cambridge University in England, and his best-known works on economic issues are *The Treatise on Money* (1930) and *The General Theory of Employment, Interest and Money* (1936). He rose to prominence advocating macro-economic theory that focused on the interaction of large economic variables: the Gross National Product, business investment, government spending, and the scale of employment. Looking at business practices that contributed to economic recessions like the Great Depression of 1929–33, with its overproduction and large-scale unemployment, Keynes focused on stimulating the economy through government spending. Keynes discredited the belief that unemployment was voluntary, and argued that adjusting interest rates alone could not generate the equilibrium mechanism that was needed to reinvigorate the economy. Keynesian economics influenced President Roosevelt's decision to use social policy and public works as actions of the government designed to raise employment and national income levels. Hence, Keynesian economics accorded the State with a view of the big picture, an encompassing and long-term perspective on the economy and its relationship to overall social development. Later, in

1944, economist Keynes was crucial in the creation of the International Monetary Fund at the Bretton Woods conference.

20. For instance, monetarists insist that public industries are inefficient, and that taxes such as payroll taxes and employer contributions, which pay for the social benefits of the welfare State — toward education, health, pensions, unemployment, and benefits for the disabled, at-risk children, etc. — constitute a serious burden on employers.

21. J. M. Roberts, *Twentieth Century: The History of the World, 1901–2000* (New York: Viking, 1999), 611.

22. Sarah Anderson and John Cavanagh, "The Top 200: The Rise of Global Corporate Power," www.ips-dc.org/reports/top200text.htm (accessed January 15, 2004); see also, Aziz Choudry, "Neoliberal Globalization: Cancun and Beyond," *Action for Social and Ecological Action*, Green Paper no. 4, www.asej.org (accessed January 15, 2004); and Sarah Anderson, John Cavanagh, Thea Lee, and the Institute for Policy Studies, *Field Guide to the Global Economy* (New York: New Press, 2000).

23. See Jerry Mander and Edward Goldsmith, eds., *The Case against t he Global Economy* (San Francisco: Sierra Club Books, 1996); Bruyn, *A Civil Economy;* Civicus, *Civil Society at the Millennium* (West Hartford, CT: Kumarian Press, 1999); Susan George, "A Short History of Neoliberalism," paper presented at the conference on Economic Sovereignty in a Globalising World, March 24–26, 1999, www.globalpolicy.org/globaliz/econ/histneol.htm (accessed February 10, 2004); Michael Albert, "The Movements against Neoliberal Globalization from Seattle to Porto Alegre," *Z Magazine,* www.zmag.org/albertgreecetalk.htm (accessed February 10, 2004); Executive Summary, "Global Transformations," www.polity.co.uk/global/executiv.htm (accessed February 10, 2004); Wagaki Mwangi, "A Report on Forum 2000," *Montreal International Forum: Forum 2000* 2, no. 1 (2001): 6–10; Charles Abugre, "Global Conferences and Global Civil Society in the 1990s: New Arenas of Social Struggle or New Illusions?" *Montreal International Forum: Forum 2001* 3, no. 1 (2002): 10–17; Renu Mandhane and Alison Symington, "Facts and Issues: Ten Principles for Challenging Neoliberal Globalization," *Association for Women's Rights in Development* 6 (December 2003): 1–7; Friends of the Earth, "Towards Sustainable Economies: Challenging Neoliberal Economic Globalization," www.foe.co.uk/campaigns/sustainable_development/publications/trade (accessed February 15, 2004).

24. Srilatha Batliwala, "Grassroots Movements as Transnational Actors: Implications for Global Civil Society," *Voluntas* 13, no. 4 (2002): 393–410; Civicus, *Civil Society at the Millennium.*

CHAPTER THREE

Claiming Global Power: Transnational Civil Society and Global Governance

Kumi Naidoo

Introduction

The last decade of the twentieth century has seen an explosion of civic activism, much of it coordinated across national borders. International campaigns on issues ranging from famine to debt relief, from fair labor standards to peace and environmental protection, have drawn widespread attention. Ordinary citizens, using the power of the Internet and other more traditional forms of organizing, have joined together in transnational movements aimed at promoting social justice, sustainable development, and equitable forms of globalization.

This phenomenal growth of citizen action has been described in various ways. In 1997 Jessica Mathews, the president of the Carnegie Endowment for International Peace, wrote about a "power shift" in which governments and intergovernmental organizations were being forced to acknowledge that nongovernmental organizations (NGO) and other non-State actors had become real power brokers in various political, social, and economic processes.[1] Lester Salamon, the director of the Center for Civil Society Studies at Johns Hopkins University, called it a "global associational revolution," a process as significant to the twentieth and twenty-first centuries as the development of the nation-state system in the preceding two centuries.[2] In recent years, the idea of a global civil society has moved beyond the realm of academics and specialized practitioners and into the mainstream; in February 2003, following the massive, worldwide protests against the imminent invasion of Iraq, the *New York Times* editorial page hailed civil society as the world's "second superpower."[3]

This chapter examines one facet of this global superpower — that of transnational civil society (TCS) movements. It offers ways of defining and understanding these movements, and places them in a historical context. The chapter also considers the main opportunities and challenges facing transnational movements, with particular attention to the dynamics that prevail in a post–September 11 world. Finally, it will attempt to answer the following questions: What kind of impact have transnational movements had? And what are the internal and external factors that both encourage and limit their influence?

Civil Society and Transnational Civil Society Movements

What is civil society, what constitutes a transnational civil society movement, and how is it different from the idea of global civil society?

The tens of millions of ordinary citizens who took to the streets in February 2003 in opposition to war in Iraq; the grassroots action witnessed at the periodic meetings of the World Bank, the International Monetary Fund (IMF), the Group of Eight (G8), the European Union heads of State, and the World Trade Organization (WTO); and the vibrant, transnational organizing that takes place around the clock and across the globe through the Internet are all reflections of the phenomenon known as civil society. The concept of civil society is not a new one — in fact, it dates back hundreds of years — but it has been rediscovered over the past decade with the rise of citizen activism, which ushered in and strengthened the democratic revolutions of the late 1980s and early 1990s in former Communist countries and other parts of the world such as Latin America and South Africa.

Although the term is being used with increasing frequency, there is yet no universally accepted definition of civil society. In fact, civic activists in different parts of the world may each have a quite different understanding of what civil society is, whom it encompasses, and what the values are that underpin it. However, one simple way to think of civil society is in terms of the activities that are undertaken for the public good by groups or individuals in the space between the family, the State, and the market. Civil society therefore encompasses not only ordinary citizens exercising their right to protest and dissent but also a diverse array of groups and elements such as trade unions, foundations, faith-based and religious groups, nongovernmental organizations, community-based organizations, and social movements. In some countries and in the discourse that has emerged around civil society in the last two decades, political parties and business associations are sometimes seen to belong to civil society.

Civil society operates at multiple levels and on a wide variety of issues. Historically, much of the work of civil society organizations (CSO) has occurred at a micro level, where they are involved in providing important services to vulnerable communities in areas as diverse as health care, education and professional training, legal advice, humanitarian relief, women's empowerment, technical assistance in agriculture and environmental protection, and so on. Civil society groups are often among the first to enter into difficult postconflict situations to deliver needed assistance and to contribute to reconstruction efforts. In recent years, as this chapter explores, civil society groups have become increasingly involved in advocacy efforts and policy work, in an attempt to get at the root causes of social ills rather than simply addressing their visible symptoms on the ground.

While many civil society groups still focus their work on local and national problems, and are limited by geography to a particular context, over the past decade a growing number of civil society actors and organizations have internationalized their work. Some nonprofit organizations historically based in one country have expanded their efforts into other regions by setting up operational infrastructures in other countries, hiring local and international staff, and working side by side there with local governments and civil society groups. In other cases, civil society activists continue to work in their own countries, but have constructed loose networks of like-minded individuals and organizations in other parts of the world in order to share information and coordinate activities around a particular area of concern.

Although some believe that this recent growth of cross-border activism has successfully created a *global* civil society, it is more accurate to describe the current situation as one dominated by TCS movements, because no organizations can truly claim representation in all the countries of the world. For example, many otherwise global organizations do not have any significant representation in Indonesia, Japan, Russia, Brazil, Nigeria, or China, all countries with large populations. Rather, what we have witnessed is the emergence of loosely organized cross-border relationships between CSOs and actors who are interested in similar issues and who to a greater or lesser extent coordinate their activities "in more than one country to publicly influence social change."[4]

The Jubilee 2000 debt relief campaign and the International Campaign to Ban Landmines are prime examples of TCS activism. In both cases, CSOs in different regions, working at the national level, continued their own campaigning efforts under the auspices of their individual organizations while simultaneously coordinating their activities with counterparts in other areas of the world. Thus, TCS coalitions, in the sharing of information and streamlining key tactics, processes, and goals, allowed for participating groups and individuals to pursue broadly compatible and overlapping objectives while retaining sufficient autonomy in the design and implementation of their work.

Transnational movements are often difficult to grasp conceptually because it is not always evident how they are organized or led. This characterization is particularly true in the case of broad movements, such as the movement for global justice (often referred to as the antiglobalization movement), which are amorphous in shape, encompass a great diversity of actors, and are not always guided by a clear leader or leaders. Movements such as these are perhaps best understood as networks of loose, nonhierarchical structures that unite like-minded groups, while allowing room for a great variety of tactics, approaches, and goals.

These characteristics are simultaneously the greatest strength and greatest weakness of the TCS phenomenon; while transnational movements are powerful because of their diversity, flexibility, and dynamic creativity, they can also be accused of incoherence, fragmentation, and intellectual confusion.

Historical Evolution of Transnational Movements

Transnational organizing is not a result of globalization, as is sometimes suggested. During the last several decades, many such efforts grew in response to specific needs: the trade union moment, movements for political change, and faith-based movements as well as solidarity movements such as the antiapartheid movement have all predated the current wave of transnational initiatives. However, some of the features of globalization have certainly accelerated this process — for example, new communication and information technologies, and cheaper and more options for global travel.

Since the early 1990s, transnational movements have come into their own as a powerful political force as the number, capacity, scope, reach, and public profile of citizen groups has grown. It is difficult if not impossible to identify any clear point of origin for the evolution of transnational movements, since there have been a number of seminal events over the past fifteen years that can be seen as having initiated this phenomenon. However, the rise of transnational movements has clearly emerged as part of a broad-based effort to democratize political space and to overcome the democracy deficit exacerbated by the processes of globalization.

Globalization is simultaneously bringing the world's people closer together and reminding them of the distances that separate them. The instant connectivity characteristic of the age in terms of communications, trade, financial flows, and so on, has meant that globalization has succeeded in reducing barriers, loosening borders, and bringing people into closer and more direct contact with one another. Yet globalization's unevenness and harsh contradictions also remind us of the huge gaps that separate the world's people in terms of economic and social inequalities, the cultural divides and misconceptions that lead us to mistrust and misunderstand one another, and the growing number of transnational challenges that increasingly affect us all.

This connectivity between people in very different parts of the world is transpiring in a particular kind of social space — one that transcends territories and borders. Even as traditional, nation-state forms of governance have become increasingly ineffective — unable on their own to regulate scourges such as AIDS, drug trafficking, environmental degradation, terrorism, money laundering, and other problems that cannot be contained by national borders — attempts to address these challenges through intergovernmental structures at the supranational level are growing. The range of acronyms that describe these attempts are dizzying: UN, EU, WTO, MERCOSUR, OECD, OSCE, APEC, AU, G8, and so on. While some of these institutions may be household names, many of them are not — yet they wield great power over the lives of ordinary people around the world.

Herein lies the crux of the democracy deficit: decisions affecting the lives and well-being of people around the world increasingly lie with supranational institutions that are neither directly accountable to those people nor accessible to citizen voices. Decisions about trade rules, intellectual property rights, macroeconomic restructuring policies, privatization of vital services, and debt relief are made behind closed doors in ways that are largely perceived to be undemocratic. National governments continue to be key political actors, but they are no longer the primary locus of power. Decision making has fragmented over multiple levels and political venues; although State sovereignty is still very important, power in the decision-making process is increasingly located at the supranational level with regional institutions such as the EU or global institutions such as the United Nations or the WTO. Issues of trade, environment, aid, and debt, for example, are increasingly addressed multilaterally.

This present system of global governance lacks representative legitimacy; at the same time, democracy at the local and national levels is also in trouble, even in many established democracies. Surveys reveal declining levels of citizen trust in political institutions. In many democratic systems, form has largely overtaken the substance of democracy: elections may be held, but fewer and fewer people are choosing to vote, and the meaningful interaction between citizens and their elected representatives is minimal between election periods. Affiliation with traditional political parties is on the decline as the parties themselves are characterized by a lack of internal democracy, or a failure to address issues that citizens believe are important. The influence of moneyed interests in many political systems is also turning citizens away from traditional engagement in favor of new forms of participation.

Given these deficiencies in the democratic process and the inadequacy of State mechanisms to resolve them, it is understandable that increasing numbers of citizens have considered civil movements as a way to enhance public participation, consultation, transparency, and accountability in governance. At the same time that traditional political engagement is on the decline, civil society and peoples' movements are growing. What these groups and movements have come to represent for many people around the world are spaces where the voices of average citizens are heard in discussions on social, political, and economic justice. They are venues where people and groups who feel increasingly alienated from the prevailing political system can join together to explore alternative visions for a more ethical form of governance that works for the benefit of average people, rather than simply for the benefit of powerful interests. By globalizing these efforts, transnational movements are pushing for a new configuration of relations between society and the political system, attempting to reclaim the social and political space for citizens to shape the world in which they live.

One of the earliest major manifestations of TCS was the Earth Summit held in Rio de Janeiro in 1992, where thousands of environmental and community activists gathered at the parallel NGO forum. As Peter van Tuijl and Lisa Jordan have noted, TCS largely arose from the need for civil society groups to engage in more than one political arena, given the growing fragmentation of decision-making processes under globalization.[5] By the time of the Rio summit, it was clear to environmental CSOs that it was no longer adequate to lobby their national governments prior to the start of international summits. Important decisions on the global environmental framework would be made in Rio, largely behind closed doors where it would be difficult to track the process by which decisions were finally taken. Individual national delegations would play their roles for their own ends, and bargains (perhaps detrimental to weaker countries) would certainly be struck. Therefore, it was not only necessary for civil society groups to press their agendas at home but also in Rio, during the summit itself. This realization additionally provided an important networking opportunity for environmental groups from around the world, who came into direct contact with one another in Rio for the first time, laying the groundwork for future communication and cooperation. Since Rio, major UN summits have seen greater and greater participation by CSOs, which are gradually being incorporated into formal proceedings rather than being relegated to separate and parallel sessions.

The years since Rio witnessed a broadening and deepening of transnational movements, whether on single-issue matters such as debt relief and land mines or on more diffuse aims such as the global justice movement.[6] As the use of the Internet and new technologies grew during the early to mid-1990s, activists from around the globe got together at international meetings of activists and through specific campaigns such as the Zapatista liberation movement[7] during the 1990s; the many campaigns against the Multilateral Agreement on Investment (MAI), which began in 1995 and ended in 1998; and the meeting of the G8 heads of State in Birmingham, UK, in 1998, for which seventy thousand campaign activists gathered.[8]

By 1999, this nascent international web of civil society activists had strengthened considerably, and the momentous events now known as the Battle of Seattle occurred during the WTO's ministerial meeting in December 1999. Seattle represented the convergence of a broad spectrum of aims, championing, among others, environmental, economic, and fair-labor standards; indigenous peoples' issues; and human rights. Since Seattle, transnational movements have spread and consolidated, with activity now on every continent, and developments highlighted and examined annually at the World Social Forum (WSF). The WSF has emerged as a venue for planning, coordination, and information sharing, as well as a viable platform for developing alternative visions for social and economic transformation.

The past decade of activism has revealed that popular perceptions of democracy are changing; it is no longer seen as bounded by the confines of a nation-state. Rather, it has taken on a global character, where transnational communities of interest form, work together, and disband around areas of shared concern. While there are undoubtedly "uncivil" elements, such as those that espouse racism and religious intolerance, to global civil society, for the most part transnational movements are characterized by their nonhierarchical and democratic structures and by principles of horizontal accountability, collective responsibility, and concern for the common welfare. Perhaps as a result, CSOs in general enjoy high levels of trust among ordinary citizens — significantly higher than do government institutions or multinational businesses.[9]

Current Trends in Transnational Civil Society: Opportunities and Challenges

Transnational civil society movements are facing critical opportunities and important challenges at the start of the twenty-first century, particularly given the volatile and rapidly changing global context following the terrorist attacks on the United States in 2001 and the subsequent rise of US unilateralism in prosecuting a war on terror in Iraq.

The first major opportunity facing transnational movements is that of advocacy work on policy issues. As noted above, much of the credibility that civil society groups enjoy derives from the work that thousands of organizations have undertaken at the grassroots level in communities around the world. However, with the passage of time many civil society groups have recognized the need to rethink the well-known slogan "think globally, act locally." Experience has shown that, in and of itself, acting locally will not get to the root causes of many social and economic problems; if the real locus of power is global, there is a need to think locally and act globally as well. As a result, many civil society groups have become actively engaged in advocacy activity, campaigning, and policy work, linking the experience and perspectives gained on the ground with the larger policy debates that shape important aspects of the world in which we live.

The growing acceptance of civil society as a legitimate actor — not only in service delivery but also in policy formation — presents an important opportunity for those CSOs that want to help shape broader development agendas. This is eminently logical and extremely necessary; as the prime policy initiators, political leaders can thus avail themselves of the knowledge that civil society actors acquire from working directly with vulnerable communities. Engagement with citizen voices leads to more effective policies that better address the concerns of primary and secondary stakeholders, that integrate innovative ideas and knowledge from the local level, and that result in greater effect and ownership within communities.

Related to this, it is also critical that TCS continues to advocate for the priorities that are important to ordinary citizens around the world: sustainable development, health care and sanitation, gender equity, and the eradication of poverty. In the post–September 11 context, where militarization and neoliberal economic agendas have combined into a powerful transformative force, there is a real danger that the concerns of average people can be lost or ignored. Transnational movements have already proven their ability to shape agendas and to put issues of popular concern into the public realm, and this role will become even more critical in the future.

A second important opportunity for TCS, especially at this juncture, is that of public observer and champion for accountability at multiple levels. CSOs have a key role to play in monitoring the actions of governments, the media, public institutions, and private businesses insofar as their policies and practices affect the lives of ordinary citizens. Civil society groups have played leading supervisory roles on issues ranging from human rights abuses to environmental protection, from monitoring corruption to documenting progress on gender equity. In doing so, civil society has attempted to make transparent and to publicize the extent to which governments and other institutions are meeting (or falling short of) their own publicly pronounced goals and commitments. As such, civil society can serve as an additional, popular restraint on systems of power and influence.

A decade after its first great demonstration of solidarity in 1992, the opportunities open to civil society in terms of advocating for change, shaping public policy, and serving as a public monitor are tremendous. As civil society has matured, its credibility with the people it seeks to serve has mainly grown. Transnational alliances of citizens are coordinating their messages and actions with a greater degree of professionalism. These coordinated campaigns are starting to have real effect and impact, as has been seen in the defeat of the MAI because of the power it would afford to multinational corporations to the detriment of national governments;[10] the Jubilee campaign for debt relief, which sought to liberate the poorest countries from debilitating debt; the global anti–land mines campaign; and even in the global public opposition to the war in Iraq early in 2003.

However, there are also serious risks and challenges that accompany civil society's enhanced stature: as civil society has grown in prominence and influence as a public actor, it has attracted a new level of scrutiny. Coalescing now into a permanent entity, it is being forced to grapple with both external and internal challenges — from those who are seeking to make civil society stronger and more credible as well as from those who question its right to play certain roles.

The first challenge is the belief held by some critics that transnational citizen activism is essentially undemocratic — that it threatens to undermine the nation-state and formal democratic systems by short-circuiting established procedures for decision making. They argue that direct civil society involvement in many types of decision making is unnecessary and redundant because democratic societies are predicated upon representative institutions that provide channels through which citizens' concerns can be fed into decision-making processes. According to them, even the World Bank and the WTO are accessible to citizen voices through the national governments that constitute the institutions' membership and governing structures. The message seems to be that citizens should continue to operate within (what is perceived to be) the democratic channels that already exist, rather than trying to chart new territory and new forms of engagement through the collective strength of CSOs.

This reaction has been voiced with increasing vehemence since the terrorist attacks on the United States in 2001 and the start of the United States–led war on terror. New legislation passed in the United States and in a number of other countries threatens to limit the space for civic engagement, opening the door to expanded government surveillance and even prosecution of citizen activity suspected of being directly or indirectly linked to terrorism. In the four years following the September 11 attacks, the United States has been characterized by an atmosphere openly inhospitable to dissent and criticism. Nongovernmental organizations have also come under direct attack from conservative US thinkers and politicians, who are concerned that NGOs have come to wield undue influence on the political process and that organizations funded by the government should be more comprehensively guided by government policy.

The idea that civic activism threatens democracy rather than strengthens it is one that civil society activists vehemently reject. Their view is that an active, engaged citizenry is essential for a healthy, democratic society. Civic activism complements democratic practices, makes them more effective by drawing citizens more fully into public life, and provides a constant check on official accountability. Against the backdrop of a democracy deficit at the global level that was described earlier, citizen activism must be seen as an essential construct in the proper functioning of democracy, no matter from which position this process is viewed.

Perhaps the greatest challenge facing global civil society at the moment is the challenge of legitimacy, or what some have called "political responsibility."[11] As civil society organizations have grown more vocal, visible, and influential, an increasing number of governments, think tanks, and governance institutions have been questioning the right of the unelected few to be playing the role they have come to assume. It is frequently said or implied that civil society groups do not represent the views of anyone but themselves, and that if they are accountable at all it is usually upward to their funding superiors, rather than downward to those they purportedly serve. Whereas governments are accountable to electorates and derive their mandate through electoral processes, and businesses are accountable to their shareholders, from where do CSOs derive their mandates?

Even at the national, provincial, and local levels, this charge is sometimes difficult to respond to, since those CSOs engaged in advocacy work cannot always show that their positions derive from a significant body of opinion, that they have a mandate to pursue that work, and that they are not acting in the interests of a small number of individuals who hold strong views and are able to raise resources for that work. Needless to say, this challenge for transnational networks is even more acute given the complexities of language, culture, and diversity of membership.

The question of civil society legitimacy is intimately connected to that of representation:

> The emergence of global civil society brings with it inherent dangers of representation and legitimacy. It is sometimes a temptation for those within civil society — who acquire access to institutions of local, national and global governance — to assume the role of information and opinion gatekeepers. The righteousness of their cause — not necessarily driven by bad intentions — can sometimes lead them to ignore the realities of citizen struggles in everyday life. There is a real danger of disconnectedness between an emerging elite in civil society and the base units of civil society, where the voices of millions are expressed. Not only are elites in civil society talking to their counterparts in the state and the market, but sometimes have more in common (materially at the very least) with these other elites than they do with their own members whose interests they seek to advance. While there are no absolute solutions to this conundrum it is imperative that CSO leaders remind themselves constantly from whence they came and of the inherent contradictions that exist in the complicated interrelationships that constitute the web of global humanity.[12]

Another issue that transnational movements must confront is the extent to which civil society has come to broadly mirror the power and resource structures of globalization. Although this tendency is slowly changing, many Northern civil society groups still speak on behalf of Southern interests at conferences and other international events. Moreover, because they often provide funding or access to donors for Southern groups, they are seen as having a certain paternalistic influence on civil society activities in the South. Northern languages — primarily English, but also French and to a lesser extent Spanish — have become the lingua franca of TCS, effectively sidelining civil society activists and groups that cannot communicate in those dominant languages. Access to the Internet and new technologies is much more widespread in the North than it is in the South, or in transitioning countries. In this respect, TCS is still characterized by a considerable degree of internal domination between its Northern and Southern counterparts. Participation in TCS is also uneven, with certain countries and regions such as China, the former Soviet Union, and the Middle East significantly less involved in global activity than groups from other regions.

Conclusion

There is little question that TCS has had some clear successes in setting goals and agendas. It has also served notice that it intends to check the misuses of power and practice within the nation-state global governance systems. The limited number of very concrete victories following upon broad-based international campaigns cannot be overlooked. However, there are important internal questions that remain to be addressed if TCS is to be taken as a legitimate player in the global public sphere. Are the agendas being pursued derived in a meaningful and legitimate way through genuine efforts at dialogue with a broad spectrum of citizens? Are TCS movements resourced in transparent and accountable ways? Are transnational movements attempting to overcome technological and linguistic divides that threaten to marginalize authentic voices?

The answers to these questions are not readily available given the fluid moment in the growth of transnational civil society movements. What is clear, though, is that these questions are very much on the agenda and are being addressed already. For example, with regard to giving voice to citizens' aspirations and views, many advocacy campaigns and strategies are shaped by consultative processes with the affected constituencies of citizens. The issues of resourcing, transparency, and accountability are under constant review, with many organizations investing considerable energy in improving their internal and external accountability mechanisms; a recently formed informal network of leaders of several international advocacy NGOs has focused its attention on these very subjects. While the problems of the digital divide and linguistic barriers are acknowledged by most organizations as requiring urgent attention, in reality the constraints of cost have thus far militated against addressing these issues forcefully.

Since September 2001, skeptics of TCS have been quick to announce the demise of cross-border activism, particularly the public protests that have become associated with the antiglobalization movement. They suggest that the movement has lost any momentum it might have built up in the late 1990s, and that we now live in a new era in which the imperatives of the war on terror have defined the global discourse.

While transnational activism has been somewhat subdued since September 11, 2001, there have also been attempts at sharpening its focus and vision. The events since September 11 have clearly spelled out the dangers of a unilateralist world order, and have strengthened public support for the rule of law and multilateralism. In this atmosphere, the peace movement and the global justice movement have been reinvigorated. The annual World Social Forum has moved beyond its dynamic and fluid early days to emerge as a serious, thoughtful platform for transnational organizing and campaigning. The fact that tens of millions of ordinary citizens took to the streets in peaceful antiwar demonstrations in dozens of countries on February 15, 2003, suggests that TCS movements are, in fact, alive and well.

Notes

1. Jessica Mathews, "Power Shift," *Foreign Affairs* 76, no. 1 (1997): 50.

2. Lester M. Salamon, "The Rise of the Non-Profit Sector," *Foreign Affairs* 73, no. 4 (1994): 109.

3. Patrick E. Tyler, "Threats and Responses: A New Power in the Streets," *New York Times*, February 17, 2003.

4. Sanjeev Khagram, James V. Riker, and Kathryn Sikkink, eds., *Restructuring World Politics: Transnational Social Movements, Networks and Norms* (Minneapolis: University of Minnesota Press, 2002), 8.

5. Peter van Tuijl and Lisa Jordan, "Political Responsibility in Transnational NGO Advocacy," Bank Information Center, www.bicusa.org/bicusa/issues/misc_resources/138.php (accessed October 31, 2003).

6. The evolution of the antiglobalization movement is well summarized in Jose Seoane and Emilio Taddei's article "From Seattle to Porto Alegre: The Anti-Neoliberal Globalization Movement," *Current Sociology* 50, no. 1 (2002): 99–123.

7. The roots of this movement date back to the early sixteenth century. The name Zapatista comes from its founding member Emiliano Zapata, who started recruiting supporters around 1909.

8. The vision of the Jubilee 2000 debt relief campaign was a world in which the people of the poorest countries were liberated from the crushing burden of debt, and in which the future financial arrangements between rich and poor nations were founded on fairness, accountability, and transparency. The Birmingham protest was a major boost for the campaign; unfortunately, it received limited media coverage since the protest was devoid of violence.

9. Survey conducted by the Canadian firm Environics and launched at the World Economic and the World Social Forums in January 2003. See World Economic Forum, "Results on the Survey on Trust," www.weforum.org/site/homepublic.nsf/Content/Annual+Meeting+2003%5CResults+of+the+Survey+on+Trust#II (accessed October 31, 2003).

10. The text of the agreement made provision for an effective transfer of decision-making power to unaccountable, private, multinational corporations, thus obstructing the working of democracy by infringing

on the rights of elected governments to pass and apply laws in the interests of their peoples. Many feared that the passage of the MAI would consequently be accompanied by grave social and environmental consequences.

11. van Tuijl and Jordan, "Political Responsibility."

12. Rajesh Tandon and Kumi Naidoo, "Civil Society at the Millennium," in *Civil Society at the Millennium,* ed. Kumi Naidoo, 193–207 (West Hartford, CT: Kumarian Press, 1999), 199.

CHAPTER FOUR

The Rise of Civic Transnationalism

Sanjeev Khagram and Sarah Alvord

Introduction

This volume offers an introduction and overview, a primer, of what is being called transnational civil society. More specifically, the contributors examine the collective and/or coordinated advocacy of cross-border, progressive, largely voluntary, nonprofit, nongovernmental organizations (NGO) and social movements (SM) attempting to publicly influence social change in the recent or contemporary historical period.[1] This chapter provides a mapping of the current organizational forms and institutional arrangements of transnational civic society actors, including NGOs, non-State actors (NSA), and (nation)-state and inter-State actors (SA and ISA), as a way to locate transnational progressive civic advocacy actors (TPCA).[2] To best understand TPCAs, it is helpful to focus on their relations to these other actors as well as to the way they are embedded in the broader structures and dynamics of power and meaning. The mapping is done utilizing four comparative approaches: functional, political, modal motivation and power, and historical. These comparisons begin to generate far more complex and revealing accounts of the world than do the increasingly widespread use of tri-sectoral (government, business, and nonprofit) and tri-level (international, national, and local) images of the contemporary associational world.[3]

While there are many ways that academics, policymakers, and practitioners currently frame and define the activities of actors, organizations, and phenomena that cross boundaries and borders, it is important to clarify the meaning and use of "transnational" in this chapter and to briefly suggest why "transnational" is used rather than "global" or "international." At the same time, there is little agreement in the current literature on the definition of "transnationalism" and its units of analysis. The definition of "transnational" utilized in this chapter builds on the work of several others in the field and argues for a broad, inclusive view.[4] Transnational activities are phenomena and dynamics that cross, alter, transcend, and even transform borders and boundaries. By defining these activities transnationally, they stand in contrast to dominant types of ostensibly bounded and/or bordered units, actors, structures, and processes that are typically associated with notions of the local, regional, or global but especially the nation, State, nation-state, and nation-state system.

The term "transnational" is more apt to the context and arguments outlined in this chapter than the terms "global" or "international" for the following reasons. First, most cross-border or cross-boundary civic organizations and activities are probably not global in scope, orientation, or mind-set. Second, even those campaigns, organizations, networks, and/or movements that claim to be global do not involve or reach all corners of the planet. Third, the term "transnational" directs our attention to activities and organizational forms that may cross levels (local, national, regional, international, etc.) as well as *borders*.[5] "International" most often connotes a more "strict sense of involving nations — actually, states — as corporate actors" and many of the "linkages [and dynamics] in question are not 'international,' in the strict sense."[6] A similar explanation is needed for the use of "civic" in reference to organizations and activities that are often referred to as "civil society." "Civic" is used throughout this chapter to suggest an alternative and more inclusive terminology for what is traditionally known as civil society for two reasons: civil society has its roots in Western traditions which are often not inclusive of Southern scholarship, and civil society may also suggest an implication of civilization vis-à-vis barbaric or uncivil social phenomena.

Over the last decade and a half, much attention throughout the world has been focused on contemporary transnational *progressive* civic advocacy actors, activities, accomplishments, and challenges. By progressive we mean a broad political orientation toward promoting equitable, sustainable, peaceful, and culturally nurturing practices that advance human rights and social justice. While the breadth of attention is more recent, efforts of this kind became more visible and increasingly efficacious at least from the 1970s on. If a worldwide poll had been taken in the 1970s and then again in 2000 asking respondents whether they were familiar with an organization like Amnesty International or Greenpeace, it seems highly likely that the percentage of the global population aware of such groups would have grown dramatically in the intervening years. While perhaps less known in some contexts, organizations like the Third World Network or DAWN are now well recognized in the fields and issue areas in which they conduct their work. A World Social Forum or a transnational organization like CIVICUS, devoted to the protection and advancement of civic organizations and activities worldwide, did not seem imaginable prior to the end of the Cold War.

As evidence of the expansion of progressive civic advocacy that crosses borders, we can point to the remarkable growth of transnational nongovernmental advocacy organizations. For example, in 1953 there were 33 transnational nongovernmental organizations working on human rights. The number at least doubled each decade between 1973 and 1993, growing from 41 to 190. Similarly, in the areas of environment and development, the number of transnational nongovernmental organizations grew gradually between 1953 and 1973, but then dramatically increased. Between 1983 and 1993, advocacy groups promoting development grew by over 500 percent, while the number of transnational environmental organizations swelled immeasurably. The numbers of transnational coalitions, networks, and movements also grew dramatically during the latter part of the twentieth century.[7]

Simultaneously, progressive transnational civic advocacy became seemingly more efficacious during this period. Notable examples of their success are the campaigns and struggles to reform multilateral development banks (the "50 Years is Enough" network), to ban land mines (the International Campaign to Ban Landmines), to reduce the public debt of States in the Third World (the Jubilee 2000 campaign), to stigmatize and ultimately end corruption (led by Transparency International), to empower women (so visibly advanced at the Beijing Conference), to halt the construction of destructively large infrastructure projects (particularly large dams), and so on. Less well known are efforts to advance the social protection of women workers in the informal sector (led by Women in the Informal Economy Globalizing and Organizing [WIEGO]), to achieve the right of prior informed consent for indigenous peoples to control incursions into their territories (Right to Prior Informed Consent), and to ensure that all information about activities affecting communities be made public through the adoption of right-to-know laws or policies (Right to Information). Indeed, what some of the chapters in this volume do is highlight the important self-organized progressive transnational civic advocacy of various communities at the grassroots that far too often get overlooked (such as Shackdwellers International or Via Campesina).[8]

The goal of this chapter, in a synoptic but hopefully illuminating way, is to locate contemporary progressive transnational civic advocacy relative to:

- *Historical analogues and antecedents* of various kinds that cross borders and boundaries, as well as the institutional arrangements, political-economic systems, and social fields that they shaped and were shaped by in the contemporary as well as previous historical time periods.

- *Service-oriented NGOs* that cross borders and boundaries, such as groups that contribute to humanitarian relief, conflict prevention/negotiation, and peace-making/building work as well as groups that contribute to reconstruction and development efforts of various kinds.

- *Politically conservative NGOs and SMs* that cross borders and boundaries and publicly advocate for social change (often the social status quo), utilizing types of tactics and relying on forms of power that are quite similar to those of their progressive (whether transformative or reformist in orientation) counterparts, such as mass mobilization, representation, moral persuasion, expertise, and so on.

- *Non-State actors* of various kinds that cross borders and boundaries, such as philanthropies, professional associations (scientific, technical, or otherwise), private-sector companies and business organizations, ethnic communities/diasporas, religious groups, organized criminals, and "terrorists" whose modal motivations (causal ideas, profit, salvation, liberation, etc.) and/or modal strategies (violent or nonviolent) are quite different from the members of contemporary progressive civic transnationalism.

- *(Nation)-State actors and formal inter-State actors* of various kinds, such as international organizations that have global or regional mandates as well as novel transnational policy or action networks that are governmental or cross-sectoral in membership, that cross borders and boundaries.

The next five sections of this chapter elaborate on each of these claims by offering a comparative perspective. The new meaning gained from these comparative perspectives, in turn, may suggest that we need to rethink conventional wisdom on the subjects at hand and may require an inversion of contemporary understandings of governance, power, and authority.

A Comparative Historical Perspective

Before addressing the contemporary context of TPCAs, it is important to consider the historical contexts of these activities. The focus on actors that cross borders and boundaries, even if it were comprehensive, might be misleading if it were viewed as a purely contemporary phenomenon. Such transnational non-State actors have clear transborder and transboundary historical analogues and antecedents, ones that often predate contemporary (nation)-states; thus, the terms "non-State" and "transnational" are themselves partly misnomers. Moreover, the broader institutional arrangements, political-economic systems, and social fields, which the NSAs, ISAs, and SAs (or state-like actors) have shaped and been shaped by in the contemporary as well as in previous historical time periods, are often underemphasized.

These historical precursors and social structures include, among others, transcontinental capitalism, imperialism and colonialism, religious formations, antislavery and workers' rights movements, illegal pirating networks, and scientific discourse. Indeed, contemporary States and the State-system itself are relatively recent creations in comparison to these older transnational actors, structures, and processes. In other words, the world has always been in some sense transnational — even States, nations, nation-states, and the sovereign nation-state system have been transnationally constituted and shaped over time and space.[9] For example, approximately 130 territorially demarcated political units or countries, of which only 55 were formally governed by sovereign central States, including 14 empires, existed as of 1900. The rest — more than 65 percent of the total number of political units — were colonies or protectorates. Taking a retrospective view, 112 of the 192 countries recognized as of the year 2000 could be classified as having been formed within the last one hundred years (and a large proportion in the last fifty years) under colonial or imperial domination, and thus relative newcomers in the world's history. Looking at transnational phenomena and dynamics across time and space serves to ground the following contemporary mapping exercise. The range of actors with different motivations, capacities, strategies, and so on, that cross borders and boundaries (or sometimes attempt to maintain, enforce, and create them) in various ways are discussed in the next several sections. Combining historical context with the following mapping exercise, one can construct various and layered functional, political, sectoral, and institutional architectures of the current world. These maps illuminate transnational distributions and interactions of power and meaning among these actors.

A Comparative Functional Perspective

The first distinction that should be kept in mind when comparing TPCA groups with other actors is a functional one. Service-oriented NGOs that cross borders and boundaries, such as groups that contribute to humanitarian relief, conflict prevention/negotiation, and peace-making/building work, as well as groups that contribute to reconstruction and development efforts of various kinds, have expanded, and become more active and more visible during the recent historical period.[10] These groups and activities are prime candidates for being included in any notion of transnational civil or civic society.

These transnational service civic groups do not directly advocate for broad changes in policies, institutions, or social change. Rather, they often focus on providing material forms of support directly to recipient individuals or communities in the form of cash or loans, vaccines, literacy programs, job training, technology, infrastructure, and so on. Indeed, they often not only espouse but pride themselves in claiming positions of political neutrality, which is a very distinct stance from that of their advocacy counterparts. However, both are committed to nonviolent activities and work — a crucial and fundamental similarity that should not be overlooked.

Notable examples of transnational civic service groups are such organizations as the International Red Cross or Plan International. Less visible, but much greater in number, are the countless groups, often very ad hoc and informal, that are inspired to become involved in such activities as disaster relief or capacity building of various kinds (human, organizational, etc.). These groups, such as the *turuq* (Sufi networks) in West Africa or the Ismailis (followers of the Aga Khan) around the world, are usually motivated by cultural connections or religious beliefs but focus their energies on providing material and other forms of support to people and communities that may or may not be located in their immediate territorial space.

Nevertheless, the difference between transnational progressive civic advocacy as opposed to service groups should not be overstated. As mentioned above, both sets utilize nonviolent means in their work. Both sets are by and large motivated by principled beliefs and moral commitments. However, by providing material support of particular kinds, transnational civic service groups are implicitly acting politically even though they are not formally engaged in political advocacy. The choice to contribute to child survival by providing medicines as opposed to educating mothers is a political one, whether the political basis of the decision is made explicit or not. The deployment of funds, time, skills, and other resources toward building houses for shack dwellers rather than marshaling them to advocate for changes in public policy and governmental practices is certainly a politically motivated choice.

The choices and activities of transnational civic service groups also have a political impact, whether intended or not. This becomes all the more evident when humanitarian groups attempt to work in conflict situations. It is almost impossible to feign ignorance of political implications or espouse political neutrality when, for example, the act of providing food to displaced victims of war also provides sustenance to one or more of the militias involved in the armed struggle. Similarly, if supporting reconstruction efforts implicitly or explicitly justifies foreign military occupation, then a claim to political neutrality is highly suspect. Indeed, the separation between transnational civic service and advocacy groups has become increasingly blurred as service groups have recognized that their goals are often not being achieved due to these political realities. They have consequently added or even begun to prioritize lobbying and/or mobilizing work in their repertoires.

A Comparative Political Perspective

A second source of variation that must be kept in mind is a political one. Contemporary transnational progressive civic advocacy should be distinguished from politically conservative groups and activities that cross borders and boundaries and publicly advocate for social change. The latter promote conservative or traditionalist agendas of various kinds (a social status quo, for example), but utilize types of tactics and rely on forms of power that are quite similar to those of their progressive counterparts, such as mass mobilization, representation, moral persuasion, and expertise.

A prominent example of conservative transnational civic advocacy is the groups and activities that constitute the Christian right. This advocacy movement has become more consolidated and powerful over the years, and has further formalized a set of strategies such as those that emerged from the second World Congress of Families held in Geneva in 1999. At the heart of the Christian right's agenda is a globally conceived project for spreading a particular notion of family values and religious behavior while opposing a range of progressive causes (women's rights, population control, sexual and reproductive rights, gay and lesbian rights, etc.) that are seen as opposed to this political vision. They have become a more organized force at the United Nations and in other international arenas, and have forged coalitions from time to time with other conservative groups that are not consistently a part of their networks.[11]

The Christian right, while a visible example, is by no means the only conservative transnational civic advocacy group that exists. So that scholars, policymakers, and the broader public can better understand the motivations, reach, and agendas of these groups, much more public and intellectual attention must be focused on the growth, increasing power, and visibility of these actors. Moreover, even transnational progressive civic advocacy groups are far from politically homogenous, as can be seen from the gamut of critical perspectives with respect to corporate-driven or neoliberal economic globalization. These range from the large numbers of transnational civic advocacy groups who are reformist in orientation, advocating a more ethical approach to globalization, to the many transformationalists who mobilize against economic globalization altogether. Similarly, there are any number of other political positions being advocated that can arguably be considered as progressive. Comparative political perspectives such as these are likely to result in a more finely grained analysis and consequently a more effectively directed praxis.

A Comparative Non-State-Actor's Perspective

Whatever their functional and political orientations, voluntary NGOs and SMs are only some of the non-State actors of various kinds that cross borders and boundaries.[12] Such transnational groups include philanthropies, professional organizations (scientific, technical, or otherwise), private-sector companies and business associations, ethnic communities/diasporas, religious groups, and organized criminals and terrorists, among many others. Many of these groups have become as visible and effective, if not more so, as those that engage in transnational progressive civic advocacy.

One way of distinguishing these various transnationals is to identify their modal motivations. For example, transnational civic groups of various kinds (whether service- or advocacy-oriented) are driven by principled ideas and moral beliefs, professional associations by causal ideas and scientific/technical knowledge, businesses by earnings and profits, diasporas by cultural connections, and religious groups by worldviews and notions of salvation. While such explications are useful as an entry point, it is clear that each of these types of groups is motivated by multiple goals: business associations, for example, do much more than attempt to increase the competitiveness and profitability of their members. The moral beliefs of transnational civic groups are often part of a larger worldview and understanding. All of these groups need to sustain themselves financially (or mobilize material resources of some kind) even if they may not be driven to maximize profit.

The various transnational groups can also be distinguished by the predominant kinds of power capabilities and partly related types of strategies they adopt. It is often claimed, for example, that the power of transnational civic advocacy groups is linked to their ability to deploy information, lobby officials, alter public opinion, and/or mobilize mass protest. Corporations, on the other hand, can utilize their superior financial resources to advance their goals and interests (without necessarily using any of these other strategies, although they often do employ multiple tactics). But firms are also often members of larger business associations that attempt to publicly and nonviolently advocate for social change, such as the World Business Council for Sustainable Development, or the International Chambers of Commerce. And leveraging funds are what philanthropies (which are nonprofit and nongovernmental), particularly large ones, do well; in this sense, a large foundation would seem to be more akin to a large transnational corporation than a grassroots transnational social movement. Transnational religious and identity-based communities of various kinds can, and often do, deploy both edicts and money — as, for example, the Catholic Church. Finally, the mass-communication capabilities of the press and media in a world powered by images cannot be disregarded. For example, the changing relations between CNN and Al Jazeera vividly demonstrate these powerful influences as they depict the dynamic situation in the Middle East.

Of course, labor organizations and various mobilizations by workers that cross borders and boundaries, such as the International Public Service Union, or the growing number of joint campaigns by the trade unions of Brazil, South Africa, and South Korea, are potentially crucial elements (or allies) of contemporary progressive transnational civic advocacy. These transnational worker groups are certainly motivated by complex combinations of material interests (higher wages, better benefits, etc.) and principled beliefs (freedom to organize, universal health care, etc.). They can, and do, wield a range of power capabilities, from mass organization and mobilization to financial resources deployed through political contributions, pension funds, and media campaigning. While much has been written about the declining strength of unions and worker organizations, neither their historical global significance nor their transnational political potential should be deemphasized.[13]

Transnational professional associations concerned with scientific and technical knowledge are even more underappreciated in any analysis of this topic.[14] Indeed, by some estimates, these groups constitute the largest proportion of cross-border nonprofit, nongovernmental organizations in the world. Most of these, like the International Association of Impact Assessment or the International Electro-Technical Commission, keep a low profile, while others, like the International Standards Organization or International Hydropower Association, are more visible. But their power, which derives from claims to expertise in a world in which science and technical knowledge are held in high esteem, makes these groups critical players in any transnational civil society.

Of course, the most prominent, although not numerically the largest, of contemporary cross-border groups are those identified as transnational terrorist networks. These groups are distinguished from contemporary transnational progressive civic advocates by their use (or threat of use) of physically violent means to achieve their ends.[15] Other clandestine transnational actors (CTA), such as drug traffickers, mafias, human smugglers, and other organized criminals of various kinds, often utilize violence and generally illicit means as well.[16]

Yet CTAs can be driven by very similar motivations as their nonviolent, public, and generally lawful opposites. Transnational mafias are motivated first and foremost by profit, similar to transnational corporations. Indeed, corruption is a criminal activity utilized by many individuals in each of these ostensibly different organizational forms. Transnational terrorists are also driven by principled ideas and worldviews analogous to the most ideological of transnational social or religious movements. They are also able to provide organizational spaces that attract members seeking political liberation and individual salvation. The dramatic growth of cross-border, profit-motivated, private protection firms, all ostensibly legal, complicates the situation all the more.[17]

Before concluding this section, it is necessary to direct attention to one very important grouping that is often linked with virtually every other category of transnational actors. Generally called diasporas, and more recently understood as transnational communities (more than half the people of Guyana live outside the country, for example), transnational migrants are involved in various types of cross-boundary and cross-border organizations and activities, including hometown associations, advocacy- or service-oriented nonprofit activities, transnational business (more than half the direct foreign investment in China comes from overseas Chinese),[18] political parties, liberation movements, as well as transnational criminal networks. While some of these groups pursue the creation of nation-states for their ethnic communities through long-distance nationalism[19] (consider the trans-territorial supporters of the Irish Republican Army), most are not so Statist in their orientation that they seek to create new nation-states and secede from the countries in which they reside. Diasporas, therefore, most certainly deserve to be included in any notion of transnational civil society, to the extent that one exists.

A Comparative Actor's Perspective

One goal of this chapter is to highlight those transnational groups and activities that are often not given enough attention in discussions of transnational civil society. For example, not much space has been devoted to transnational corporations, even though the power of these actors is unquestionable. However, not all transnational corporations are the same, and the kinds of distinctions (functional, political, etc.) offered in this chapter (as well as many others) can be utilized to disaggregate the transnational actors in this category as well. BP should certainly be distinguished from Exxon Mobil based on its quite different political orientation toward global climate change, even though both defend their individual actions on the principle of maximizing shareholder value or profits.

The focus of this chapter thus far should not be read, however, as a claim that State actors or formal inter-State actors of various kinds, such as international organizations that have global or regional mandates, are not important or are fading away. Rather, one of the objectives thus far has been to delineate and map the extraordinary range of actors that cross borders and boundaries in relation to what has been identified as contemporary transnational progressive civic advocacy, and one that might be included in our notions of transnational civil society.

State actions, policies, and structures certainly condition the environment in which non-State transnational actors are organized and act.[20] For example, there is no shortage of acronyms for the innumerable groups that are backed directly by the State (GONGO — government-organized nongovernmental organizations), often only to undermine more independent actors. The World Movement on Democracy is one such GONGO, sponsored by various agencies (such as the National Endowment for Democracy), which is funded by the US government. State resources are often provided to these non-State actors through contracts, subsidies, tax-relief measures, and various other mechanisms for the conduct of their activities.

Equally, States can limit the possibility for transnational non-State organizations and activities to exist, as in the case of the governments of China, Japan, and Korea, particularly from the 1950s through the 1970s, allowing groups inspired by transnational religions to operate only if they severed all foreign ties, communicated outside the country only through State channels, and accepted State control over finances.[21] More recently, these policies are slowly being relaxed. States can attempt to control and police their territorial borders and national cultural boundaries in other ways as well: the increasing control over Islamic charities in many countries of Western Europe after September 11, 2001, offers a clear example of this form of potentially rights-limiting State behavior.

In the contemporary world, however, the nature of States is not homogenous; we have everything from more legitimated States with a greater monopoly over the use of violence within their territories (Sweden or Brazil, for example); highly contested States where military capabilities are distributed amongst various contenders for control (Sudan or Afghanistan); super-States (like China); administratively failing States (Somalia or Haiti); wide-open and highly porous States (like Lesotho);

and physically and culturally sealed States (consider Bhutan). There is no singular type of State in the world, and States change dramatically over time. States also die — most arrestingly, the disintegration of the Soviet Union after the fall of the Berlin Wall.

States are also transnational actors in themselves, to a greater or lesser degree: they not only interact with each other but also engage with non-State transnational actors as well as non-State actors in the territories of other States. In this regard, it cannot be denied that the government of the United States is *the* transnational State actor that has a virtual (although not complete) global reach. But within geographical regions, many States are dominant transnational actors (Japan, India, South Africa, Brazil, etc.).

But to speak of any current, territorially recognized State being a singular nation, even as an "imagined community," seems a stretch.[22] Finding a true nation-state seems even more phantasmal. Whether because of the nonintegration of extant ethnic groups, the cyclic movements of peoples, the emergence of entirely new identities and communities, or the lack of fixity and the continual flux of territorial borders and cultural boundaries, nations that are coterminous with formally recognized States do not exist anywhere.[23]

The various transnational actors identified previously are certainly shaped by this variability across States, and often strategically adapt to the type of State or States they engage. On the other hand, various transnational actors also shape the environment, nature, structures, capabilities, and actions of States (consider our category of transnational technical and professional associations). These relationships are sometimes competitive but also potentially cooperative, or simply separate and parallel; they are certainly dynamic. Consider, for example, the transnational Ismaili community, whose members are located in virtually every part of the globe and yet willingly pay "taxes" to the Aga Khan, receiving benefits in return, while still being law-abiding citizens of the countries in which they reside. In contrast, consider Al-Qaeda, which forged a cooperative relationship with the Taliban government of Afghanistan in order to wage a war against the government of the United States.

We also now have numerous ISAs that can be more or less relatively autonomous from the States that constitute them, from the International Telegraph Union that was founded in 1865 to the United Nations. These organizations vary widely in terms of their categories and levels of resources and capacities as well as in their motivations. They are also more or less open to, and engage with, transnational non-State actors of various kinds. For example, the United Nations is a sprawling organizational entity that is arguably a hybrid between a multilateral agency and a transnational organization. Its Intergovernmental Panel on Climate Change is ostensibly organized around government-appointed representatives, but these delegates are also members, and in some sense trustees, of transnational scientific and technical communities.

It has been forcefully argued lately that what holds the world together and offers the greatest potential for planetary stability are the different types of transnational action, policy, or authority networks. In the transgovernmental version of this argument, horizontal and vertical networks of government officials and agents (central bankers, judges, mayors, legislators, ministers, generals, etc.) from organizationally disaggregated States share information, increase capacity, and coordinate activity to manage global affairs.[24] In the multi-stakeholder version, waxing and waning networks of relevant actors from across sectors (public governmental, private business, and private nonprofit/nongovernmental in particular, but also others) join together in loose institutional arrangements to address challenges and seize opportunities in different domains of cross-border and cross-boundary social life. Policy or action networks such as the Global Reporting Initiative or the World Commission on Dams assemble groups from across multiple sectors, and are themselves potentially linked together to reconstitute global governance. States and inter-State organizations are still important, but to varying degrees and not always predominantly.[25]

Conclusion

In sum, when we consider the role of contemporary progressive transnational civic advocacy in governance and social life more broadly, we must take into serious and systematic account both the full range of transnational relations of power and meaning that exist currently, as well as the historical structures and dynamics from which they have emerged. By doing this, we might infer the following conclusions that: (1) transnational civil or civic society (as well as uncivil society) is not simply a recent addition to the world of nation-states or global capitalism (think of transnational religions or the antislavery movement); (2) contemporary transnational civil society includes a far greater range of actors, formations, functions, political orientations, motivations, and capacities than is conventionally assumed; (3) there are more similarities and dissimilarities between these various actors and categories than is conventionally assumed (for instance, large, international, nongovernmental organizations often have a very similar organizational structure and procedure to those of the Fortune 500 multinational corporations); (4) the range of challenges and opportunities to transnational progressive civic advocacy groups is far greater than is often assumed (it is not just States, international organizations, or multinational corporations that they must engage but also transnational religions, diasporas, and professional associations); and (5) future possibilities for governance and associational life — both negative and positive — are far more plural than most contemporary progressive civic advocacy groups often recognize (including everything from a world of warring parochialisms to a world State). In particular, it would make great sense to consider a multi-stakeholder, cross-sectoral, and trans-scale vision for future global governance that supersedes the ultimately unappealing binary opposition between unilateralism and multilateralism. Contemporary progressive civic advocacy can do much to help create such a future.

Notes

1. For example, Kumi Naidoo's and the empirical chapters rightfully stick to the general purpose of the volume and the mandate that they were given, but some chapters in the book certainly address some of the themes I highlight here.

2. By "State" I mean, depending on the context, an actor or a set of institutions, although it is better to argue that governments and government officials are the actors who deploy State authority. Following Alfred Stepan and others, the State as a set of institutions is generally understood as "the continuous administrative, legal, bureaucratic, and coercive systems that attempt not only to structure relationships between civil society and public authority in a polity but also to structure many crucial relationships within civil society as well." See Alfred Stepan, *The State and Society: Peru in Comparative Perspective* (Princeton, NJ: Princeton University Press, 1978). See also Atul Kohli, ed., *The State and Development in the Third World* (Princeton, NJ: Princeton University Press, 1986); and Donald Rothchild and Naomi Chazan, *State and Society in Africa* (Boulder, CO: Westview, 1988).

3. For an explication of such an approach, see Joseph S. Nye Jr. and John D. Donahue, eds., *Governance in a Globalizing World* (Washington, DC: Brookings Institution Press, 2000).

4. This definition of transnationalism is built on one that Sanjeev Khagram and Peggy Levitt espouse in "Towards a Sociology of Transnationalism and a Transnational Sociology," working paper no. 24, Hauser Center for Nonprofit Organizations Working Paper Series, Harvard University, Cambridge, MA, April 2004). The definition also incorporates the work of several others writing about transnationalism, including Alejandro Portes, Luis Guarnizo, and Patricia Landolt, "Introduction: Pit-

falls and Promise of an Emergent Research Field," *Ethnic and Racial Studies* 22, no. 2 (1999): 217–37; Rainer Baubock, "Towards a Political Theory of Migrant Transnationalism," *International Migration Review* 37 (Fall 2003): 700–23; Michael Kearney, "The Local and the Global: The Anthropology of Globalization and Transnationalism," *Annual Review of Anthropology* 24 (1995): 547–65; and Nina Glick Schiller, "Transmigrants and Nation-States: Something Old and Something New in the U.S. Immigrant Experience," in *The Handbook of International Migration,* ed. Charles Hirschman, Philip Kasinitz, and Josh DeWind (New York: Russell Sage Foundation, 1999): 94–119.

5. At a higher level of abstraction, we can identify transnational civic activity that is entirely local in territorial manifestation but crosses cultural borders and boundaries.

6. Ulf Hannerz, *Transnational Connections: Culture, People, Places* (London: Routledge, 1996): 6.

7. For an explanation and elaboration of these trends and patterns, see Sanjeev Khagram, James V. Riker, and Kathryn Sikkink, eds., *Restructuring World Politics: Transnational Social Movements, Networks and Norms* (Minneapolis: University of Minnesota Press, 2002).

8. For a review of some of the key texts on progressive civic transnational advocacy, see Richard Price, "Transnational Civil Society and Advocacy in World Politics," *World Politics* 55, no. 4 (2003): 579–606.

9. Even in a volume that made perhaps one of the strongest cases for focusing on the central importance of States, the editors clearly and unequivocally acknowledged that States are embedded and thus shaped by different types of transnational political, economic, social, and cultural structures. See Peter Evans, Dietrich Rueschemeyer, and Theda Skocpol, eds., *Bringing the State Back In: New Perspectives on the State as Institution and Social Actor* (Cambridge: Cambridge University Press, 1985).

10. For a good analysis of several Northern-based but transnational relief and development service organizations and how they are increasingly conducting advocacy work, see Marc Lindenberg and Coralie Bryant, *Going Global: Transforming Relief and Development NGOs* (Bloomfield, CT: Kumarian Press, 2001).

11. See Doris Buss and Didi Herman, *Globalizing Family Values: The Christian Right in International Politics* (Minneapolis: University of Minnesota Press, 2003). To be clear, there are multiple "Christian rights" and there are many "right-wing" transnational civic groups that are not explicitly Christian and vice versa (a prominent example of Christian "left-wing" transnationalism is liberation theology).

12. For a good general overview, see Daphne Josselin and William Wallace, eds., *Non-State Actors in World Politics* (New York: Palgrave, 2001).

13. Beverly J. Silver, *Forces of Labor: Workers Movements and Globalization Since 1870* (Cambridge: Cambridge University Press, 2003).

14. For a thorough introduction to these types of transnational actors, see John Boli and George M. Thomas, eds., *Constructing World Culture: International Organizations Since 1875* (Stanford, CA: Stanford University Press, 1999).

15. Walter Enders, "Is Transnational Terrorism Becoming More Threatening? A Time Series Investigation," *Journal of Conflict Resolution* 44, no. 3 (2000): 307–32. For many people around the world, State-sponsored transnational terrorism is a signature tactic of various governments, and specifically, presidential administrations of the United States.

16. See Phil Williams, "Transnational Criminal Organizations and International Security," *Survival* 36, no. 1 (1994): 96–113. See also Nikos Passas, *Transnational Crime* (Brookfield, VT: Ashgate, 1999).

17. P. W. Singer, *Corporate Warriors: The Rise of the Privatized Military Industry* (Ithaca, NY: Cornell University Press, 2004).

18. "Diaspora Philanthropy: Perspectives on India and China" (Global Equity Initiative Workshop, Harvard University, Cambridge, MA, May 7–8, 2003).

19. Nadje Al-Ali and Khalid Moser, eds., *New Approaches to Migration: Transnational Communities and the Transformation of Home* (London: Routledge, 2001).

20. See Thomas Risse-Kappen, ed., *Bringing Transnational Actors Back In: Non-State Actors, Domestic Structures, and International Institutions* (Cambridge: Cambridge University Press, 1995).

21. See Susanne Hoeber Rudolph, "Dehomogenizing Religious Formations," in *Transnational Religion and Fading States,* ed. Suzanne Hoeber Rudolph and James Piscatori, 243–61 (Boulder, CO: Westview, 1997).

22. The terms and ideas of nation and State are often conflated but should be kept analytically distinct. For the definition of "State," see n. 2 above. A nation, or national community, shares with an ethnic community a set of (perceived to be real) shared characteristics that members of that collectivity understand to be what connects them together and separates them from other groups — in other words, an imagined collectivity of descent. See Benedict Anderson, *Imagined Communities: Reflections on the Origin and Spread of Nationalism* (London and New York:

Verso, 1991). One of the key distinctions between ethnic communities and nations is the greater degree of institutionalized political self-organization exhibited by the latter. To the extent that the type of political organization a nation has established is a State as previously defined, we might call it a nation-state. But as suggested in the main text, virtually no contemporary country organized as a State is mono-ethnic or mono-national. This is precisely why the term "transnational" can refer to phenomena and dynamics that cross State borders and/or phenomena and dynamics that cross national/cultural boundaries, depending on the way the term is being used.

23. The extensive and growing literature on the fallacy and myth of the nation-state is impossible to cite here, but see, for example, Matthew Sparke, *Hyphen-Nation-States: Critical Geographies of Displacement and Disjuncture* (Minnesota: University of Minnesota Press, 2003).

24. Anne-Marie Slaughter, "The Real New World Order," *Foreign Affairs* 76, no. 5 (1997): 183–98. See also Robert O. Keohane and Joseph S. Nye Jr., "Transgovernmental Relations and International Organizations," *World Politics* 27, no. 1 (1972): 39–62.

25. See Jan Martin, Wolfgang H. Reinicke, and Thorsten Benner, "Beyond Multilateralism: Global Policy Networks," *International Politics and Society* 2 (2000): 176–88. Steve Waddell recently enumerated and described four different types of "global action networks (GAN)": (1) internal collaboration, (2) associative, (3) supportive, and (4) adaptive in his paper, "Global Action Networks: A Global Invention to Make Globalisation Work for All," *Journal of Corporate Citizenship* 12 (Winter 2003): 1–16.

PART TWO

Movements That Changed the World

CHAPTER FIVE

Transnational Pioneers:
The International Labor Movement

Dan Gallin

Introduction

In the most common acceptance of the term, especially in the United States, the labor movement refers primarily to the trade union movement. It is actually far more than that. Historically, it also comprises the political parties created by workers to defend their interests, such as labor, socialist, and social-democratic parties, as well as the many institutions created for specific purposes: workers' cooperatives (both of producers and of consumers), workers' banks, educational associations, schools and colleges, health and welfare institutions, cultural institutions (theaters, libraries, chorales, brass bands, book clubs), leisure activities (sports and hiking clubs), women's organizations, youth organizations, solidarity and defense organizations (including armed militias), radio and television stations, newspapers and review magazines, publishing houses, and bookshops. All of these, taken together, constitute the historical labor movement.

The full range of such institutions and organizations rarely exists all at the same time in any one country. The important point is that all these institutions taken together are not only meant to support workers in all aspects of their lives but also to constitute an alternative society and a counterculture. The labor movement is thus a multifaceted social movement with a cause and a vision of society.

The trade union movement is the most important component of the labor movement in its wider sense. It is the first, and often the last, line of resistance that workers have to defend themselves, and without it none of the other institutions of the labor movement would survive. It is also the most representative part of the labor movement; it exists in every country in the world except in those with the most extreme dictatorships.

From the very beginning, the labor movement has been inspired and organized by many different ideologies: Marxism in various (sometimes contradictory) interpretations, revolutionary and conservative syndicalism, Christian social doctrines, radical liberation movements, and others. Each ideology derives its values and objectives from its own traditions, but they share a common cause, which by now constitutes the culture of the mainstream labor movement. The basic elements of this culture are reflected in the movement's values and goals.

The labor movement is the oldest social movement seeking to transform society in the name of universal values, with the objective of creating a society that meets the needs and aspirations of all human beings. The fundamental value, from which all others are derived, is a sense of *dignity* of the human being — a value stronger than even survival, since people are prepared to die for it. A related value is that of *equality*; all human beings are of equal worth, and therefore should have equal rights. From this derives the value of *justice*; it is unacceptable that, because of the way power is distributed in society, some should enjoy wealth and privilege while others, the greater number, should be circumscribed by poverty, starvation, and early death. Finally, all human beings aspire to *freedom* — freedom from exploitation and oppression. These values have driven every movement of resistance throughout history, and they are driving the modern labor movement.

What differentiates the modern labor movement from the many earlier liberation movements is that it is international in nature. The transnationality of the labor movement is rooted in the perception that workers constitute a class with a common cause. Because it has a vital interest in the abolition of exploitation for all people, the labor movement is not only a self-help movement of workers but also a liberation movement for all humanity.

The values of the labor movement explain its concept of democracy as a process and method, not just as an ultimate goal. This concept is based on the understanding that ends and means are closely linked: for example, undemocratic means cannot lead to democratic outcomes. Therefore, democracy is a living process and a continuous work in progress.

The goals of the labor movement naturally derive from its values. They are several, and include:

- The defense of the immediate interests of its members on the job: decent wages, security of employment, working conditions that are not threatening to the mental and physical health of the workers, and basic social protection;

- Socially progressive legislation in the interests of all workers and, indeed, for humanity as a whole;

- A political society where the rights of workers and of all citizens are guaranteed;[1]

- International solidarity, since its achievements are under threat as long as injustice and oppression exist anywhere.

The enduring strength of the solidarity principle is demonstrated by the resilience of the international labor movement, which survived the wars and totalitarian dictatorships of the twentieth century. Dictatorships establish themselves by breaking unions; churches and businesses have survived and flourished in dictatorships where labor activists have been sent to jail, concentration camps, and death.

This chapter first outlines the history of the birth and growth of the labor movement, from its optimistic beginnings in Europe in the mid-nineteenth century to a powerful entity worldwide a century later. It then analyzes the setbacks to the movement, stressing particularly the ideological, and subsequently the economic, factors that have challenged it in the last fifty years. In conclusion, the chapter highlights the issues of immediate urgency that have to be faced and addressed by the labor movement if it is to fulfill its historic mission.

History

A brief overview of the inception and growth of the labor movement in different parts of the world is described below. The labor movement was a powerful engine for social change, and it played a significant role in the freedom movements of many developing nations.

The Social-Democratic and Communist Labor Movement

Origins to World War I. The modern labor movement began in Europe at the turn of the nineteenth century with the rise of the Industrial Revolution, the emergence of capitalist mass production, and the formation of an impoverished working class. The brutal injustice of the emergent society inspired social reformers to propose a more rational and fairer social order. By the end of the 1830s, small groups of trade unionists, socialists, and democrats in Britain and France were planning for an "international association for the emancipation of the working class."[2]

However, it was not until 1847 that a group of workers and political exiles living in London organized a meeting, at which a declaration and a program authored by Karl Marx and Friedrich Engels was adopted. This document, which came to be known as the Communist Manifesto, eventually emerged as the basic statement of the Marxist version of socialism, and the theoretical basis of the modern mainstream labor movement.

In 1864, a meeting in London that was attended by local and national workers' societies as well as many other forms of workers' organizations (political parties and propaganda groups, unions, cooperatives, mutual-aid societies, etc.) led to the establishment of an organization that came to be called the First International. The first congress of the International met in Geneva in 1866, and for the next ten years the organization grew rapidly as unions formed in many countries and allied themselves to it. Despite its evident relevance and popularity, however, the First International was short-lived. Struggles between the Marxists and the anarchists within the organization led to several splits, and eventually contributed to its demise in 1876. As an international labor organization, the First International had an obvious weakness: geographically limited to Europe, it was supported by a thin layer of politically conscious workers in essentially conservative societies. Severe financial constraints were part of the problem as income from dues was never enough to carry out even basic tasks such as publishing a bulletin or conducting research. Despite this, its achievements were remarkable. It gave the first practical expression to labor internationalism and established the first regular contacts between labor organizations in different countries; those contacts survived its dissolution and became the basis of its successor organizations. The First International was the first to formulate general demands (such as the eight-hour day), which became common demands of unions internationally, and it provided a theoretical and political framework for later international action.

Several attempts to re-create an international labor organization in the following decade led to the establishment of the Second International in Paris in 1889. On the last day of its deliberations, the congress declared May 1 as an international day of struggle for the eight-hour day. The first May Day in 1890 turned out to be a more forceful and impressive demonstration than its organizers had anticipated. May Day immediately became the official day of remembrance of workers' struggles, and of celebration of the international labor movement.

The Second International was an umbrella organization that included political parties, trade unions, and other workers' organizations. It was soon recognized, however, that a clearer division of labor was necessary. After 1900, the Second International evolved into an association of socialist parties and other organizations developed for other functions. Some members of the International founded international organizations of workers in the same trade or industry. These became known as the international trade secretariats (ITS), the first permanently organized form of international trade union solidarity. Twenty-eight ITSs had been formed by 1911, with a total membership of about 6.3 million. Their main activities were centered on organizing worker solidarity during strikes, and exchanging information on trade and labor legislation. When in 1903 the national trade union centers in some countries felt the need for an independent international organization, they founded what became in 1913 the International Federation of Trade Unions (IFTU). In that year, the IFTU had members in twenty countries with a total membership of approximately 7.7 million.

The Interwar Years. The first phase of the movement came to an abrupt end with the outbreak of World War I in August 1914. Neither the Second International nor the IFTU survived the war intact. In the preceding decade, the socialist labor movement had developed into a mass movement with strong positions against militarism and war. Nevertheless, when war broke out, the tidal wave of nationalism and patriotic fervor swept all before it. The socialist parties largely supported the governments in most European countries and voted for the war.

After one year of hostilities, the labor movement split into the parties and unions that supported the Allies, those that supported the Central Powers, and those of the neutral countries. Only a minority of revolutionary socialists and syndicalists opposed the war in all European countries, but this opposition gained in strength as the war dragged on and revulsion against the mass slaughter on the battlefield spread throughout Europe.

In 1917, revolution broke out in Russia; the czar was overthrown and replaced, first by a center-left Constituent Assembly and later by a coalition government of revolutionary socialists (led and eventually taken over by the Bolsheviks). They established a government based on Councils (Soviets) and took Russia out of the war. They nationalized the land and the main industries, created a Red Army, and in the ensuing civil war repressed political opposition through terror. The impact of the Bolshevik revolution on the labor movement was twofold: it greatly strengthened the agitation for peace and for political, social, and economic reforms, but it also caused a deep rift in the socialist movement. Most socialist parties and unions rejected the Bolshevik concept of political dictatorship supported by terror, and stressed political democracy as an inseparable part of socialism.

In March 1919, the Bolsheviks convened an international conference in Moscow to establish the Communist or Third International. The conference, called in haste to preempt the reconstitution of the Second International, was hardly representative of the wider movement, but it adopted provisional statutes and elected a provisional executive committee. In its sessions it called on workers to rise and establish Soviet republics on the Russian model, and for an uncompromising struggle against socialist parties and movements that did not accept their leadership. Two years later a congress of trade unionists in Moscow established the Red International of Labor Unions (RILU), an international coalition of communist and syndicalist unions, with a close connection to the Communist International.

Meanwhile, the IFTU had been revived at a congress in Amsterdam in 1919, and had a representation of 23 million members in twenty-two countries. The Second International was reconstituted in 1923 as the Labor and Socialist International. Also in 1919, the Allies constituted the International Labor Organization (ILO) as a part of the Treaty of Versailles. It was initially intended to be a reformist alternative to the revolutionary threat from Russia. The ILO, a tripartite institution with representation from government, employers, and workers, survived World War II and is now part of the United Nations system. It prepares social legislation in the form of conventions that are then ratified by the member states to form the basis of national legislation.

The period from the 1920s to the outbreak of World War II in 1939 was dominated by the bitter and increasingly irreconcilable split between the social-democratic and communist movements. Antifascist and popular-front "unity" policies promoted by the communist parties proved to be tactical foreign policy maneuvers of the USSR, as Russia was now known. Stalin's intervention in the Spanish civil war demonstrated that the communist parties would accept unity only on their terms, involving total control.

These political struggles formed part of a historical catastrophe of huge proportions. Fascism had wiped out the labor movement in Italy, Germany, Austria, Portugal, and Spain, and then in most of Europe as the German armies occupied nearly the entire continent.[3] Hundreds of thousands of socialists, anarchists, and communists in Russia and later in Eastern and Central Europe perished in the Stalinist forced-labor camps. In the three decades following the Russian revolution, two generations of labor activists and leaders disappeared. In 1939, as a result of the USSR and Nazi Germany signing a treaty of nonaggression, the communist parties had denounced Britain and France for declaring war on Germany. In 1941, however, Germany attacked the USSR, and the communist parties now declared that this was no longer an imperialist struggle but a war for democracy and freedom. The USSR joined the war on the side of the Allies, and in May 1943, the Communist International was dissolved to reassure the Allied powers that the USSR no longer harbored revolutionary ambitions.

The Cold War Period. The social-democratic labor movement emerged from the war in a strong political position but actually greatly weakened by its losses and far more dependent on the State than in the past. This dependence grew from its wartime alliance with the Allied governments, the weakened state of economies devastated by the war, and the fact that many postwar governments were now ready to support the legislative agenda of the labor movement.

Although the Socialist International was reconstituted in 1951 it gradually lost its relevance, evolving over time into an open forum with weak links to the trade union movement. Attempts to broaden its constituency beyond Europe reduced its political substance, and by the end of the twentieth century it had ceased to exercise a significant influence in international labor politics. At the end of the war, there was a widespread assumption that the wartime alliance of the Allies could be reflected in trade union terms, and that a united international trade union organization could include the Soviet as well as the Western social-democratic unions. After several exploratory international meetings, the World Federation of Trade Unions (WFTU) was established in 1945, and the IFTU was formally dissolved by its General Council. Soon, however, differences developed between the social-democratic and communist unions. In Eastern Europe the social-democratic, independent left, and dissident communist cadres quickly disappeared into jails and labor camps. Trade unions were replaced by State organizations for labor administration on the Soviet model. In Western Europe, the European Recovery Program was welcomed by the social-democratic unions and opposed by the communist unions. The ITSs broke off relations with the WFTU. By 1949, escalating tensions led to the noncommunist unions leaving the WFTU and establishing the International Confederation of Free Trade Unions (ICFTU) by the end of that year.

The Cold War, which began in 1949, cast its shadow over the trade union movement, but many factors in the split were a result of earlier tensions over issues such as whether "bourgeois democracy" was preferable to no democracy at all; whether unions should be accountable to their members or to a State; and whether this State represented a new class exercising control over society, including the working class, by means of terror. The beginning of the Cold War meant that the antifascist alliance that had briefly held together organizations with fundamentally opposed views, could no longer bridge these divisions.

The newly formed ICFTU was less grounded in the socialist tradition than the IFTU had been. Anticommunism was a far stronger driving force, even though this sometimes limited its agenda for workers' and human rights. The main achievement of the ICFTU was to become a truly worldwide organization, whereas all previous international labor organizations had been essentially Eurocentric, in practice if not in intent.

The Christian Unions

The spread of socialist and anarchist ideas among workers at the end of the nineteenth century caused concern in the Catholic Church and prompted it to create its own trade union movement. Christian trade unions, made up largely of Catholic workers, were formed in a number of European countries. The International Federation of Christian Trade Unions (IFCTU) was established in 1920. Like other trade unions, they were suppressed under fascism and Nazism in the 1930s and early 1940s. In 1945, the IFCTU reorganized and expanded outside Europe, with affiliations in the former French colonies in Africa, and in Latin America and Asia. It broadened its membership to include other religious affiliations, and in 1968 changed its name to the World Confederation of Labor (WCL), positioning itself somewhere to the left of the ICFTU. Although the WCL had maintained its international trade federations, these could not compete with the global union federations (GUF), as the ITSs were now known, at any level of activity.

Labor Unions in Other Parts of the World

Since the labor movement originated in the workers' revolt against exploitation in the early capitalist economies, it first developed in Europe and North America, where the capitalist economy was most advanced. The First and Second Internationals and the IFTU were essentially European organizations. It was easy to establish and maintain international organizations in a relatively small, densely populated area. Maintaining regular contact with organizations that could be reached only after weeks of travel was a different matter. The early labor internationals were worldwide in intent, but remained largely (with some US participation) European in practice.

In the United States, unions developed at the same time as in Europe. The first lasting federation of national unions, the American Federation of Labor (AFofL), was established in 1886. Massive immigration from Europe radicalized American unions, creating socialist organizations. Socialist ideals greatly influenced the US labor movement in the first decades of the twentieth century: Eugene Victor Debs, founder of the American Railway Union, gained 6 percent of the popular vote as Socialist Party candidate for president in 1912. The Industrial Workers of the

World (IWW), a revolutionary trade union federation founded in 1905, had close to two hundred thousand members in the United States, and branches in Australia, Britain, Canada, Chile, Germany, Mexico, New Zealand, Norway, and South Africa at its peak. In the 1930s, the mass-production industries were organized under the leadership of the Congress of Industrial Organizations (CIO). (The AFofL and the CIO eventually merged in 1955.)

Although the labor movement began in response to the capitalist economies of the West, its ideas spread rapidly to other parts of the world, often through seamen or immigrants. This was particularly so in the colonies of the European countries; unions as well as workers' parties and other labor movement institutions formed in Latin America and Asia in the second half of the nineteenth century, and in Africa a few decades later.

In Latin America, anarcho-syndicalist unionism from Spain, Portugal, and Italy was predominant. Social struggles were often violent, with military repression by employers and conservative governments a common response to strikes in most countries. In the 1940s, other powerful actors intervened. In Argentina, for example, General Perón combined an authoritarian ideology with pro-labor policies (while suppressing socialist, communist, and syndicalist unions) to create a unionism that survived the second Perón presidency and a military dictatorship to remain the dominant force in the Argentine labor movement. In Brazil, the trade union movement linked to a socialist mass party emerged as a strong social and political force in the 1990s, with a former union organizer gaining the presidency in 2003.

In the British Empire, trade unionism spread to Australia, New Zealand, Canada, and South Africa, often retaining its affiliation to the British parent organization. General unions also arose in Australia and Canada. In many of these early industrialized democracies, the rise of trade unionism followed patterns quite similar to those of European and North American labor movements.

In the British colonies, however, labor movements were often closely linked to political struggles. In India, for example, organized strikes were frequent at the end of the nineteenth century, particularly in the textile industry and the railways, even in the absence of unions. The arrest in 1908 of Bal Gangadhar Tilak, a prominent nationalist leader, resulted in a six-day general strike by the Bombay textile-mill workers, the first politically motivated mass strike in Indian history. The All India Trade Union Congress was founded in 1920; following independence in 1947, however, the trade union movement began to fragment as different groups formed alliances with the various political parties.

Labor organizations in the African colonies of the United Kingdom also took on critical political roles. The movement often first came into being in those areas that were closely linked with the plundering activities of the colonizers: mining and plantations, railways, harbors, and administration. The mineworkers in the copper belt in Zambia, for example, struck in 1935, 1940, and again in 1957, finally winning a wage increase. In many countries the labor movement became a training ground for national leaders, since it provided opportunities for building leadership skills and learning ways to prevail upon the colonialists via economic pressure. In South Africa, discrimination against blacks created race-based unions that became major political actors in the struggle against apartheid.

In the French colonies, the trade union movement started as branches of the French trade unions, especially after 1944, when the freedom to organize trade unions was extended to the colonial territories. Here as elsewhere, the trade unions were soon linked to nationalist movements. In 1952, the unions in French West Africa called a general strike for the enactment of a forty-hour week, with a 20 percent increase in the hourly wage rates. The strike was totally effective throughout the colony, an unprecedented event, and it forced the French government to pass the bill. In 1955–56, the African unions severed their links with the French trade unions and constituted themselves as independent, African organizations.

In Asia, European immigration and colonization played a lesser role in the rise of the labor movement, although contacts between the Asian intelligentsia and European and American radicals influenced the direction of the early Asian labor movements. In Japan, the trade union movement emerged from radical intellectuals concerned with challenging an authoritarian regime, though the organizers of the early Japanese unions had gained their expertise by organizing Japanese workers in San Francisco with the AFofL. Sun Yat Sen, the leader of the Chinese democratic revolution of 1911, and other progressive Chinese intellectuals maintained friendly relations with the Second International. Chinese anarchist groups were in touch with their counterparts in Paris and Tokyo in the same period. Indonesian labor leaders learned their trade from Dutch unionists, while progressive Filipino intellectuals discovered socialism and anarcho-syndicalism in Spain in the late nineteenth century.

It is clear from the above that organized labor was a reality in nearly all parts of the world by the early twentieth century, even in the absence of effective international organizations. The universality of the ideas and the interests of the labor movement preceded its organizational expression. By 1945, the elements of a global international movement were in place, though it would take several decades before such a movement arose in a recognizable form.

By the end of World War II, most European powers had given up their colonial empires, sometimes with destructive military rear-guard actions (France in Indochina and Algeria, the Netherlands in Indonesia, later Portugal in its African colonies). The labor movement in this "Third World" was initially strong, benefiting from its alliance with the liberation movements that formed the first postcolonial governments. In the 1950s and 1960s, however, the Cold War became the new global political reality. Each of the two superpowers deployed tremendous financial and political resources to control the labor movement in support of their respective blocs. The movement thus became polarized, and the position of those who tried to maintain an independent trade union movement based on class interest became very difficult. The contending blocs in the Cold War were trying to buy allies, thereby introducing widespread corruption.

Other factors contributed to the gradual erosion of the labor movement's position of strength. In Africa and Asia particularly, regimes that were initially democratic became tyrannical and authoritarian, confronting the labor movement in their countries with the choice of submission or repression. From the 1980s onward, the structural adjustment policies imposed by the international financial institutions all over the world undermined the public sector, and therefore an important membership base of the trade union movement.

Many Third World unions tried to maintain solidarity by forming regional organizations such as the Organization of African Trade Union Unity (OATUU), but because their member unions had for the most part become State-controlled, these regional organizations served mainly the political purposes of the governments that financed and controlled them. Much the same can be said for the European Trade Union Confederation (ETUC), which is largely dependent on the European Union for its budget.[4] The ideological basis of this new regional organization was a strong sense of European identity, which some perceived as European nationalism. This new, inward-looking orientation of many European unions strained relations between the ETUC, the ICFTU, and the GUFs. The ETUC includes the European Trade Union Federations (ETUF), which correspond largely to the GUFs in their jurisdictional scope. In some cases, two competing organizations reflecting internationalist or Europeanist priorities existed side by side and only unified after several years of protracted conflict.

European separatism also affected trade union positions when the European works councils (EWC) were formed by EU directive in 1994, wherein transnational corporations (TNC) are obliged to establish works councils in which workers are represented. Although hailed by unions as enforcing that corporations meet with representative bodies of their employees at least once a year, the directive is greatly inhibiting in that it only covers EU countries; defines the purpose of the EWCs as "information and consultation" (not negotiation); and does not refer to unions but to "workers' representatives" (who could be handpicked by management). The directive, however, also provides that the management and the workers can together negotiate changes.[5]

Thus, by the end of the twentieth century, the labor movement the world over had clearly been weakened by a series of political factors. However, the worst was yet to come, in the form of economic compulsions that were as devastating to workers' interests as they were widespread. The labor movement now had to face the onslaught of globalization.

Globalization

The onset of globalization since the 1980s, while undermining the economic and political base of regional exclusionism and separatism, has at the same time created massive new problems for the international labor movement. In a little over ten years, the world economy has undergone a fundamental change, moving from an aggregate of national economies linked together by a network of trade, investment, and credit, to an integrated, borderless, global economy. Revolutionary changes in telecommunications and transport, driven by transnational capital, have immensely increased its power by increasing its scope. Meanwhile, the autonomy, power, and resources of national States have been steadily shrinking.

Transnational capital has emancipated itself from national States and is reordering the world economy in its own interests, with support from the governments of the United States and the European Union, and the international financial institutions. States in the developing and transition countries[6] underbid each other to attract foreign direct investment, which results in a downward spiral of wages, cuts in social welfare, mounting unemployment, and restrictions on human rights. The immediate consequences of globalization have been growing social inequalities, social disruption, reduced social protection, spreading poverty, and growing threats to the environment. The traditional, core workforce with permanent and regulated employment is shrinking in industrialized countries, as the opportunities to outsource and subcontract grow. Relocation of industrial production and services cascades down from high-wage to low-wage countries, much of it ending up in China, where free trade unions are banned and workers earn as little as USD 20 per month.

The labor movement at the end of the twentieth century was badly prepared for this situation. Its priorities had been distorted by the Cold War, and decades of complacency had diluted its ideological and political heritage. Many powerful trade unions had leaderships geared to administering the gains of earlier struggles rather than organizing for new challenges, while the rank and file were educated to bureaucratic routine and passivity. To date, few international labor organizations have a strategy to meet these challenges. They remain loose associations of national unions, which think and react in local terms at a time when transnational capital thinks and acts globally. Most union organizations have not yet developed a common global strategy.

Nevertheless, the domination of the world economy by the TNCs has set new priorities for the ITSs, insofar as they are the natural vehicle for coordinating activities and mobilizing support for unions facing difficulties within a TNC. Such support can make a significant difference to the outcome of union campaigns, as the accompanying box illustrates.

BOX 5.1
International Food Workers and Coca-Cola in Guatemala

In Guatemala under a brutal military dictatorship, the manager of a Coca-Cola plant owned by a franchise holder tried to destroy the union by having its leaders killed by death squads. The International Food Workers (IUF) held Coca-Cola responsible and organized boycotts, strikes, and other protest actions in seventeen countries in 1979–81. This campaign forced Coca-Cola to buy out the franchise and appoint new directors, who then recognized the union and signed a collective agreement.

At the end of 1983, however, the directors closed the plant and disappeared after declaring bankruptcy. The workers then occupied the plant; when Coca-Cola refused any responsibility in sorting out the issue, the IUF organized a second international campaign that was more forceful than the first. It took over a year to reach a settlement, end the occupation, and reopen the plant. Coca-Cola eventually sold the plant to a Guatemalan businessman, who recognized the union and signed a new collective agreement. Today, the union is still there and the agreement is still in effect.

International campaigns can also be conducted at the level of a global industry. For example, the International Transport Workers' Federation has conducted a campaign for more than fifty years to regulate wages and working conditions for seafarers working on ships flying "flags of convenience," a ploy that allows lax or substandard regulations and exploitation of workers. The campaign has sought to establish a regulatory framework for the shipping industry irrespective of the flag flown. Many ships are now covered by these agreements, giving direct protection to over 140,000 seafarers.

The growing internationalization of companies makes corporate management, not governments, responsible for decisions that have a major effect on local workplaces; therefore, workers' representatives must now bargain directly with international management. An exchange of experiences and information with unionists in other countries may thus be critical to their effectiveness. To meet this need, some GUFs have sought to establish permanent coordinating structures in leading TNCs. This coordination with some companies prepared to enter into a formal relationship with them has led to the negotiation of international framework agreements (IFA). These agreements deal with general questions of principle, such as workers' rights and international labor standards. Typically, they commit the company to respecting freedom of association and collective bargaining, and are designed to ensure fundamental workers' rights in the company's various workplaces. Like all collective agreements, they recognize mutual obligations between the parties, including negotiated procedures for monitoring, verifying, and handling grievances and disputes. The local unions usually conduct the monitoring. Not all IFAs, however, are equally monitored and enforced, and therefore some have little impact at the level of the workplace. Also, given that there are more than sixty thousand TNCs, their number is still too small to make a significant difference in global social relations.

Conclusion

Although the IFAs represent the first form of collective bargaining at an international level, the international labor movement still faces critical challenges. While some of these are emerging in the context of a globalizing world, others pertain to old and unresolved issues. Whatever their causes, it is vital that the labor movement recognizes these issues and initiates serious, long-term measures to address them if it is to carry out the tasks for which it was created.

The Changing Nature of the Working Class

The changing composition of the working class, the growth of the informal economy, and the gender issue have all affected the labor movement. Trade unions over the years have championed women's rights, and many women have been charismatic union leaders, but the movement has been dominated since its origins by the industrial sector, in which men predominate. Much of the movement still remains male-dominated, even though this tradition threatens the movement's survival as well as its progress. The growth of economic sectors with weak union traditions, deregulation of the labor market, and privatization of the public sector have combined to create a new working class, largely composed of women, in unregulated and unprotected jobs. A growing proportion of this new working class is in informal employment, without secure contracts, benefits, or social protection. It includes self-employed workers in informal enterprises as well as paid workers in informal jobs. The concept of informal work is spreading in industrialized countries and is particularly widespread in the developing countries. Organizing these workers at the local level is onerous enough, and at present represents a huge challenge on a global scale. Interestingly, women in some areas of informal employment have taken the lead and formed their own unions;[7] the traditional trade union movement is very weak in this field and in fact has found it difficult to relate to these unions of a new kind. Yet, for the trade union movement to have any meaning and survive, it must make organizing in the informal economy a priority and especially form partnerships with women's movements for success in this field.

Human Rights as Workers' Rights

A second challenge is the issue of human rights. Repression can take extreme forms, as in the killings of fifteen hundred Colombian trade unionists in the last ten years, or in the tight control or outright prohibition of trade unions, as in China or Saudi Arabia, respectively. Often it takes subtler forms, as in the legal restrictions on trade union formation in the United States: many thousands of workers in the United States are excluded by law from the right to organize themselves into unions. Employers routinely violate the law in aggressive antiunion campaigns, and legal redress is slow and uncertain. In many advanced industrial democracies, international solidarity strikes are restricted — which is precisely the form of action needed to defend union members in a globalized economy. The international labor movement has been campaigning for the recognition of workers' rights as human rights, but with declining support from its traditional political allies, the unions must now join forces with human rights organizations to raise public awareness of these issues.

Newer Social Movements

A major social and political development over the last two decades has been the emergence of new social movements that champion a variety of single-issue causes and protest movements against globalizing capitalism. Collectively described as the global justice movement, it is filling the void left by the labor movement's retreat from broader social concerns and responsibilities. The international labor movement must decide if it will join this coalition to call for an alternative globalization, or remain suspended in a lobbying activity with the international financial institutions, the European Union, and other intergovernmental institutions.

Ineffectual Political Allies

A fourth challenge involves the relationship between the movement and its historical allies, the social-democratic and labor parties. The old allegiances with political parties, given the declining autonomy of States with respect to transnational capital, are no longer viable. The relationships of the past have become more difficult to maintain and are increasingly less productive, yet the trade union movement needs a political dimension. In the present situation, restoring the political dimension cannot mean reestablishing allegiances, much less dependencies, with existing political parties. All trade union activity is political by nature, but the old politics have to be overhauled. One might say that democratic socialism itself has to be reinvented, from and by the trade union movement, as an alternative to the new world order of transnational capital.

The labor movement entered history as the carrier of an alternative social order to that of capitalism. Today, most of its leadership no longer focuses on fundamental social change. Yet the movement remains, stubbornly and irreducibly, the world's largest movement, made up of thousands of daily struggles to resist oppression by the dominant social order. Today, millions of people rally to the vision that "another world is possible": the most powerful anticapitalist movement the world has seen since historical socialism left the scene. When organized labor joins once again in this vision of global justice, another, better world will certainly become possible.

Notes

1. The earliest battles of the labor movement were conducted to achieve universal suffrage as well as universal and free education, freedom of association, and a free press — in most countries via political power exercised through its own parties.

2. Lewis Lorwin, *The International Labor Movement: History, Policies, Outlook* (New York: Harper, 1953), 4.

3. The Jewish Labor Bund was destroyed as its entire membership (the Jewish working class in Poland, the occupied parts of the USSR, and in other Eastern European countries) was exterminated.

4. Corinne Gobin, *L'Europe Syndicale* (Brussels: Editions Labor, 1997), 186.

5. *European Trade Union Information Bulletin,* no. 4 (1994).

6. These refer to the former communist countries in Eastern and Central Europe, including the successor States of the USSR.

7. In India, the Self-Employed Women's Association (SEWA) has over the years organized seven hundred thousand poor women in seven Indian states. They have developed approaches that are being imitated by others in the informal sectors around the world.

CHAPTER SIX

Spinning the Green Web: Transnational Environmentalism

Wendy E. F. Torrance and Andrew W. Torrance

Introduction

The three and a half decades between 1957 and 1992 have been called the "formative years of the global environmental era."[1] The period began with the International Geophysical Year (IGY) in 1957, which witnessed a remarkable collaboration between scientists around the globe to produce baseline data on the state of the Earth, including its oceans and atmosphere, as well as its sun. By the time of the United Nations Conference on Environment and Development (UNCED) in 1992, scientists had been joined by official national delegates from countries around the world, including the largest gathering of heads of State ever assembled in one place, all of whom attended for the purpose of negotiating agreements to embody basic principles governing responsible care of the Earth's environment. Beyond the official UNCED participants was a vast penumbra of nongovernmental organizations (NGO), there to champion the interests and groups purportedly underrepresented by the official delegates. These two years serve as useful bookends to a watershed period during which awareness of the effect of human activities on the planet pierced public consciousness worldwide, and the number and scope of international environmental agreements grew at a prodigious rate.[2]

A number of factors have together pushed environmental issues onto the international agenda. Chief among these have been the marked growth in international scientific collaboration (begun during the IGY), which has often generated quality information about the Earth's condition, and an explosion in the number of nongovernmental organizations operating or collaborating on environmental issues whose causes or effects cross national boundaries. Together, these factors have highlighted the gravity of such international environmental issues as acid rain, the depleting ozone layer, global climate change, and loss of biodiversity in the minds of citizens around the world.

This chapter first traces the history of transnational environmentalism. A detailed analysis of two important environmental concerns then highlights the activities of transnational civil society as well as the nature of their role as agenda setters, information providers, and advocates for solutions to these problems. The chapter concludes with an assessment of the fundamental importance of transnational activism in spreading awareness of the impact of human activity on the health of the Earth, and the challenges that activists face in the pursuit of this goal.

History

Transnational environmentalism has used every kind of transnational activity to draw attention to its issues. Science and scientists have played a prominent role in the early history of environmental networks, as they continue to do in existing networks and negotiations on environmental concerns. Nongovernmental organizations, networks, and coalitions have galvanized the public, the media, and governments on numerous environmental issues. The activities of the United Nations and other institutions such as the World Trade Organization have provided important focal points for the development of international networks. And, though themselves largely the result of transnational activity, international conferences and negotiations have also contributed greatly to fostering further transnational connections.

Scientific networks were the first important transnational networks, and their influence remains strong to this day. These "epistemic communities,"[3] whose scientific results are often the first to reveal environmental problems, are credited with helping to raise a number of environmental issues to the international agenda by bringing them to the attention of governments and the public.[4]

The International Council of Scientific Unions (ICSU), whose origins date back to 1919, is an important example of an early transnational network. Over the years, the ICSU has succeeded in attracting funding from its members' home governments, creating a transnational environmental effort spanning sixty-seven participating countries. Most significantly, the ICSU helped to accumulate the data and interpretive knowledge upon which many subsequent actions in global environmental protection were built. The IGY was one of the ICSU's early programs, and its success illustrated the importance of a collaborative and interdisciplinary approach to the gathering of scientific information. The ICSU was largely responsible for building and encouraging transnational networks on environmental issues, while the IGY stimulated research that might not otherwise have been conducted by enabling extensive cooperation among scientists and generating enthusiasm for a wide range of scientific studies on the state of the Earth.[5] Along with the ICSU, the International Union for the Conservation of Nature and Natural Resources (IUCN) and the Friends of the Earth (FOE) were active participants at the 1972 United Nations Conference on Human Development, commonly known as the Stockholm Conference in recognition of its host city. Both organizations are part of what the IUCN, a transnational network of NGOs, calls a "green web" of partnerships on environmental issues.[6]

Early international cooperation on environmental issues did not attract widespread attention from other nongovernmental actors, though naturalists and conservationists were active in seeking agreements to protect certain aspects of it — for instance, wildlife.[7] Nongovernmental organizations made their presence felt for the first time at the Stockholm Conference by being "involved in the preparations for Stockholm [and sending] official observers to the Conference."[8] This conference was a watershed event in the development of international environmental politics. Where the IGY had laid the foundation for international exchange of scientific information on the state of the environment, the Stockholm Conference now spurred an era of greater political awareness of international environmental issues.

The Stockholm Conference produced a strong legacy of collective action. Of the 463 international environmental treaties negotiated over the past 120 years, the vast majority — roughly two-thirds of the total — date from after the Stockholm Conference (see Box 6.1).[9] This conference articulated a plan of action for the environment and also established the United Nations Environment Programme (UNEP), a new UN agency intended to serve henceforth as the primary focal point for coordinating international responses to environmental issues. The formation of many national environmental ministries or agencies also dates from this time.[10]

During the Stockholm Conference, an official parallel conference called the Environment Forum was set up as a venue where NGOs could discuss issues of common concern.[11] The Environment Forum also arranged "lectures, exhibits, parades, and engaged in other attention-gathering activities, which were covered in the world press."[12] NGOs cooperated with each other to start *ECO*, a daily report on the proceedings of the conference that was distributed to NGOs and government delegates. Today, *ECO* still serves as an important means of communication between networks of environmental NGOs and delegates at international environmental negotiations. Since Stockholm, parallel conferences have become a common feature of international conferences, environmental or otherwise.

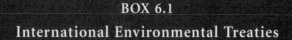

BOX 6.1
International Environmental Treaties

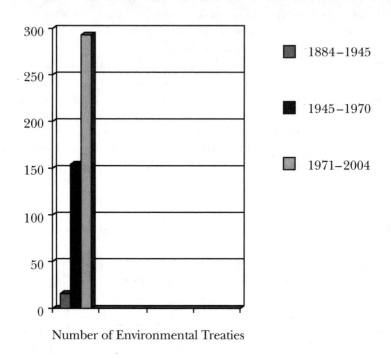

Number of Environmental Treaties

Influences and Changing Agendas

The rise in international cooperation on the environment has occurred alongside the growth of myriad transnational connections between scientists, governments and their agencies, businesses, NGOs dealing with other issues, and individual citizens. Scientists and NGOs, and, later, governments played key roles in encouraging the earliest of these connections. Businesses and individual citizens have since followed suit, and have been of influence themselves.

Environmental awareness grew during the 1970s mainly in the developed countries, where issues like those raised by Rachel Carson in *Silent Spring* and a focus on local concerns involving pollution, wildlife, and nuclear power spawned domestic environmental regulation. This new awareness of environmental issues spurred a growth in environmental organizations. These groups were initially focused on

BOX 6.2

ECO: An Example of Transnational Environmentalism

Since its debut at the Stockholm Conference in 1972, *ECO* has sought to provide participants of climate conferences with updates on the negotiations and the issues affecting them. As well as being distributed to the press, delegates, and NGOs by hand every morning, fast electronic distribution by fax and e-mail makes it possible to distribute *ECO* to a large unseen audience around the world. Fax copies are sent daily to six distribution nodes in Australia, Brazil, Belgium, Kenya, the United Kingdom, and the United States, from where they are faxed on in turn to other organizations, newspapers, national government representatives, and decision makers. It is also faxed directly to twenty-five World Wide Fund for Nature (WWF) organizations.

local and "visible" environmental problems, including "cleaner rivers, less air pollution, the closing down of a nuclear plant or polluting factory."[13]

The 1980s saw a significant rise in awareness of a wide range of environmental issues among the media and the public, and during this period transnational environmentalism grew by leaps and bounds. Environmental organizations, particularly those in the developed countries, began to focus their attention on global environmental issues such as acid rain, the depletion of the ozone layer, and global warming; trans-boundary issues such as trade in hazardous waste; and threats to endangered species worldwide.

Scientific networks, organizational alliances, and other coordinated organizational movements helped to propel environmental issues onto the international agenda during this period. By identifying problems that merited attention and urgent action, transnational alliances and scientific and other nongovernmental networks played an important role in highlighting the beleaguered state of the environment. Transnational alliances in many cases also provided other services: they contributed to the development of policy recommendations, identified stakeholders, and highlighted how policy change benefited, or at least lessened the damage to, the environment. These services often assisted in the formation and cohesion of coalitions of countries by helping them achieve a consensus on issues, with high attendant informational benefits.[14] Large transnational environmental organizations (WWF, Greenpeace, and IUCN, for example) developed strategies for spreading environmental concerns worldwide and played a crucial role in promoting transnational coalitions and networks.

By the 1980s, the environmental movement had spread to the developing countries as well, and with this came an understanding of the close ties between the environment and social development, and political and economic opportunity, particular to the Third World. *Our Common Future*, a report published by the World Commission on Environment and Development (created in 1983 and popularly known as the Brundtland Commission) drew direct connections between environmental and developmental issues, citing for the first time the need for "sustainable development" as a goal for the international community.[15]

The tremendous rise in media, public, and government attention on environmental issues culminated in 1992, when the international community gathered in Rio de Janeiro for the United Nations Conference on Environment and Development. Generally referred to as the Earth Summit, this meeting attracted over one hundred heads of State and more than fifteen hundred accredited NGOs. The culmination of a five-year preparatory process, the Earth Summit achieved five international agreements: the Framework Convention on Climate Change (FCCC), the Convention on Biological Diversity (CBD), a declaration on sustainable development entitled Agenda 21, the Rio Declaration on Environment and Development, and an effort to address forest resources in the Forest Principles.

The Earth Summit was a momentous event for environmental organizations worldwide. The NGOs actively participated at all levels throughout the preparatory process and indeed the entire duration of the conference, speaking and submitting written statements at the various forums. Furthermore, many of them served on national delegations to the conference, as governments valued them as an important source of information and experience.

This level of participation was greater than that at any previous international conference.[16] Transnational environmentalism had not up till then taken the form of a vast coordinated movement; the activities of the NGOs at the Earth Summit arguably represented a unique moment for transnational environmentalism, and the enthusiasm and idealism this generated continued to resonate for some time thereafter, fueling hope that the environment would receive greater attention worldwide. A large number of NGOs also came together at the Global Forum, the parallel NGO conference, and produced "people's treaties": thirty-nine alternative treaties in nine different issue areas ranging from consumption and poverty to marine and biodiversity protection. The NGOs declared that:

> We, the people of the world, will mobilize the forces of transnational civil society behind a widely shared agenda that bonds our many social movements in pursuit of just, sustainable, and participatory human societies. In so doing, we are forging our own instruments and processes for redefining the nature and meaning of human progress and for transforming those institutions that no longer respond to our needs.[17]

The Earth Summit brought together diverse environmental organizations with concerns ranging from development to the rights of indigenous people and women. Agenda 21, a major component of government resolutions at the Earth Summit, also reflected a broader environmental agenda. Women's organizations mobilized in advance of the Earth Summit and developed the Women's Action Agenda 21. They successfully lobbied for the recognition of the role of women in the environmental arena and the importance of their participation in achieving the aims of the Earth Summit. Chapter 24 of the Rio Declaration directly addresses the role of women in sustainable development.

The decade since the Earth Summit has witnessed a marked deceleration in environmental achievements at the international level. After the great promise of the 1980s, "both public attention to global environmental risks and the rate of production of new international conventions [has] dropped off from its Rio peak."[18] There have been notable achievements, such as the 1997 Kyoto Protocol of the Framework Convention on Climate Change aimed at reducing emissions contributing to global climate change, but, in the main, many of the issues raised at Rio have remained unaddressed, particularly those concerned with ensuring that economic development is environmentally sustainable.

In 2002, the United Nations again sponsored a major meeting of governmental and nongovernmental representatives at the World Summit on Sustainable Development in Johannesburg, South Africa, to review and revise the issues raised in the Agenda 21. The Johannesburg Conference attempted to develop plans of action to alleviate poverty worldwide while promoting environmentally sustainable development practices,[19] but did not generate the same degree of enthusiasm or commitment. It is too early to judge the success of the Johannesburg Conference in attempting to revive some of the goals of the Earth Summit; however, it did mark a new high-water mark in participation by business interests, such as Alcan and HSBC, much to the dismay of some environmental NGOs, who saw these interests as potential competitors for influence and direct opponents to their environmental aims.[20]

The Problems of Definition and Structure

Environmental issues vary a great deal. The problems may be local (drinking water contamination), trans-boundary (air pollution), or truly global (ozone depletion). They may involve just two countries or fifty. They may involve use of common resources (fisheries) or private land (biodiversity), or renewable (timber) and nonrenewable (oil) resources. The issues may be those of preservation (whaling agreements), conservation (debt-for-nature swaps),[21] sustainability, or development. They may be issues primarily for developed countries (acid rain) or those that largely concern developing countries (tropical deforestation). Governments, NGOs, or industry may spearhead solutions to problems. Environmental issues may be presented in ethical terms — harm to nature or humans — or as problems that involve market failure or economic disincentives. This great variation in the environmental ambit gives rise to different constellations of interests, and means that one environmental perspective and an accompanying unified movement are unlikely to arise. Moreover, as one scholar of global environmental movements has observed, the diversity of circumstances between the liberal, developed democracies and the developing countries means that environmental concerns and discourses are unlikely to be "universally appropriate or accepted."[22] As discussed below, a developing country's environmental concerns are more likely to be rooted in local needs, and those related to economic development and sustainability, rather than in the conservation ideals that drove early environmental action in the West. In addition, conflicts have emerged between developed and developing countries over the responsibility for solving existing environmental problems, funding the implementation of obligations, and even the relative importance of particular environmental issues.

Transnational coordination and cooperation can be divided into three broad categories: transnational networks, coalitions, and movements. Transnational networks are common in the international environmental arena, coalitions less so, and movements characterized by mass mobilization and coordinated tactics even rarer. Scientific and advocacy networks are easily identified in a wide range of issues, and many effective transnational coalitions have emerged in a number of issue areas. However, the great variation in environmental concerns, along with a fundamental division in outlook between the developing and developed countries, has prevented a unified environmental movement from emerging. Nevertheless, transnational organizations have been important contributors to the success of various campaigns in developing countries. Local environmental organizations pair with transnational organizations (such as Greenpeace or WWF) to bring issues to the global stage. An example of this is the reform of funding considerations by the World Bank for development projects: in the late 1980s, for example, a transnational campaign halted a development project in Brazil's rainforest and brought environmental and social considerations into the World Bank's decision-making process. Transnational coalitions "clos[ed] the circle between the highest levels of public international finance, the Brazilian national government, and local concerns. It was a novel form of international political action, linking formerly isolated constituencies."[23]

The Role of Nongovernmental Organizations

While IUCN and FOE were joined by nearly two hundred NGOs at Stockholm, nearly fifteen hundred NGOs were accredited to the Earth Summit at Rio de Janeiro in 1992.[24] These and other NGOs have over the years engaged with growing frequency in transnational campaigns to raise awareness of environmental issues worldwide, lobby governments, and provide information and expertise on international environmental issues to governments, international institutions, and the public. Their participation in international environmental negotiations as well as their contribution to the implementation and monitoring of international environmental agreements is now well documented.[25]

Though it is difficult to measure the magnitude and form of their influence, NGOs are certainly considered to have played an important role in raising a general awareness of international environmental issues and persuading governments to negotiate agreements and protocols to address these concerns. Several major transnational organizations have been crucial to the dissemination of environmental concerns and action. The IUCN, FOE, the WWF, and Greenpeace have grown into large and wealthy organizations with a truly global reach. These organizations form important constituent parts of the green web, whose aim is to influence the opinions and actions of governments, international institutions, the public, and even other NGOs.

The structures and strategies of these NGOs shed some light on the roles and influences these organizations have had on international environmental issues, and explicate the array of organizations, strategies, and tactics that shape the broad outlines of environmental transnationalism. These organizations (along with many others) have contributed to the spread of environmental awareness worldwide through a variety of strategies. The IUCN exercises its influence most notably through its dissemination of high-quality information about the state of the Earth's environment, and through its direct involvement in implementing conservation plans rather than through coordinated tactics or social mobilization. The work of its largest commission, the Species Survival Commission, has contributed immensely to international conservation efforts. For example, the IUCN maintains a "Red List" of threatened species of living organisms, which has long been an essential reference both for governments and NGOs involved in the conservation of biodiversity. The IUCN has also been active in a wide range of other environmental issues of international importance, including climate change, trade in endangered species, and sustainable development.

Greenpeace engages in direct action worldwide, using its members to protest against what they perceive to be objectionable practices by blocking whaling vessels, hanging banners on prominent buildings, chaining themselves to trees, and other such maneuvers. The aim of these highly publicized actions is to "induce people to engage in . . . environmentally sound practices."[26] In addition to influencing the cessation of nuclear testing in Alaska and French Polynesia, Greenpeace has been actively involved in campaigns to end whaling and the indiscriminate dumping of toxic waste as well as in highlighting the hazards of acid rain, ozone depletion, and climate change.

FOE's strategy is to focus its attention on the activities of States in the international arena in an effort to make them "more accountable to environmental protection." FOE lobbies governments and tries to "corner states into environmentally sound behavior."[27] It does this by working at the local level (by persuading local municipalities to adopt

Earth-friendly policies) while simultaneously applying pressure at the national level through international organizations (by participating in delegations to environmental negotiations). It also monitors whether States are complying with the international agreements signed by them, and generates potentially embarrassing publicity in the event of a State's noncompliance. FOE's sphere of activity has included transnational campaigns to pressure States to comply with the International Convention for the Regulation of Whaling, restrictions in the emission of chemicals that cause acid rain and ozone depletion, and protection of tropical rainforests. It has also organized networks of NGOs to lobby against multilateral banks, including the World Bank and the International Monetary Fund, organizations long seen as ignoring the environmental consequences of development projects.[28]

The WWF has always focused its efforts on the preservation of biodiversity. Its initiatives have included protecting tropical forests, promoting the establishment of marine sanctuaries, and protecting flora and fauna on the verge of extinction, such as its own symbol, the giant panda. Its strategies tend to be less confrontational than those of Greenpeace or FOE; rather than criticize the international trade system as a whole, the WWF has long supported working within that system to minimize its effects on biodiversity. To that end, is has been a strong proponent of TRAFFIC (Trade Records Analysis of Fauna and Flora in Commerce), a body created by the IUCN to monitor trade in endangered species and the products derived from these.[29] By focusing campaigns around "charismatic mega-fauna" like tigers, elephants, sea turtles, and whales, it has pioneered effective techniques for raising public awareness of, and money for, conservation issues. In recent years, the WWF campaigns have extended into additional environmental issues such as ozone depletion and climate change.

While environmental activism originated almost exclusively in the developed world, there is now increasing participation in local and transnational environmentalism from the developing world, and particularly in Latin America and Asia.[30] Alliances with large transnational environmental organizations have helped in the development and propagation of environmental groups in this region. Their campaigns are generally not limited to conservation or preservation concerns, and often encompass wider issues such as demands for social justice or economic reforms. They attract their supporters from rural areas and include young people, and particularly women.[31] The presence of Third World environmental organizations in the international arena has helped to reinforce the focus on sustainable development,

BOX 6.3
Ozone Depletion

Scientific collaborations to study the problem of ozone depletion accelerated in the 1980s with the discovery in 1985 of the
ozone hole above the Antarctic. As scientific consensus began to
coalesce around the severity of the damage being done to the
ozone layer, the transnational network of scientists originally
formed just to study the phenomenon began to expand its role
into a crucial disseminator of scientific information.

Networks of scientists were able to provide not only critically
important scientific theories and empirical discoveries but also
to achieve scientific consensus: "The best scientists and the most
advanced technological resources had to be brought together in
a cooperative effort to build an international scientific consensus." [32]

Transnational coalitions of environmental organizations also
played a role in mobilizing interest and action on the ozone
issue. Environmental organizations in the United States swung
into action from the early 1980s on, with the crucial support of
industry and the US government.[33] Since European environmental organizations were showing little interest at the time the
"[US] State Department encouraged American environmental
organizations to motivate their European counterparts to offset
the influence of industry."[34] Greenpeace and FOE, so often
adversarial in their relationships with the US government, were
especially effective in alerting European environmental organizations to the threat of ozone depletion. By 1988, British environmental organizations were not only mobilizing public
support but were also pressing for parliamentary hearings to discuss the threat.[35] In September 1987, twenty-four countries,
along with the Commission of the European Communities,
signed the Montreal Protocol on Substances That Deplete the
Ozone Layer.

---

explore funding mechanisms for developing nations, and, interestingly, to bring environmental concerns back to the local level by putting developing-country concerns for clean water, sanitation, and food
also on the international agenda.

BOX 6.4
Climate Change

Although extensive scientific observation of the earth's climate began after the 1952 IGY, and crucial observations of atmospheric CO_2 began in 1958, not until the mid-1980s did fears over changing climate patterns explode onto the international environment agenda. In 1985, relying for their material on a scientific assessment of global climate change authored by the SCOPE (Scientific Committee on Problems of the Environment) committee of the ICSU, a group of scientists at an international gathering in Villach, Austria, determined that "substantial warming" of the Earth's surface was likely to occur as a result of significant increases in the concentration of CO_2 in the atmosphere. It further noted that these increases "were attributable to human activities," and noted that the problem of "global warming" merited urgent international political attention.[36]

Acting as a transnational coalition, this group drew considerable attention to issues of global climate change in policy-making circles by conveying its conclusions to home governments, and urging governments worldwide to heed its warnings. It stressed the need for dissemination of information about greenhouse gases (i.e., gases such as CO_2 that can cause global warming) and called for further scientific research into the issue. The 1988 Toronto Conference on the Changing Atmosphere gathered together scientists and government delegates to discuss the evidence for global climate change and what actions could be taken to reverse it. This conference prompted the establishment of the Intergovernmental Panel on Climate Change (IPCC), consisting of a group of about three hundred climate scientists from around the world who were given the task of reviewing and disseminating scientific information on global climate change. In addition, the governments of many industrialized countries represented at the Toronto Conference voluntarily committed themselves to reducing their emissions of greenhouse gases by 20 percent by 2005. The text of the Framework Convention for Climate Change was adopted in 1992, and the Convention itself entered into force on March 21, 1994. The Kyoto Protocol of 1997 established specific, binding targets for reductions in emissions of greenhouse gases.

Two Case Studies: Ozone Depletion and Climate Change

An analysis of two major international environmental issues illustrates the achievements and limitations of the roles of transnational networks, coalitions, and movements. Epistemic communities, which fall within the category of transnational networks, have been instrumental in catalyzing action on these two environmental issues. Networks of scientists were integral to developing agendas, providing essential information to countries and NGOs involved in negotiations, and suggesting remedies to the underlying environmental problems. Supported as they were by these networks, environmental NGOs were able to close the circle on ozone depletion by spurring agreement on the means of reducing emissions of ozone-destroying substances.

The case of ozone depletion is one that also highlights the importance of the influence of governments and industry in moving the issue forward. Success in this case may not be entirely ascribed to the role of transnational environmentalism. It is axiomatic that economic considerations play a crucial role in whether and to what extent industry and governments support environmental issues. In this case, it was in the interests of a US industrial giant, DuPont, to promote international limits on chlorofluorocarbons (CFC), the ozone-destroying substance present in widely used products like refrigerators and aerosol cans; they were already facing a domestic ban in the United States and held a significant lead in the development of CFC substitutes. While scientific consensus and transnational civil society concerns may have been a condition precedent to the Vienna Agreement in 1985 and the Montreal Protocol in 1987, the strong support of industry and the US government contributed significantly to these agreements becoming a reality.

The process has been similar for global climate change, but the outcome not nearly as successful. Transnational environmentalism has been present in the case of climate change, but limits on the development of a consensus, and the activity of significant industry interests against action to reduce carbon dioxide (CO_2), have contributed to a slower progress. The effort to prevent or reduce global climate change has become a highly contentious international environmental issue.

As awareness of the dangers of climate change spread in the wake of the Toronto Conference of 1988, many environmental NGOs and industry groups readied their strategies to deal with the problem. By 1990, eighty-eight NGOs were in attendance at the second World Climate Conference in Geneva, held to pave the way for an international climate change treaty.[37] By 1991, FOE had developed a strong campaign to combat global climate change. Greenpeace also pursued several simultaneous climate change strategies: First, it attempted to mobilize countries predicted to suffer the worst damage from global warming, especially low-elevation island States at risk from rising sea levels, and African States at risk from accelerated desertification. Second, it sought to politicize the issue among citizens and governments of the industrialized countries that formed the Organization for Economic Cooperation and Development (OECD). Third, by attempting to interpret scientific information itself so as to highlight the possible adverse effects of climate change and the "high-risk side of science," it tried to highlight the immediacy of the problem in contrast to the more neutral and balanced analysis of the IPCC.[38] In 1995, Greenpeace International alone spent USD 4.35 million on its climate campaign, making it the third most expensive protest campaign after antinuclear and disarmament issues.[39]

The Toronto Conference catalyzed the formation of the Climate Action Network (CAN), a transnational network of environmental NGOs. CAN is an important example of such a network and thus merits detailed attention. CAN was created in March 1989 with the purpose of

> strengthen[ing] communication and co-ordination with respect to: (1) information exchanges on science, policy, and events such as intergovernmental meetings concerning the greenhouse effect; (2) attendance at and preparation for relevant intergovernment and other meetings, including prior circulation of draft position-statements; (3) facilitating national effort through the sharing of expertise and information between network members; and (4) stimulating joint or simultaneous actions where appropriate.[40]

Originally established by twenty NGOs, CAN now has a membership of 287 NGOs and regional offices in Africa, Europe, Latin America, North America, South Asia, and Southeast Asia.[41] CAN has assumed the role of an umbrella organization for NGOs concerned with the climate change issue: the founders of CAN describe it as a "transnational system of information, communication, and coordination."[42]

The similarities and differences between the two campaigns against ozone depletion and climate change are instructive. Especially during the early years of climate change as an international environmental issue, NGOs from developed countries (developed NGOs) largely viewed participation by NGOs from developing countries (developing NGOs) as a useful reinforcement to their demands on governments in their own industrialized countries. Such cooperation was seen as helpful because it demonstrated worldwide support for reductions of greenhouse gas emissions. However, the presence of these developing NGOs may have actually complicated rather than aided the effectiveness of the developed NGOs' message on this issue, because a schism soon emerged between the goals pursued by these two types of NGOs. Rather than being confronted by a united NGO position on global climate change, country representatives heard instead a cacophony of positions, wherein aims often differed from region to region. This stood in stark contrast to the relatively united stand articulated by transnational networks of climate scientists such as the IPCC.

Although NGOs did manage to champion a set of expectations and goals that came to dominate rhetoric about the overall targets for reductions in emissions of CO_2, they achieved few consensus positions. The areas in which NGOs had the most difficulty in reaching unanimity often involved national policy choices that would have imposed significant costs or benefits on particular countries, regions, or interest groups within them. Even today, a consensus among NGOs on certain issues at the international level may be impossible: "NGOs from different parts of the world will always hold different views and different predilections for action based on their own individual and national interests."[43] Often, there is no concord even among NGOs within the same country. These constraints on the development of a universal agreement limit the extent of the transnationality of their message as well as the extent to which CAN could be considered anything more than a transnational network.[44] In contrast, ozone depletion was an issue in which the scientific evidence was relatively clear, and the solution uncontroversial.

Attempts to bring about legislation to retard climate change were also limited by interests that mobilized against elements of the climate agreement. The Global Climate Coalition (GCC), an organization of private companies and business/trade associations representing more than 230,000 firms (many from the fossil-fuel industry), was established in 1989 to coordinate participation by business interests in the science and policy debates on climate change. The GCC then represented industry at Rio, and spent USD 13 million in an advertising campaign to oppose the Framework Convention on Climate Change. Again in contrast, influential industrial actors, such as DuPont, supported international action to ban ozone-depleting substances, in part because they already faced domestic regulation and desired a level playing field internationally.

Challenges

As noted above, international interest in environmental issues seems to have peaked in the 1990s; little progress towards concrete international action has been made in the years since the Earth Summit. The United States has recently sought to roll back its obligations to the Montreal Protocol, and has refused to sign the Kyoto Protocol (though Russia has ratified it, bringing it into effect in spite of US hesitation). Current international priorities center around security issues; these developments in domestic and international politics mean that it will be difficult to introduce or keep environmental issues on the international agenda.

Scientific inquiry will be crucial to the future of transnational environmental action, as scientific evidence that human activity has an effect on the environment has, time and again, spurred international agreement. In a number of issue areas, scientific networks have been even more important than those concerned with advocacy: the Intergovernmental Panel on Climate Change has helped to clarify the importance of international agreement to reduce CO_2 emissions, for example. Future research may reveal evidence of environmental fragility that is too compelling to ignore. Anti-environmental interests have already mobilized in a number of issue areas. Such activity might be expected to increase as environmental considerations become increasingly influential. To combat this, transnational organizations will need to broaden and deepen their own transnational networks, and more effectively bridge internal divides — such as those between Northern and Southern perspectives on environmental priorities. They will also have to work with business and other interests to incorporate environmental concerns into business practices. This is not as difficult as it seems: despite strong and deep opposition from the fossil-fuel industry to acknowledge that climate change was an issue of real concern, concern for the environment has penetrated several companies. British Petroleum (BP), for example, has turned its attention to the development of cleaner fuel and has sought to reduce emissions in its own operations; "Beyond Petroleum" is its slogan in television advertisements. In 1998, BP joined the World Resources Institute in an initiative to combat climate change.[45] As seen from the ozone-depletion case, alliances between business and environmental organizations may serve to advance environmental aims in the future.

In an international climate that may be less hospitable to environmental issues in and of themselves, linkages between the environment and other issues have also become very important. Environmental side-agreements and provisions for environmental protection have been integrated into international agreements, particularly those concerning trade. This may be a fruitful way to ensure that the environment does not disappear from the international agenda. The North American Free Trade Agreement, as well as the European Union and the World Trade Organization, all provide for overseeing mechanisms and cooperation for addressing environmental concerns. At another level, however, these institutions also present challenges for transnational environmentalism as their missions are not primarily environmental; critics fear that the pursuit of global free trade will have environmental consequences, and tensions have developed when environmental considerations have clashed with the ideals of barrier-free trade. The WTO (and its predecessor GATT) have ruled against environmental concerns in two well-known cases.[46] Whether environmental considerations will ever prevail remains to be seen.

Conclusion

Consciousness of international environmental issues has increased markedly among both governments and their citizens over the last quarter of a century. In large part, this reflects the political globalism practiced by transnational networks of scientists such as the ICSU, and by NGOs such as WWF, Greenpeace, and FOE, that has lifted environmental issues to the top of the international agenda by mobilizing both the citizenry and high-level officials in nations around the world.

There is little doubt that vast transnational networks have contributed in myriad ways to species conservation, biodiversity protection, pollution prevention, and the ecological health and integrity of the Earth. Transnational networks and the communication they foster have served to provide information to citizens, organizations, and governments worldwide on the full range of environmental issues. This green web has supplied information and inspired action: in some instances, transnational networks and coalitions, by bringing unified pressure for environmental action to bear, have been able to change the practices of government, industry, and international institutions. As the current crop of international environmental issues continues to evolve and new issues arise, the participation of transnational networks and coalitions will likely continue to increase.

Notes

1. The Social Learning Group, *Learning to Manage Global Environmental Risks*, 2 vols. (Cambridge, MA: MIT Press, 2001), 1:3.

2. Multilateral treaties that could be broadly construed as environmental, in the sense that they dealt with transnational efforts to manage or protect wildlife, date as far back as the 1880s (for example, the Regulation of Salmon Fishery in the Rhine River Basin [Berlin], 1885). Several treaties were signed before 1945, including the Convention for the Protection of Birds Useful to Agriculture (Paris, 1902); North Pacific Fur Seal Treaty (1911); Convention for the Regulation of Whaling (Geneva, 1931); Convention Relative to the Preservation of Fauna and Flora in Their Natural State (London, 1933).

3. This term was articulated for environmental politics by Peter Haas in *Saving the Mediterranean* (New York: Columbia University Press, 1990), 18. See chap. 2 in particular.

4. The Social Learning Group has documented the pioneering role of science in highlighting international environmental issues. It tracked the coverage of three atmospheric areas of concern — acid rain, ozone depletion, and climate change — in *Nature*, a leading international scientific journal, and Reuters World Newswire. Coverage of all three issues peaked in scientific circles prior to the same concerns being voiced in the popular press. Social Learning Group, *Learning to Manage Global Environmental Risks*, 1:27.

5. Currently known as the International Council for Science, ICSU has over one hundred constituent members, including individual scientific unions and other scientific organizations. Academy of Sciences, www.nas.edu/history/igy/ (accessed January 7, 2004); J. Eric Smith, "The Role of Special Purpose and Nongovernmental Organizations in the Environmental Crisis," *International Organization* 26, no. 2 (1972): 308.

6. International Union for the Conservation of Nature, "Welcome to IUCN — World Conservation Union," www.iucn.org/about/index.htm (accessed September 1, 2004).

7. Margaret E. Keck and Kathryn Sikkink, *Activists beyond Borders: Advocacy Networks in International Politics* (Ithaca, NY: Cornell University Press, 1998), 122.

8. Anne Thompson Feraru, "Transnational Political Interests and the Global Environment," *International Organization* 28, no. 1 (1974): 32.

9. Program of the Center for International Earth Science Information Network (the Socioeconomic Data and Applications Center, database 1885–2004), www.ciesin.columbia.edu/ (accessed September 1, 2004).

10. Michael Grubb, Matthias Koch, Abby Munson, Francis Sullivan, and Koy Thomson, *The Earth Summit Agreements: A Guide and Assessment* (London: Earthscan, 1993).

11. Two unofficial parallel conferences were also set up: the Peoples Forum and Dai Dong. These were more radical in nature than the Environment Forum, and were inspired, in part, by opposition to the Vietnam War. See P. Haas, M. Levy, and T. Parson, "Appraising the Earth Summit: How Should We Judge UNCED's Success?" *Environment* 34, no. 8 (1992): 6–11, 26–33.

12. Feraru, "Transnational Political Interests," 48.

13. Hein-Anton van der Heijden, "Environmental Movements, Ecological Modernisation and Political Opportunity Structures," in *Environmental Movements: Local, National and Global,* ed. Christopher Rootes, 199–221 (London and Portland, OR: Frank Cass, 1999), 202.

14. There are many accounts of the role of transnational environmentalism in influencing local practice, government policies, and international agreements. See, for instance, M. Finger, "The Ivory Trade Ban: NGOs and International Conservation," in *Environmental NGOs in World Politics: Linking the Local and the Global,* ed. T. Princen and M. Finger, 121–59 (London: Routledge, 1994), for an account on the ivory trade; Keck and Sikkink, *Activists beyond Borders,* for tropical deforestation; B. Rich, *Mortgaging the Earth: The World Bank, Environmental Impoverishment, and the Crisis of Development* (Boston: Beacon Press, 1994), for World Bank reform; M. J. Peterson, "Whalers, Cetologists, Environmentalists, and the International Management of Whaling," *International Organization* 46, no. 1 (1992): 147–86, for whaling; and J. P. Manno, "Advocacy and Diplomacy: NGOs and the Great Lakes H_2O Quality Agreement," in *Environmental NGOs in World Politics: Linking the Local and the Global,* ed. T. Princen and M. Finger, 69–120 (London: Routledge, 1994), for trans-boundary air pollution.

15. G. Brundtland, ed., *Our Common Future: The World Commission on Environment and Development* (Oxford: Oxford University Press, 1987), 16.

16. Grubb et al., *The Earth Summit Agreements,* 44.

17. The NGO Alternative Treaties, "People's Earth Declaration," article 23, habitat.igc.org/treaties/ (accessed November 14, 2004).

18. Social Learning Group, *Learning to Manage*, 1:25.

19. United Nations Johannesburg Summit 2002, www.johannes-burgsummit.org/html/basic_info/basicinfo.html (accessed November 14, 2004).

20. "The Bubble-and-Squeak Summit," *The Economist*, September 4, 2002.

21. An example of a debt-for-nature swap is the purchase by a nongovernmental organization of discounted foreign debt followed by the forgiveness of that debt in exchange for conservation activity.

22. Christopher Rootes, "Environmental Movements from the Local to the Global," in *Environmental Movements: Local, National and Global*, ed. Christopher Rootes, 1–12 (London and Portland, OR: Frank Cass, 1999), 6.

23. Rich, *Mortgaging the Earth*, 132.

24. A. Doherty, "The Role of Nongovernmental Organizations in UNCED," in *Negotiating International Regimes: Lessons Learned from the United Nations Conference on Environment and Development*, ed. Bertram I. Spector, Gunnar Sjostedt, and I. William Zartman, 199–218 (London: Graham and Trotman, 1994), 199.

25. See, among many others, Princen and Finger, *Environmental NGOs in World Politics*; and K. Raustiala, "States, NGOs, and International Environmental Institutions," *International Studies Quarterly* 41, no. 4 (1997): 719–40.

26. P. Wapner, *Environmental Activism and World Civic Politics* (Albany: State University of New York Press, 1996), 14.

27. Ibid., 15, 126.

28. Ibid., 118; Also see Robert Lamb, *Promising the Earth* (London and New York: Routledge, 1996), 134.

29. World Wide Fund for Nature, www.panda.org/about_wwf/who_we_are/history/seventies.cfm (accessed November 14, 2004).

30. Jeff Haynes, "Power, Politics and Environmental Movements in the Third World," in *Environmental Movements: Local, National and Global*, ed. Christopher Rootes, 222–42 (London and Portland, OR: Frank Cass, 1999), 223.

31. Ibid., 223.

32. Richard Benedick, *Ozone Diplomacy: New Directions in Safeguarding the Planet* (Cambridge, MA: Harvard University Press, 1991), 5.

33. This support resulted from the development of competitive alternatives to CFCs by an American company, DuPont, whose interests the US government wished to promote. See Scott Barrett, *Environment and Statecraft: The Strategy of Environmental Treaty-Making* (Oxford: Oxford University Press, 2003), 234–35.

34. Benedick, *Ozone Diplomacy*, 27.

35. Ibid., 114.

36. International Council of Scientific Unions, United Nations Environment Programme and World Meteorological Organization, *Report of the International Conference on the Assessment of the Role of Carbon Dioxide and of Other Greenhouse Gases in Climate Variations and Associated Impacts*, WMO document no. 661 (Geneva: WMO, 1986).

37. J. Jaeger and H. L. Ferguson, eds., *Climate Change: Science, Impacts and Policy: Proceedings of the Second World Climate Conference* (Cambridge: Cambridge University Press, 1990).

38. Bill Hare, Greenpeace International policy director, interview with Wendy E. Franz, February 27, 1997, Bonn; Greenpeace International, *Climate Campaign Archives 1990–1997*. Notes on file with the authors.

39. Greenpeace International, *Annual Report*, 1995.

40. Climate Action Network Charter, working document, dated March 12, 1989.

41. Climate Action Network, "What Does CAN Hope to Achieve," www.climatenework.org/pages/aboutCANInt.html (accessed November 13, 2004).

42. A. Roncerel and Navroz Dubash, "Needs, Challenges and Opportunities for Environmental Action: The Case of Climate Action Network," paper presented at a workshop on *The New Europe Conference: Opportunities for Foundations*, Paris, July 9, 1992.

43. A. Rahman and A. Roncerel, "A View from the Ground Up," in *Negotiating Climate Change: The Inside Story of the Rio Convention*, ed. Irving M. Mintzer and J. Amber Leonard, 239–72 (Cambridge: Cambridge University Press, 1994), 248.

44. Wendy E. Franz, *Changing the Climate? Non-State Actors in International Environmental Politics* (doctoral dissertation, Harvard University, 2000).

45. British Petroleum, "Environment and Society," www.bp.com (accessed September 1, 2004).

46. United States Restrictions on Imports of Tuna, August 16, 1991, GATT BISD (39th Supp.) at 1SS (1993), 30 ILM 1594 (1991) [commonly known as Tuna/Dolphin I]; and GATT Dispute Settlement Panel Report on United States' Restrictions on Imports of Tuna, 33 ILM 839 (1994) [commonly known as Tuna/Dolphin II].

CHAPTER SEVEN

Dot-Causes and Protest: Transnational Economic Justice Movements

John D. Clark

Introduction

Transnational civil society (TCS) movements have witnessed a dramatic growth in recent years, of which the rise of what is variously called the economic justice movement (EJM) or the global social justice movement is one of the most spectacular examples. However, these terms are imprecise because, unlike others, this is not strictly a single movement: it is not a coherent network of people and groups uniting in solidarity around common conditions or common aims.[1] As Kumi Naidoo observes, it is "not always evident how [it is] organized or led."[2] Some describe it as a movement of movements as it encompasses diverse issues and aims,[3] from those seeking specific reforms (for example, regarding Third World debt) to those who want to smash capitalism. Its bonds stem often from what its constituents *don't* like, rather than what they call for. The characteristics of the EJM owe much to it being the first political movement to be organized essentially through the medium of the Internet. These terms are, however, more rigorous than the name many establishment journalists and others know it by — the antiglobalization movement.

This chapter seeks to illuminate the phenomenon of EJM using social movement analysis. Of particular significance is the prominence of an eclectic array of Web-based civil society organizations (CSO) (called "dot-causes") that largely mobilize the movement's followers and disseminate its diverse messages. We then look at the various ways in which the EJM is forcing a reshaping of global governance, and draw parallels with the governance reforms that the international community often presses Southern governments to adopt. We start by asking why the movement is achieving such wide support and managing to define a set of democracy deficits inherent in intergovernmental processes today.

Civil Society and the Democratization of Democracy

The history of democracy is about the evolving ways through which citizens shape government policies and hold officials to account. The potency of democratic tools, therefore, is the degree to which they close the gap between citizens and the decisions that affect them. Civil society has other roles, but the one that is gathering most momentum is that of strengthening democracy through advocacy — particularly as international arenas are fast becoming the crucibles in which new policies are forged, and traditional instruments of democracy hold little sway in that realm.

This trend is particularly powerful because of the increasing interconnectedness of the world we live in. An important paradox is unfolding: while a great deal of the substance of politics has been globalized (trade, economics, climate change, HIV/AIDS, the SARS pandemic, terrorism, etc.), the process of politics hasn't. Its main institutions — elections, political parties, and parliaments — remain rooted at the national (or local) level. Civil society organizations, on the other hand, have proved well able to adapt to working in strong global organizations and networks.[4]

This emerging capacity indicates that democracy can now mean more than the opportunity for citizens to vote every few years for politicians who sit in assemblies or parliaments representing their constituents' concerns across the spectrum of political matters, which could be called traditional or representative democracy. While this form remains important, it has become greatly eroded in much of the world as citizens are increasingly disenchanted with electoral politics. Now, the more politically active citizens (a minority, but traditionally those who have driven societal change) are able to take part in growing numbers in participatory democracy as well. By joining NGOs, pressure groups, social movements, protests, etc., they are entering directly the debates that most interest them.

It could be argued that participatory democracy is not new: the earliest form of democracy existed in ancient Greece, in which all native-born citizens (except slaves and women) could gather in the forum to speak and vote on any issue that concerned them. This was rule (*kratein*) of the people (*demos*). As city-states grew, such decision making became unwieldy, and the practice of electing delegates to represent a constituency was born.

In traditional democracy we are grouped according to where we live; our neighborhoods form the constituencies for which we elect our representatives. Political parties often assume that our class, income, and locality are the main determinants of our politics. Participatory democracy is now changing the geography of politics: it allows us to aggregate differently, with others who share our burning concerns wherever they live. In other words, community of neighborhood is being supplemented by community of interest — and thanks to modern information and communication technologies (ICT), such communities can be global as easily as local.

Civil society today cannot be put into any nutshell. In structural forms it ranges from the organized nongovernmental organizations (NGO) for public benefit (such as Amnesty International, Oxfam, Greenpeace, and CARE) and associations for member benefits (such as trade unions, consumers' groups, professional associations, and sports clubs) to faith-based organizations and antiwar protestors. Its characteristics and impact vary from country to country. As with the private sector and the natural world, diversity is a cornerstone of its strength. A vibrant civil society is packed with organizations and causes competing for the attention of citizens.

Given this diversity, it is dangerous to generalize about the sector or imply homogeneity. For every cause espoused by some CSOs there is a counter-cause waged by others. However, within this emerging sector is located a strong segment of very diverse organizations that all critique globalization in different ways. Their combined impact has been to outline a common set of values and aims, one that has come to dominate civil society advocacy in international policy debates. This constellation comprises NGOs, unions, protest groups, religious organizations, and others — what is very loosely called the EJM.

This movement flourishes on the growing malaise with the institutional fabric of democratic political systems, a subject to which we return later. It has also become popular because it has exposed the unethical framework of today's globalization. This chapter is not the place to discuss the arguments on globalization and its economic and ethical impacts; these are well discussed earlier in this book and elsewhere.[5] Suffice it to say, there is a widespread view among those who are concerned about world poverty that the current management of globalization widens inequalities between and within most countries. As such, the problem may not be with globalization per se, but with the selective kind of globalization in practice today. This is the root of economic injustice.

The EJM and other civil society pressures have done much to trigger a mounting disquiet in, and challenge to, the traditional institutions of democracy. This contestation has brought into sharp relief at least five democracy deficits:

The ideological deficit: Political parties, especially in rich countries, have become less relevant to the political cleavages that concern most people today. They often seem stuck in the old political rivalries of socialist versus capitalist theories of ownership of the means of production. Contemporary voters are increasingly interested in other issues, concerning not just who owns the means of production but also what is produced, how this is done, who decides on these issues, what impact this has on society, what are the alternatives, and so on. Pressure groups and social movements are natural leaders in these newer and more diverse debates.

The deficit of integrity: Political parties in much of the world are seen to have lost their integrity, largely because of their fundraising activities and corporate links. Politicians too seem increasingly mired in sleaze, nepotism, and corruption, willing to bargain priorities ruthlessly in political coalitions in order to cling to power for today.

The deficit of representation: Electoral democracy allows citizens to choose representatives from among their peers to speak for them in national political forums. But increasingly, getting into office demands great wealth and powerful contacts; hence, representatives today rarely reflect the diversity of the electorate. Only 15 percent worldwide are women; few come from ethnic minorities, poor, or working-class backgrounds. Voters are increasingly disillusioned by the fact that democracy has failed to offer them the chance to be represented by their peers.

The deficiency of reach: In the globalizing world, traditional institutions of democracy no longer hold sway over the many decisions affecting everyday life. These are increasingly forged in regional forums (such as NAFTA and the European Union), in intergovernmental forums (such as the International Monetary Fund or World Trade Organization), and in global corporations. These forums may be accountable to some governments for some things, but they do not regularly come under the purview of national parliaments or other traditional democratic instruments as would forums at the national level, and no supranational parliaments yet fill the void.

The deficiency of sovereignty: Most national governments experience dwindling autonomy as they become powerless to buck trends set by global powers, particularly in the economic realm. For example, developing countries find that they now have little latitude to set tariffs, exchange rates, or interest rates at levels that differ substantially from what the market indicates. Similarly, they must increasingly conform to received wisdom when it comes to currency controls, labor market policies, and taxation regimes. Paradoxically, just as formal democracy has spread into new areas of the globe for the first time, substantive democracy — the ability to participate in decisions affecting everyday life — has been eroded by this loss of autonomy of national States.[6]

These deficiencies combine to provoke a widespread public image (perhaps unfair to the many politicians who are genuinely committed to international justice issues) that elected representatives are irrelevant to the global debates, and are obsessed by nimbyism and pork-barrel politics.[7] Just as many voters are prioritizing issues of world justice and the environment that are long-term and global, they see parliamentarians as consumed by matters that are short-term and parochial.

The evidence of the democracy deficits is clear to see.[8] Voter turnouts have fallen in most Western democracies (except Scandinavia). In the United Kingdom and the United States, for example, the turnouts in national elections averaged about 80 percent since World War II until the last few years; in the most recent elections, they were 59 percent and 51 percent, respectively — even though advertising budgets for elections have rocketed. Even in the new democracies of Eastern Europe, voter turnouts are falling steeply. More marked still is the fall in the membership of political parties: in a range of Organization for Economic Cooperation and Development (OECD) countries (again, not Scandinavia), party membership has declined to between one half and one fifth of the levels prevailing in the 1960s. As an example, the British Conservative Party dwindled from 2.2 million members to just 350,000 today. In contrast, membership of cause-specific NGOs has risen sharply: in the United Kingdom, more people now belong to the Royal Society for the Protection of Birds than to all political parties combined.

In developing countries also, there are similar manifestations of democracy deficits. Only 20 percent of Mozambique's population voted in the last election. Indian elections have more stable turnouts, but are extremely costly because of the largesse showered by political parties come election time on important sectors (such as farmers) to gain or stay in power. Further, these deficits may lead to more serious consequences, such as failing States, authoritarian regimes, rising fundamentalism, human rights violations, and so on.

The world over, people no longer trust politicians and are increasingly disinclined to join political parties. A similar skepticism extends towards multinationals: people flock to buy branded goods manufactured by the large corporations because they trust the products, not the institutions. A forty-country survey, commissioned by the World Economic Forum in 2002, showed that of seventeen leading institutions of influence in these countries, those *least* trusted were parliaments, large corporations, and the International Monetary Fund (IMF), and those most trusted were NGOs and the military.[9]

To summarize: People speak passionately about democracy. Many are prepared to lay down their life to defend it, but fewer than ever can be bothered to use it. We have become so cynical in much of the OECD that electoral democracy means little more than the chance to choose every four or five years between one white millionaire or another to run our country. At the same time, a revolution is under way — a mounting crescendo of diverse voices — as NGOs and pressure groups gain confidence and members. Through active support of specific CSOs, we can today engage more directly in policy debates that particularly interest us. This is an invaluable benefit, as we are all interested in different issues. In participatory democracy, we make our choice by aligning ourselves with the groups that most closely speak for us. CSOs compete for our attention, as do shops in an arcade. Civil society is a veritable marketplace, but not of goods and services: it is a marketplace of interests, ideas, and ideologies. Customers don't trade with cash and shares but with their support and time. Those, and media coverage, are the assets most prized by policy activists.

The antiglobalization debate — with the EJM as its engine — has exposed these deficits and demonstrated how they together maintain the political and economic power of the privileged and check dissenting voices. It has also demonstrated the new opportunities of participatory democracy by structuring the critique and prompting an alternative framework for global governance. Before analyzing these matters of content, however, we first examine the process aspects of the EJM — its structure.

The EJM Explored

A particularly distinctive feature of the EJM is that it has been the first social movement to be orchestrated essentially through Internet-based communications, a fact that explains many of the characteristics of the movement. This is not to say that it was the first example of Web-based activism. Far from it.[10] Indeed, the International Campaign to Ban Landmines was almost entirely a Web-based endeavor (to the extent that when the Nobel Prize committee decided to give it the Peace Prize, it had no bank account into which to receive the prize money). However, this campaign essentially used the Web to coordinate action and exchange views and information between the many CSOs who had joined the campaign. In other words, it was a membership network, not a social movement.

Social scientists often analyze social movements from three different angles. They examine:

- The organizational forms and mobilizing structures;

- The political opportunities and constraints;

- The social construction or cultural framing process — that is, how and why people identify with the movement.[11]

When deconstructing more traditional social movements (i.e., feminist, peasant, and those dealing with civil liberties) these three characteristics serve well. We now analyze the EJM within this same framework, and find that it helps explain its ambiguities.

Mobilizing Structures

That the organizational forms within the EJM are largely Web-based and virtual networks is a very distinctive feature. This includes established CSOs who may have offices, staff, and defined structures, but who use the Internet as their main interface with their supporters ("clicks and mortar" organizations). Dot-causes both mobilize adherents and are the platforms for planning campaign strategies. They prove very powerful conduits of information and motivation, but are poor facilitators of complex planning — especially when this entails resolving deep differences. Hence, the major events that characterize the EJM tend to be omnibus occasions for which the location and date of action are agreed, but the myriad EJM components plan their own events within that very broad framework. The net result is less a coherent demonstration and more a protest mall, comprising hundreds of specific causes (like shop fronts competing for people's attention), with just a vague unifying theme — opposing cookie-cutter capitalism in which one Northern, market-driven culture comes to dominate the world.

The leader of the Zapatista peasant movement in Mexico, Subcommandante Marcos — one of the icons of the EJM — once famously celebrated this characteristic by explaining that it is a movement of "one big No and many small Yesses." He argued that the EJM should cease struggling to define an alternative political framework and simply promote local autonomy. In truth, it has to be a movement of "many Yesses" — because who is there to say no? The virtual nature of the movement's structure means that there are no clear leaders (or so many as to defy the possibility of leadership). There are leaders of specific components (such as the World Social Forum, or the Jubilee 2000 debt relief campaign), and there are movement stars who appear at every big event (such as Vandana Shiva from India, or Naomi Klein from Canada) — but they prefer to describe themselves as interpreters of the movement rather than its leaders.[12] Beyond this, anyone who can start a Web site and post ideas that others read becomes a leader.

It is simply not feasible to bring the leaders of the different components together for a face-to-face meeting, partly because of the logistical difficulties of what is a truly global movement, and partly because these EJM components are rapidly shifting, and — in contrast, say, with the feminist movement — there are no defined entry criteria and no bottom lines. Without such meetings, it is impossible to build up either the trust or the tacit leadership that are strong features of other social movements.[13]

The most evident consequence of these leadership dilemmas concerns political tactics. The EJM comprises groups who want to challenge policy makers face to face with their alternatives (such as Jubilee 2000 and Association for the Taxation of Financial Transaction for the Aid of Citizens), groups who think this is a waste of time and promote nonviolent protests (such as the Wombles and Ruckus Society), and those bent on the use of violence (such as anarchists and the Black Block group). For most within the movement, the adherents of violence pose a real dilemma. The majority abhor the tactic, but also recognize that it has made the EJM powerful, and so feared by officials. The Battle of Seattle (the protests at the World Trade Organization meeting in 1999) marked the movement's real birth. It is still widely talked about many years later as a momentous event, even though the number of protestors there was less than the multitude that took part in the 1988 protests at the World Bank/IMF Annual Meeting in Berlin. The two key differences that made the EJM a potent force in Seattle were, first, that activists were extremely well informed about what was going on at the WTO meetings, including about the very latest developments, thanks to CSO Web sites; and, second, the deliberate and widespread use of violence by some protestors against property and in fighting the police.

These features led to great and unresolved tension within the movement, but also to new opportunities. Taken off guard, policymakers felt compelled to dialogue with this upsurge of civil society activism. They certainly didn't want to talk with anarchists or the punks, but they felt comfortable talking with the alternative-policy advocates. This provided a powerful new political platform for the latter, but angered the protest-oriented groups, who were more concerned with capturing headlines and sparking a public uprising than in winning specific reforms.

Political Opportunities and Constraints

The EJM has emerged at a time when there is a hiatus in global governance that is both capitalized on and exposed by the movement. First, there are the mounting concerns about the democracy deficits discussed earlier in the chapter. Second, there are tensions between governments about global policymaking — which were the real reasons that the Seattle WTO talks finally broke down, and which led to the emergence of a new trans-regional bloc of developing countries (the G21) at the Cancun WTO talks in 2003. In the aftermath of the Iraq war, it seems increasingly likely that the Atlantic Divide between Europe and the United States will grow in areas of economic policy as well as the fight against terrorism. Third, the East Asian economic crisis revealed the fragility of the region's "economic miracle" — based as it was on ever-closer integration with world markets dominated by the United States (and to a lesser extent by the European Union and Japan).

The movement benefited from opportunities of a different nature too: from the arrival of new information and communication technologies and cheaper travel, from the growth of civil society networks that are helping generate a global set of cosmopolitan ideas and ideals among citizens everywhere, from the spread of democracy and enabling environments for civil society to new shores, and from an increased reluctance by Western states to repress protests.

All these factors meant that it was possible for the EJM to come of age simultaneously throughout much of the world — and specifically to flourish by making political opportunity of major high-level intergovernmental meetings, such as the G8 summits, WTO ministerials, and World Bank/IMF annual meetings. Just ten years ago it would have been too expensive to mount global protests, and too dangerous for most Southern activists to take part in them. Now the calendar is packed full of such events. To dampen this opportunity, summit organizers increasingly look for hard-to-reach locations, or ones where protestors can easily be held at bay, such as Sea Island, Georgia, in the United States, or Doha in Qatar.

ICT may have managed to defeat distance, and to some extent have helped overcome language barriers.[14] However, it hasn't yet been able to overcome barriers of mistrust, especially between those from different class and cultural backgrounds. While the webs of interconnection are strong within social movements whose adherents have common personal connections with it, they are weak and shifting in the EJM.

The movement has also been much more successful at pointing to what is wrong in the world than what might be right. Its main meeting point — the World Social Forum (set up in counterpoint to its nemesis, the World Economic Forum) — attracts large numbers but defines no new manifesto or common endeavors (beyond further meetings). In contrast, the World Economic Forum — for all its elitism — is increasingly inviting civil society and intellectual leaders, as well as political leaders, to take part in its meetings, and so is becoming the very sort of multiconstituency forum that can forge new breakthroughs by bridging divides on tough policy issues and by galvanizing new and surprising partnerships.

The end result of the anything-goes foundation of the movement is that it can lead to problem identification, but largely fails (at present) to lead to problem solution.

The Framing Process

Unlike other social movements, there is no unifying or shared cultural framing, no single community of interest within the EJM. How could there be? Its activists include environmentalists and the unemployed of Northern countries; peasants and nationalists from the South; and leftists, intellectuals, union activists, and students everywhere. Some join it because they think their livelihoods are threatened, others to protect their national culture from a homogenizing McTakeover, and others because of a sense of justice denied.

Paradoxically, its strength is also its weakness. Its multifaceted nature and diverse strategies encourage and empower a wide range of adherents, but these connect personally with it in very widely differing ways. The young middle class of the United States or Europe may fret about an approaching global environmental Armageddon, or feel alienated from political processes over which they have no say. Union activists feel threatened by the drift towards flexible labor markets and the global mobility of jobs in transnational corporations. Peasants in the South feel threatened by the pressure for agricultural markets to be opened to (probably subsidized) foods from rich countries, while Northern protectionism denies them the chance to export reciprocally. Southern factory workers fear that introducing labor and environmental standards in world trade will present an excuse for banning importation of their products. Each group connects with the movement in its distinctive personal way, but these are so diverse as to be often contradictory, presenting problems for the EJM's capacity to propose alternatives.

Much of the framing process is achieved through ICT; since these tend to be dominated by younger, better-educated activists (particularly those in the global North) who provide leadership of the dot-causes that are embedded in or close to the mass movements, there is an emerging tendency towards elite leadership, with little of the framing being achieved in practice by the mass-based organizations of the poor and marginalized.

The diversity of framings further explains why it is so difficult to define what the EJM is and what it stands for. Even the "one big No" is not clear: for some it means No to globalization, to others it means No to capitalism, while for yet others it stands for No to this particular type of globalization. Clearly there are many Nos.

Action: Civilizing Global Governance . . .

How can the EJM and its mobilizing CSOs use their assets to win reforms in how globalization is managed — in effect, to civilize global governance? The ingredients can be found in the prescriptions that the donor community urge on developing and transition countries for reforming their governments and their institutions. These measures are designed to ensure that governments are honest, fair, responsive, and efficient; that they concentrate on citizens' priorities; and that citizens are well informed about their rights and are politically empowered. These same pillars of good governance apply equally to the intergovernmental realm:

Transparency: CSOs are powerful not just as conduits to disseminate information about what intergovernmental agencies, transnational companies (TNC), and others are doing (based on their research, evidence gathering, and eyewitness experience — anecdotal as this may be). They also inform citizens about how these institutions work and make decisions. During the WTO ministerial talks in Seattle and Doha, for example, millions of people logged on to the Web sites of various dot-causes every day to find out what was going on and what it all meant. CSOs have also campaigned successfully for organizations such as the World Bank to bring into the open swathes of documentation that was previously confidential, and they continuously press for observer-access and public minutes for all intergovernmental meetings.

Accountability: By pressing national media and national parliaments around the world to give serious attention to how the IMF, WTO, and other global bureaucracies are behaving, and to tackle the excesses of corporate greed and sleaze, CSOs working transnationally are dragging these powerful global players into national accountability structures. By setting up their own watchdogs and international campaigns, they are also introducing new (albeit informal and self-appointed) accountability mechanisms. In the absence of regional or global parliaments, these are the only effective international mechanisms for citizen accountability.

Rule of law: Good governance requires a comprehensive framework of clear and well-understood laws that are predictably applied to protect citizens and all their legitimate interests. But there is little in the way of international law, and even that is generally subservient to national judiciaries. Hence, only national concerns are well protected by laws; global ones are mostly ignored or are covered by exhortative but toothless treaties. Many global social justice CSOs campaign for globally rigorous laws, regulations, and rules for intergovernmental processes and TNCs. The treaties on climate change, land mines, and whaling are examples of their achievements, as are the International Court for Criminal Justice and the inspection panels or ombudsman offices within intergovernmental organizations. The latter afford due process to those who have been disadvantaged by the actions of those organizations.

Citizen voices: The right to know what is going on is one thing, but CSOs seek more active citizenship. They want seats in intergovernmental deliberations, public consultations on issues that affect societies, and participatory approaches in programs and projects. They advocate public and legislative hearings to which CSOs can give evidence. And — through their public campaigns and media coverage — they make sure that citizen voices are heard (well . . . a select sample of them).

Level playing field: Good governance must embrace equality of opportunity, which entails the right of minorities, not just the elite, to be heard on the global stage. CSOs who reflect those minority views therefore want a right be heard — "a voice, not a vote" — in international forums.[15] Global social justice CSOs are also campaigning for a greater voice for the South in international forums, and are increasingly vocal in campaigns to curb the power of the "G1" — the United States.

In these ways, civil society — especially when globally networked — is helping to reshape global governance. This phenomenon has been studied by the Panel of Eminent Persons on UN–Civil Society Relations — a panel set up by the UN secretary-general and chaired by President Cardoso, the former president of Brazil.

Today's multilateralism is different from that of thirty years ago. In those days, governments would come together to discuss an emerging issue until there was sufficient consensus for an intergovernmental resolution. Then governments and intergovernmental organizations would work on implementing this agreement. Today, as the EJM demonstrates, it is increasingly likely that a civil society movement and a crescendo of public opinion put a new issue on the global agenda; next, a few like-minded governments become first among their peers to recognize the power of the case and start pressing for global action. Together with leading civil society protagonists, they form an ad hoc coalition on the issue, which builds public and political support for global action through iterative processes of public debate, policy dialogue, and perhaps pioneering action to demonstrate ways to redress the problem. Such global policy networks have shaped responses to issues as diverse as climate change, gender relations, poor country debt relief, affordable treatment for AIDS, land mines, the trade in small arms, and the campaign for the International Court for Criminal Justice.

These shifting informal and opportunistic alliances of governments and non-State actors around specific policy issues constitute an exciting new phenomenon. Even the moves made by a powerful group of developing countries to stand up recently against the world's strongest trading powers displayed this striking new reality. The group grew and shrank as some countries joined and others were pressed by their Northern trading partners to desist. Hence it was variously called the G20, the G21, and even, at one point, the G24. (I hope it will eventually settle on calling itself the G21 — not because of the number in the group, but for the new hope Southern unity offers for economic justice in the twenty-first century.) What was constant, however, was the active support the group received from some of the leading NGOs and trade unions attending the WTO Ministerial. The CSOs were clearly giving useful advice to the trade negotiators about the latest developments in the meetings and about media strategy. The benefits were mutual: while the countries gained from their in-depth knowledge and experience of the issues, the CSOs gained credibility by appearing on G21 platforms, and the close links enhanced their media-worthiness.

As such policy networks are coming to shape the deliberative processes, we are similarly witnessing the increasing importance of partnerships (often including the private sector, civil society, and local authorities and governments) for getting things done. Hence, as concluded by the Cardoso panel, civil society has become as much part of global governance today as governments. To adapt to this new multilateralism, it urged, Secretary-General Kofi Annan must continue to transform the UN's institutional culture from a rather inward-looking institution to an outward-looking, networking organization.[16]

The United Nations has played a major role in consistently engaging CSOs in its deliberative processes — particularly in the big conferences of the 1990s. This has helped shape an emerging set of cosmopolitan political rules and norms, which transcend national sovereignty and which are enforced (albeit imperfectly) by international institutions, especially in the areas of human rights, gender relations, and the environment. Although some governments resist these trends, the Cardoso panel concludes that constructive and strategic engagement with civil society is a vital defense against the challenges the United Nations itself faces today. A United Nations that is more attuned to global public opinion, that is strongly connected with leading CSOs, and that is strategic in its ability to broker dialogue with diverse stakeholders is better able to ensure that challenges come into the open and are satisfactorily dispatched, and that global governance is strengthened. In short there is a symbiosis: civil society is strengthened by the opportunities the United Nations affords, and this in turn gives a new raison d'être that empowers the United Nations and makes it seem more relevant.

... and Reaction: The Backlash against Transnational Civil Society

As we have discussed, global civil society is starting to have an effect on the management of global change. No longer can a group of seven finance ministers spend a weekend in a hotel near the White House, announce a "Washington Consensus" on a monetarist approach to international economics, and escape with little public controversy. Moreover, corporate CEOs are now routinely challenged to demonstrate corporate social responsibility. Today, citizens everywhere are more economically literate and more politically savvy than before the Internet age. They want to know what's going on and what it means to them, and they want to have a say. We're all in the debating chamber now, and with transnational CSOs as the well-trusted crack forces of this new civic consciousness, the potential is almost unlimited. As Jodie Williams said on receiving the Nobel Prize on behalf of the International Campaign to Ban Landmines, "We should be proud we are a superpower!"[17]

Superpowers, however, are inevitably resented. The clear ascendancy of policy-oriented NGOs and interest groups over the last decade has been greeted by increasingly aggressive counter-strategies by governments, intergovernmental agencies and corporations, and the establishment media. Hence *Financial Times* journalist Martin Wolf fulminated in 1999 about "the claims of NGOs to represent civil society as a whole, and, as such, to possess legitimacy rivalling — perhaps even exceeding — that of elected governments is outrageous."[18] In the same month the *Economist* demanded to know: " Who elected Oxfam, or, for that matter, the League for a Revolutionary Communist International? . . . In the West, governments and their agencies are, in the end, accountable to voters. Who holds the activists accountable?"[19] In 2003 the right-wing think tank, American Enterprise Institute, announced that it was forming, with others, NGO Watch to monitor such "objectionable" practices of the NGOs.

Whether CSO leaders like it or not, such critics do raise important issues. In their attacks on CSOs, three words come up over and over again: legitimacy, representativity, and accountability. These are presented as the fundamental flaws of civil society organizations, but how fair is this?

CSOs must recognize that they are complements to traditional democracy, not substitutes for it. It is important not to overstate their potential. They may be more trusted than political parties and governments, but this does not mean that they are displacing traditional democratic processes; in fact, they play different roles. Indeed, to influence policy, they need well-functioning governments and parliamentary processes. Pressure groups usually focus on very specific policy issues. A vibrant civil society will generate a thousand points of pressure, but if we join those points together we don't get an alternative blueprint for governing. We still need State instruments to balance competing demands, fill in the gaps, and construct a coherent, overall policy framework.

CSOs achieve influence by persuading people to use the democracy at their fingertips — not just through their voting choices but as consumers, shareholders, lobbyists, demonstrators, educators of their children, workers, employers, and investors. Civil society is an arena for deliberation of policies and contestation, not decision making on policy matters. While every pressure group has a right to make its case, governments must, in the end, make policy decisions. Civil society can ensure that these decisions are well informed and that weaker voices are not drowned out. Governments have to reach their decisions by weighing together myriad — often conflicting — claims; if they simply appease every powerful vested interest group, politics becomes atomized and coherence is lost. They must listen to the cacophony but maintain a holistic view, which is hard.

Finally: An Emerging EJM Agenda for Ethical Globalization?

There is clearly a growing head of steam for a new departure. As the Nobel Prize–winning economist Amartya Sen says, "The real debate on globalization is, ultimately, not about the efficiency of markets, nor about the importance of modern technology. The debate, rather, is about the inequality of power, for which there is much less tolerance now than in the world that emerged at the end of the Second World War." [20] Equity of power, opportunity, and resources is the cornerstone of what could be a different course. Perhaps this could be the unifying platform for the EJM — a manifesto for ethical globalization. Civil society is the driving force for bringing moral factors into economics, the dismal science, and it has growing opportunity. Summits rarely take place these days without some involvement of CSOs, and these are no longer just optional extras after the important delegates leave. Heads of governments are keen to reach out to hear their citizens' voices. The prime minister of Belgium, Guy Verhofstadt, for example, convened a special conference for Belgians in October 2001 to ensure that civil society concerns about globalization were heard. Political leaders increasingly seek to attend (or at least to demonstrate that they are tuned into) the annual World Social Forum, and it has become standard to invite numerous CSO leaders alongside political and corporate chiefs at the World Economic Forum. The future thus holds immense opportunities for CSOs to influence international policy and alter the path of global change.

In the meantime, the informal and admittedly self-appointed account-ability roles CSOs play in matters of global governance are so far the only route through which citizens come close to the levers of transnational power. Global civil society, by itself, is not the answer, but it is vital to mak-ing an answer possible. This approach is needed all the more in the face of the mounting world polarization triggered by the Iraq War.

Civil society networks are learning to create their own widely used, noncommercial, media channels, to network globally and — equally important — to form novel alliances across sectors, with trade unions, environmental pressure groups, NGOs, human rights activists, social movements, intellectuals, and pop stars all coming together on com-mon platforms. While not presenting a total alternative, this movement is helping to introduce a set of global political values and norms and a new sense of accountability of those holding public office to a global public, thus opening the door to the possibility that perhaps politics can be globalized.

The EJM faces tough choices. One way leads to greater confrontation, more aggressive street demonstrations, more youthful hostility vented toward authority, more polarization, and unease in our societies. The other direction, equally challenging, leads to negotiations and working for institutional reform — both public and private.

There is no doubt which path will be chosen. Because of its plu-rality, the movement will surely go both ways. Participatory democ-racy knows many styles of engagement. Hence, the future of contention is largely in the hands of the official institutions them-selves. The more responsive they are to dialogue, the more confident CSOs will be in constructive engagement. But if they ignore groups who want to engage, then those groups will lose prestige and support, leaving street activists the stronger. Conversely, CSOs who get co-opted into policy dialogues that are for show only undermine more radical reform efforts.

I don't attempt any blueprint for action, but I conclude with one obser-vation. Earlier, civil society campaigns have largely sought to stop things from happening, or to oppose policies. As the global justice movement becomes more confident, we are starting to see pressure for what should be done, which is vital for building consensus about a new way of manag-ing globalization that puts the needs of poor people first. This approach reflects a maturing of global civil society, a greater willingness to take risks, and a preparedness to engage with "the establishment" and to define what it stands for — a compelling vision of ethical globalization — not just what it is against. This is the most critical challenge EJM activists face — the challenge of "Getting from No." [21]

Notes

1. Sanjeev Khagram, James V. Riker, and Kathryn Sikkink, eds., *Restructuring World Politics: Transnational Social Movements, Networks and Norms* (Minneapolis: University of Minnesota Press, 2002).

2. Kumi Naidoo, "Claiming Global Power: Transnational Civil Society and Global Governance," chap. 3, this volume.

3. Naomi Klein, "Signs of the Times: Protests Aimed at Powerful Symbols of Capitalism Find Themselves in a Transformed Landscape," *The Nation,* October 22, 2001.

4. Cardoso Panel Report, *We the Peoples: Civil Society, the United Nations, and Global Governance,* report of the Panel of Eminent Persons on UN–Civil Society Relations, A/58/817, General Assembly, 11 June 2004, United Nations.

5. See Joseph Stiglitz, *Globalization and Its Discontents* (New York: W. W. Norton, 2002); John D. Clark, *Worlds Apart: Civil Society and the Battle for Ethical Globalization* (Bloomfield, CT: Kumarian Press; London: Earthscan, 2003).

6. M. Kaldor, "'Civilizing' Globalization: The Implications of the 'Battle in Seattle,'" *Millennium,* January 29, 2000, 105–14.

7. Nimbyism (from the acronym for Not In My Back Yard) is objecting to schemes, however important for the national or global good, because of negative local consequences. Pork-barrel politics is the opposite: politicians' insistence on schemes that benefit their constituency (and hence their electoral prospects), however wasteful they may be.

8. Clark, *Worlds Apart,* 70–72.

9. GlobeScan, www.globescan.com (accessed July 31, 2004).

10. C. Warkentin, *Reshaping World Politics: NGOs, the Internet, and Global Civil Society* (Lanham, MD: Rowman and Littlefield, 2001).

11. D. McAdam, J. McCarthy, and M. Zald, eds., *Comparative Perspectives on Social Movements: Political Opportunities, Mobilizing Structures, and Cultural Framing* (New York: Cambridge University Press, 1996).

12. Klein, "Signs of the Times."

13. Peter van Tuijl and Lisa Jordan, "Political Responsibility in Transnational NGO Advocacy," *World Development* 28, no. 12 (2000): 2051–65.

14. The France-based dot-cause ATTAC has been an impressive model in this regard. It maintains, via Internet, a large cadre of volunteer translators in various countries who enable them to reproduce their newsletters, papers, and commentaries swiftly in various languages.

15. Michael Edwards, "Victims of Their Own Success," *Guardian Weekly*, July 6, 2000.

16. Cardoso Panel Report.

17. Motoko Mekata, "Building Partnerships toward a Common Goal: Experiences of the International Campaign to Ban Landmines," in *The Third Force: The Rise of Transnational Civil Society*, ed. Ann Florini, 143–76 (Washington, DC: Carnegie Endowment for International Peace, 2000), 174.

18. Martin Wolf, "Trade: Uncivil Society," *Financial Times*, September 1, 1999.

19. *The Economist*, "Anti-Capitalist Protests: Angry and Effective," September 23, 2000.

20. Amartya Sen, "Global Doubts" (commencement address, Harvard University, June 8, 2000).

21. I have parodied the title of one of the most famous books on management and negotiation: Roger Fisher, William Ury, and Bruce Patton, *Getting to Yes* (New York: Penguin, 1991).

CHAPTER EIGHT

The Personal Is Global:
The Project and Politics of the
Transnational Women's Movement

Peggy Antrobus and Gita Sen

Introduction

Women's movements have always been part of broad-based social movements. In the context of the UN conferences of the 1990s, the international women's movement emerged as a powerful political constituency, and has increasingly become part of the social movement for global justice. This chapter traces the origins of the transnational women's movement, the issues it addresses, its achievements, and the challenges it faces as it attempts to make a contribution toward the larger project for social transformation.

In tracing the history of the transnational women's movement,[1] reference is often made to three distinct phases: the first in the late nineteenth to early twentieth centuries, the second spanning the mid-twentieth century, and the third the late twentieth century onwards. Although these three phases are often depicted as separate and distinct, we believe it is instructive to look at the connections between them.

The first phase had three distinct sources. One was the emergence of social reform movements in the colonized countries that had as their primary focus the transformation of cultural practices affecting civil laws, marriage, and family life. While these reform attempts probably mobilized as many or more men as women, they were an important early strand in the transformation of social discourse and practices affecting gender relations. A second source was the major debate within the social democratic and communist organizations of the late nineteenth and early twentieth centuries, which then carried forward into the debates in the Soviet Union on the "woman question." This strand of debate was the most explicit about the connections between the institutions of private property, the control over material assets, and female–male relations within families and society. A third source was the liberal strand that combined the struggle for the right to vote with the fight to legalize contraception; this strand existed mainly, though by no means exclusively, in Europe and North America.

It is worth recognizing the presence of these different strands in the very first phase of the women's movement because they delineate in an early form the potential strengths as well as tensions that characterize the transnational women's movement to this day. The presence of multiple strands from early on has made for a movement that is broad and capable of addressing a wide range of issues. But the potential tensions between prioritizing economic issues (such as control over resources and property) or women's personal autonomy or bodily integrity existed then and continues to exist now. Some writers have noted that a number of the North American and European strands tended to be biased in terms of both race and class, although others were clearly not. Their relationship to anticolonial movements was mixed, just as the male-led sections of nationalist movements tended to downgrade and even oppose calls for gender justice.

The second phase in the mid-twentieth century was largely dictated by struggles against colonial domination, in which women were present in large numbers. Their experiences in these struggles shaped their attitudes to global economic and political inequality, even though specific issues of gender justice took a back seat at this time. Many women also went through the experience of being prominent participants in anticolonial struggles and then being marginalized in the postcolonial era.

The third phase, which is commonly recognized as the modern women's movement, had its roots, like so many other social movements in the latter part of the twentieth century, in the social and political ferment of the 1960s. The anti-imperialist and anti–Vietnam War movements, civil rights struggles, challenges to social and sexual mores and behavior, and above all, the social rebellion of young people worldwide brewed a potent mixture from which emerged many of the social movements of the succeeding decades. What was specific to the women's movement among these was its call for recognition of the personal as political.

The appearance of the transnational women's movement as part of an emerging transnational civil society was also conditioned by the processes generated by the UN Decade for Women (1975–85). The Decade provided a special context within which women from across the globe and from a diversity of backgrounds encountered each other in a sustained and ever-deepening process focused on their position and condition.[2] The official UN conferences of the 1980s and 1990s provided unparalleled opportunities for women to meet on a consistent and continuous basis. Women in large numbers, many of whom would not otherwise have had the opportunity to travel across local, let alone national, boundaries, met formally and informally through circles of friendship, and personal, political, and professional affiliations.

Women came to these conferences and meetings from different racial and ethnic backgrounds, countries, and cultures; classes and occupational backgrounds; sexual orientations; and social histories. The meetings enabled women to gain new knowledge and to learn from each other's experiences. They facilitated the organization of joint projects and collaborative efforts. They gave birth to issue-based networks at local, regional, and global levels, which in turn provided the research and analysis that served to empower women's advocacy. They helped women to develop self-confidence and leadership skills. They linked activists with researchers and, more importantly, validated and encouraged the pursuit of research among activists and activism among researchers. They forged and strengthened links between organizing at local and global levels. In this way, they facilitated the growth of a transnational women's movement of great diversity and decentralization, a movement that expanded its agenda from a narrow definition of women's issues to one that embraced a range of concerns for human welfare. In doing so, the movement transformed itself into a major alternative constituency — a hybrid of identity politics and proposals for a new social project.

Definition and Structure

One way of thinking about any social movement is to ask whether it represents identity politics focused on the needs or concerns of a particular group of people, or whether it consciously puts forward a vision for society as a whole. In the rough-and-tumble of political struggle, those who oppose a particular social movement will often try to depict it as representing a narrow and even selfish interest. Its proponents will usually argue that the good of society as a whole will flow from the benefits to its own members. Of course, the larger the group in question, the more likely it is that focusing on the needs of its members will also bring about significant social changes. However, our distinction between identity politics and a social project is more than just whether social change occurs: espousing a social project means having a vision that is inclusive of all of society, that the changes sought will be for the benefit of all. A social project also means transforming social institutions, practices, and beliefs, not simply seeking a better place within existing institutions and structures.

Some sections of the transnational women's movement see their task as a complete social project, with significant implications for all dimensions of human existence. Recognition of the centrality of the care and nurture of human beings (what feminist economists have called the "care economy") is key to this social project. It requires addressing gender relations in all the complex interplay of their economic, social, political, cultural, and personal dimensions. It also involves locating gender inequality within the context of other forms of inequality that shape and often exacerbate it. Other sections of the movement function nearer a form of identity politics, in which the project of women's organizing is viewed within a narrower calculus that pits women's well-being against that of men. Particular women and organizations often combine or move between these two approaches.

These varied views of a common task must be seen as part of the diversity and richness of a movement that seeks change in the institutions, norms, and practices that define the connection between the production of goods and services and the reproduction and care of human beings; and that seeks to transform the relationships of superiority and inferiority, domination and subordination between women and men in a male-dominated world. This diversity is valued for the issues they highlight, even though many of the tensions among women in the movement can be related to these differences.

Two decades of research and organizing on a global scale show that there are clear commonalties behind this diversity that transcend divisions of class, race, ethnicity, country, culture, age, and capacity. The experience of the past thirty years points, however, to the pitfalls of starting with an assumption of a global sisterhood, especially when that sisterhood is defined by a privileged minority. The emergence of a global movement has in fact depended on the emergence of new and different voices challenging hegemonic tendencies and claiming their own voice and space, and the acceptance of differences within the movements. As Audre Lorde put it:

> Certainly there are very real differences between us of race, age and sex. But it is not those differences between us that are separating us. It is rather our refusal to recognize those differences, and to examine the distortions which result from our misnaming them and their effects upon human behavior and expectation.[3]

She also reminds us that "there is no such thing as a single-issue struggle because we do not live single-issue lives."[4] Women understand that each of us has multiple identities and that at any point in time one may be more important than others.

In understanding the transnational women's movement, it is useful to examine some of its key features. First, it is a political movement — part of the broad array of social movements concerned with changing social conditions, rather than simply a network or coalition of women's organizations. Second, it is grounded in an understanding of women's relationship to social conditions — an understanding of gender as an important linkage within the broad structure of social relationships of production and reproduction; of class, race and ethnicity, caste, sexual orientation, age, and location. Third, it is a process, albeit discontinuous and flexible, responding to specific conditions of perceived gender inequality, inequity, or gender-related injustice. Fourth, awareness and rejection of male privilege and control is central to the politics of the women's movement. For this reason, it is energized by feminist politics[5] — whether or not the word "feminist" is used.[6] Fifth, the movement is often born at moments in which women individually or collectively become aware of their separateness *as women*, their alienation, marginalization, isolation, or even abandonment within a broader movement for social justice/social change. In other words, women's struggle for agency within other struggles is often the catalyst for women's movements.

Describing the structure of a movement as diverse and complex as the transnational women's movement is difficult. It is made up of autonomous but often overlapping organizations, networks, and coalitions focused on issues of major concern to women worldwide: peace, violence against women, trafficking of women, women's human rights, sexual and reproductive health and rights, environment, economic issues including economic development, macroeconomic policies, and trade. Some of these networks are issue-specific; many are mixed, reflecting the indivisibility of rights. Many of these transnational networks have links to national and regional networks, while others are loose affiliations.[7]

Issues Addressed

Since 1975, there has been a shift from the UN Decade's initial focus on "integrating women in development" to "empowering women for social change."[8] Throughout the decade of the 1990s, women mobilized around global issues, specifically, environment (the UN Conference on Environment and Development, Rio de Janeiro, 1992), human rights (the International Conference on Human Rights, Vienna, 1993), population (the UN International Conference on Population and Development, Cairo, 1994), social development (the UN World Summit on Social Development, Copenhagen, 1995), habitat (the UN Habitat Conference, Istanbul, 1996), and food (the UN World Summit on Food Security, Rome, 1997). This was made possible by the new ways of organizing that had evolved during the Decade for Women,[9] along with the conceptual and analytical framework adopted by the women who spearheaded the organizing around each conference. The Fourth World Conference on Women (Beijing, 1995) gave a major boost to women's presence in the global arena.

Building on the analyses and experiences of organizing across national, disciplinary, and thematic boundaries through the previous twenty years, the leadership of feminist activists succeeded in changing the terms and outcomes of many of the global debates of the 1990s. In doing this they clarified linkages between social, cultural, economic, and political processes, and pointed the way to more credible solutions to problems of environmental degradation, sustainable livelihoods, poverty, human rights abuses, and social inequality. Some illustrations follow.

Women Challenge Macroeconomic Policies

At the end of the Decade for Women, a major issue for the women's movement was the impact on poor women, particularly in developing countries, of the macroeconomic framework of structural adjustment imposed by international financial institutions (IFI), and the ways in which these policies reflected a set of assumptions grounded in women's traditional roles. Feminist analysis highlighted the ways in which this policy framework separated economic production from social reproduction and privileged economic growth rather than human development; and that in so doing, this framework jeopardized not only women but whole communities.

Feminist-led women's groups organizing to highlight the gendered nature of these policies and their negative impact on women placed the women's movement at the forefront of the challenge to the policy framework of economic liberalization and privatization contained in the "Washington Consensus."[10] To the extent that women, especially poor women, look to the State to provide or guarantee basic services in the areas of health, education, welfare, housing, water, and sanitation, these changes were to have a profound effect on women's well-being. In the two decades since the initial critique of these policies by women at the Nairobi Conference in 1985, there has been some change — although it can hardly be claimed that the core policy direction of downsizing the State has been altered, despite many other social movements joining women in challenging it. The women's movement, however, can certainly take credit for forcing policy debates to pay serious attention to the gendered nature of the framework and the implications of this, not just for women but for society as a whole.

Engendering the Environment Debate

The importance of the issue of environmental degradation in terms of consumption and production patterns and sustainable livelihoods (i.e., seeking policy frameworks capable of sustaining the livelihoods of the poor) was reflected in the major mobilization effort by the transnational women's movement prior to the UN Conference on Environment and Development (UNCED) in 1992. The formulation of a Women's Agenda 21 as a counterpart to the official Agenda 21 helped clarify women's own understanding of the issues when seen through a gender lens, and brought these gendered issues to the policy table.

Using the daily experiences of poor women as the starting point for an analysis of the environment led to a focus on health and livelihoods and to the political economy that determines their access to both. In every instance, women argued that it was impossible to understand the problem of environmental degradation without understanding economic, political, social, and cultural factors. The links between the debt crisis on the one hand, and on the other, the International Monetary Fund–influenced macroeconomic policy framework that cuts resources to the poor for health, education, and welfare, and exerts pressure on environmentally fragile land in order to boost exports, were clear to the women's movement. So too were the connections between the lucrative trade in weapons and the unequal, colonial relations that made it impossible for small island States to protect the lives of their people and their ecosystems from the destructive effects of the nuclear weapons tests conducted by the major superpowers. (See the chapter on peace movements in this volume.)

Women from the South also rejected the notion that overpopulation was a primary cause of environmental degradation. They pointed out that poor women did not have the technology to wreak the damage that could result from the use of large-scale technology and equipment, and that the often wasteful, overconsumption patterns of the people of the North exerted much greater pressure on the environment than did the consumption of those of the South.

Framing Women's Rights as Human Rights

The issue of gender-based violence against women is one of the most pervasive issues for women across nationality, race, ethnicity, class, and age. It has a long history in women's organizing, yet it was not a major issue during the UN Decade for Women.[11] In the 1990s, however, it became a central issue for women's organizing, and found major expression within the framework of women's human rights.[12]

Women's organizing in preparation for the 1993 International Conference on Human Rights in Vienna changed the historically ungendered human rights framework. Their efforts to get violence against women on the agenda brought together traditional women's rights advocates (including those focusing on violence against women) and activists from developing countries, who focused on socioeconomic issues of poverty, food, health, and education (usually referred to as socioeconomic rights).

At the conference, the presence of women telling their own stories of violation, from domestic violence to female genital mutilation and war crimes, strengthened women's advocacy and guaranteed that women's concerns would be taken into account. For the first time, violence against women was placed on the agenda of a human rights conference. In raising the veil from the violence that takes place against women in the household, the fundamentals of human rights was greatly advanced by removing the distinction between the private sphere of the household and the public sphere. In the past, both the United Nations and national governments had failed to recognize the abuses of women's bodies because they were considered private, family, cultural, or religious matters. The specific recognition in Vienna of women's rights as an integral part of human rights laid the basis for the significant advances made in the next two years in Cairo and Beijing.

Advancing Sexual and Reproductive Rights

Together with the Vienna conference, the International Conference on Population and Development (ICPD) in Cairo in 1994 saw some of the most significant advances in their cause by the women's movement. Reproductive rights had been discussed among women's organizations for at least two decades before the movement brought the issue forcefully into the global policy arena. Internationally, the population field had been driven for over forty years by a narrow agenda focused almost exclusively on reducing population growth through family planning programs. Not only did this approach give short shrift to concerns of health and disregard the question of rights, it also ignored the variation in needs and realities on the ground. While coercive family planning practices were a concern of women's groups in some regions (such as India), the acute absence of family planning services was a problem in others (as, for instance, in much of Latin America).

Transforming this situation required nothing less than a complete change in the population policy paradigm, which is what the women's movement set out to accomplish in the two years preceding the ICPD. This approach meant working through their internal differences to build a consensus for a new framework for a population-related policy that would affirm the right of women to control their fertility and meet their needs for safe, affordable, and accessible contraceptives, while recognizing the social determinants, and health and rights consequences, of sexual and reproductive behavior. Women had to clarify and advocate new and radical concepts such as reproductive and sexual health and rights in a field that had been, until then, an odd mixture of technocratic modeling and doomsday scenarios. The movement had also to build alliances and coalitions with those in the population lobbies who were open to change, to learn to negotiate with seasoned diplomats in the UN, and to ward off the tactics of religious conservatives for whom the idea of women's rights and gender equality was anathema. The ICPD Programme of Action was surely one of the most spectacular successes for the modern-day transnational women's movement.

Vienna and Cairo together represent that hybrid combination of identity politics and a larger social project that was described earlier as characterizing the women's movement. Women's advocates focused very specifically on *women's* rights in Vienna, but the opening created in Vienna emboldened the movement to push for a major shift in the entire population paradigm in Cairo. Identity politics created the space needed for the social project.[13]

At the same time, the difficulties to date in winning international consensus on sexual rights (other than a single paragraph in the Beijing Platform for Action) point to the challenges women face in building alliances that will acknowledge the legitimacy of the feminist social project, and the virulence of the opposition to it.

Achievements

Quantifying the achievements of the transnational women's movement is difficult. Reflecting as it does the emergence of women as new political actors at the international level, the global women's movement has certainly succeeded in raising awareness of women's concerns and in redefining the terms of debates on a range of issues from human rights to environment, from violence to trade, from religious and economic fundamentalisms to governance.

It is now an undeniable fact that the women's movement is today truly global, with organizations, networks, and coalitions in many parts of the world. Similarly, because every issue is a women's issue, the movement is probably linked to a wider range of struggles and movements than any other transnational social movement.

The women's movement has become closely associated with not just challenges but alternatives to the macro-economic framework of structural adjustment, neoliberalism, and trade liberalization. The International Gender and Trade Network (IGTN) is a growing network that works closely with other organizations in generating alternatives to official proposals of the World Trade Organization (WTO). The issue of unwaged work performed by women in the care economy is now recognized as a legitimate concern, and one that can and must be addressed by statisticians in national income accounts and through gender-sensitive budgets and policies. Following the International Conference on Human Rights in Vienna, the UN General Assembly adopted the Declaration on the Elimination of Violence Against Women. The Special Rapporteur appointed by the United Nations investigates and reports on violence against women to the UN Commission on Human Rights, with proposals for addressing each issue. He/she also provides a framework for monitoring progress on the Declaration. Women's rights are increasingly recognized as human rights in many forums. At the ICPD, a feminist-led network of women working with health and family planning policymakers and practitioners prevailed against a powerful alliance between religious fundamentalists to secure the adoption of a Program of Action that linked women's reproductive health to women's rights and empowerment, breaking the demographically oriented framework of the previous conferences on population. The women's movement has also withstood the backlash to these advances through the various follow-up reviews and other processes.

However, even major achievements at the level of global negotiations such as the adoption by the United Nations of women's rights as human rights, the inclusion of rape as a war crime in the protocols of the Geneva Convention, and the feminist-defined Program of Action from the ICPD have to be adopted and implemented at local levels for them to be meaningful to women in their daily lives.

Current and Future Challenges

The current conjuncture of relentless neoliberalism, virulent religious fundamentalism, aggressive militarism, and resurgent racism is one that poses enormous risks to women and to those for whose well-being they bear special responsibility. The relevance, reach, and effectiveness of the global women's movement in addressing the crises of reproduction, soaring inequality, war, human security, personal autonomy, and governance in this new scenario depends on how it deals with a set of both substantive and organizational challenges.

It is useful to recognize at the outset that all social movements face challenges, some of which are quite similar to the ones faced by the transnational women's movement. It is, in a sense, a mark of the coming of age of a movement, yet there is one core aspect of the struggle to transform gender relations that is unique. Different from every other unequal social relationship, the relations between women and men are not only deeply personal but also often involve levels of cooperation and positive emotional involvement that make critical engagement extremely difficult. Recognizing the personal as political is often easier said than done not only for men but also for women. It often involves not only material but also psychological and emotional costs. This core issue underpins a number of the challenges that women's organizing has faced from the outset and continues to face today.

Identity Politics or an Inclusive Social Project?

One of the most important challenges facing the women's movement is the balance between identity politics and a social project. As we have argued in this chapter, the modern women's movement has evolved as a hybrid of the two, but with considerable tension on this score within the movement itself as well as with other actors for social change. Those who, for reasons of their own, would wish to minimize the transforming potential of the women's movement usually seek to depict it as just another group of victims with a narrow, self-centered agenda.

But it is not only opponents of social transformation who do this. Because change in gender relations challenges people at such a personal level, many social activists (both male and female) prefer to stay within the comfort zone of the gender status quo. Given their discomfort with personal questioning of their own place in gender systems, it suits them to depict the women's movement as narrow identity politics, marginal to the economic, social, or environmental concerns of "larger" social movements. The women's movement needs to tackle this issue head on: What is its social project, and is it larger than identity politics? Does the feminist social project go beyond the project of the movement for global economic justice? If so, how?

While some women's organizations are giving this question priority in their work,[14] more analytical development and debate is required. Much more needs to be done to show the linkages between gender relations and the economic, social, cultural, and political systems and structures that serve to perpetuate the crises in reproduction and human security. There is particular need to articulate the linkages between women's subordination, homophobia, racism and the problems of poverty, the low priority given to social services in the public sector, violence, and militarism. If a human rights framework is our core analytical tool, then we need to articulate clearly the indivisibility of human rights in all its dimensions, including gender justice.

In political terms, we need to deal with the fact that there are some influential sections of the movement for global economic justice that view women's struggles for gender justice, sexual and reproductive rights, and personal autonomy as peripheral to their interests or concerns. Such groups ally themselves all too easily with the politics of religious obscurantism that implacably opposes feminism and the liberation theology of the oppressed while paying lip service to debt reduction and poverty alleviation. Clarifying the feminist social project means articulating and locating its historical and conceptual basis, as well as its political implications.

There are other challenges as well. As the lesbian/gay/bisexual/transgender (LGBT) movement grows and puts sexuality centrally on the agenda, it poses a major challenge to the feminist social project. How clearly can women incorporate sexuality into their framework of understanding and into their politics? While fruitful new work is now being done in this area, often by feminists and LGBT activists working together, much more remains to be done.

As we work to clarify the nature of the feminist social project along these lines, we must simultaneously acknowledge that it is their identity as women that gives the movement's members their commitment, energy, and sense of solidarity. Without this, the movement would lose its vitality and core strength. How to retain this sense of passion and commitment drawn from women's identity, while moving toward a clearer understanding of the feminist social project, is one of the biggest challenges that the transnational women's movement faces today.

Feminism in the Women's Movement

Not everyone in the women's movement is comfortable about feminism. There is a tension between feminists and other women within women's movements who are more ambivalent about challenging prevailing gender relations and certainly about some of the feminist language and analyses of these relations. Nevertheless, we have to acknowledge that feminist politics has been the driving force in women's organizations, often enlightening more traditional women's groups and even nongovernmental organizations and other social movements[15] by showing with greater clarity the systemic links between various kinds of oppression.

The relationship between feminism and women's movements is just one of the challenges for a global women's movement that is led by feminists. Another deals with, among other things, the power relationships inherent in differences in class, race and ethnicity, age, politics, educational levels, institutional and geographical locations, and sexuality between women within the movement. This issue of the asymmetry of power between women within the movement must be acknowledged and addressed honestly and with integrity.

Intergenerational Issues

An ongoing concern within the women's movement is the working relationship between older and younger women. While some young women in leadership positions within youth movements view the women's movement as irrelevant or alienating, many others are increasingly visible in the movement for global justice and the global women's movement, and their leadership brings new energy and creativity.

There are major issues of inclusion and exclusion between the younger and older women. This generation gap is often related to personal histories: those who took on leadership roles in the past thirty years have developed close bonds of solidarity out of the shared struggles during the Decade for Women and the UN conferences of the 1990s. Younger women feel excluded. At the same time, young women often see the world differently, and they certainly face issues that are outside the experience of their mothers and the older generation of activists. A challenge to the global women's movement is how to bridge this gap between young women in the movement for global justice and the feminist politics of women's groups. Can this be done in ways that empower younger women without negating the valuable experience of the past thirty years?

What Shall We Do about the Men?

Behind this semihumorous question lies the recognition that women cannot build a movement for social transformation without making strategic alliances with men. In any event, the relationship with men within the movement for global justice is crucial at the present juncture. One starting point may be to distinguish between men in the social movement who are open to a partnership with feminist leadership and those who are not, and to make strategic alliances with those who understand that there is no justice for anyone if there is no justice for women. Men who are willing to publicly identify with a feminist agenda are few, and unevenly distributed. A global women's movement has a special role to play in identifying and affirming these allies, and in helping to extend their skill and aid to other countries and regions where these are needed. A major challenge to the global women's movement is to work with these men to strengthen their analysis, and to help in the creation of a network of men who understand that the struggle for women's agency is intrinsic to all struggles for social transformation.

At another level, the women's movement must take the challenge of redefining masculinity and male roles in society in a positive, affirmative way, as it has done so well with femininity and women's social roles. This is particularly crucial in societies where masculinity has traditionally been defined in terms of dominance over women. Such a social project must form an integral part of the transnational women's movement.

Engaging with the State and Other Powerful Institutions

The women's movement, like many other social movements, has always been suspicious of the State and other institutions (the church, the family, etc.) that they (rightly) perceive as pillars of the status quo on gender, if not actively opposed to gender equality. For some, activism is by definition always oppositional; for other women who focus on specific goals (such as women's political participation, access to education, credit and employment, reproductive health, and ending discrimination), activism has included critical but constructive engagement with these same institutions. Critics of such engagement with mainstream institutions and policy-making processes argue that such interaction would, at best, blunt the effectiveness of feminist politics, and at worst lead to co-optation.[16]

Nonetheless, if the women's movement is to challenge and change gender power relations, and see this reflected in public policy, there is no avoiding engagement in mainstream processes. The point is to recognize that change does not occur without political pressure from outside, accepting the value of allies within mainstream institutions, and indeed acknowledging the difference that a progressive government can make (and conversely, the damage that an anti-women government can wreak).

Indeed, the strategy of working from within as well as from the outside is one of the possibilities offered by a movement that transcends the normal boundaries of class, race, nationality, and institutional location. A movement that includes a rich diversity of individuals working within and outside the system has the flexibility required for a complex strategy that draws on the access of key individuals within establishments, along with the radicalism of those who would neither seek nor receive access to the seats and centers of institutional power.

There is also no gainsaying the fact that women, especially women in the South, need the State.[17] The dilemma for the women's movement in the South in relation to the State is that on the one hand, the majority of women in these countries lack resources and must depend on the State for the provision of basic services essential for performing their multiple roles. On the other hand, women must be careful that this dependence is not used to reinforce traditional roles within the family. But while the women's movement must be wary of State power, the fact of the matter is that women's vision of a model of development that is equitable, participatory, and sustainable clearly depends at least partly on State actors for its realization. In this regard, it has been women's historic role to keep issues of equity and distribution on the development agenda.

In the past, and in the context of the global conferences of the 1990s and beyond, the engagement of the women's movement with the State has been a necessary focus for their work. In its platform for the 1995 Beijing conference, DAWN called for "transforming the state" as one part of a three-tiered strategy directed to "states, markets and civil society."[18] UN conventions, resolutions, programs, and plans of action have given women important tools for advancing their struggles. The human rights framework is particularly helpful in some countries; it has also been beneficial in providing a universal standard against which a country's performance might be judged. In the present situation, and in the context of States that seem too weak to stand up to the domination of powerful nations and financial institutions, feminist activists who have been critical of the State may have to rethink the relationship between their movement and the State.

The global women's movement has a special role to play in relation to multinational institutions such as those of the UN, the IFIs, and the WTO. While work with the United Nations involves monitoring the agreements and proposals won in the international conferences of the 1990s, the transnational women's movement must continue to challenge the ways in which the policies and programs of the IFIs and the WTO stand in contradiction to their statements on equity and global justice.

Conclusion

Today the global women's movement stands at the crossroads between protecting hard-won gains and the tidal wave of religious fundamentalism and monolithic globalization sponsored by religious groupings (Hindu, Christian, Muslim) and transnational corporations, and delivered by governments that are too weak, or too corrupt, or both, to stand up for what is in the best interests of the majority of the people in their countries. Caught between the paradigms of economic growth and human development, and offering their own unique experience and understanding on both, women today are best placed to take leadership in a movement for global justice that is long overdue.

Faced with the terrifying conjuncture of relentless neoliberalism, virulent religious and ideological fundamentalism, aggressive militarism, and resurgent racism, feminist politics and praxis seem to hold the key to addressing these threats to human security everywhere. While these forces impinge most heavily on women, it is also possible to trace their roots to the social relations of gender that is grounded in racist patriarchy; that dichotomizes good and evil, production and reproduction, rationality and intuition, and male and female; that seeks conformity; and that robs women of agency. If the resolution to the crises depends on women's agency, then the struggle for global justice must also include a struggle for women's agency.

Notes

1. Throughout this chapter, we use the terms "transnational women's movement" and "women's movement" interchangeably.

2. Where "position" connotes women's status in a society in relation to men (such as in terms of legal rights, political representation, etc.), and "condition" means the material situation of women compared to men, such as in health, education, employment, income, etc.

3. Audre Lorde, *Sister Outsider: Essays and Speeches by Audre Lorde,* 11th ed. (Freedom, CA: The Crossing Press, 1996), 115.

4. Ibid., 138.

5. That is, activism based on the core theory that men and women should be equal politically, economically, and socially.

6. There exists a considerable literature on the meaning of feminism itself, and there are many varieties of feminism. All would as their essential precept oppose male privilege and power over women.

7. There are wide variations in the strength and focus of national and regional women's movements. In this chapter we do not address these, but only look at the transnational movement.

8. The switch from Women in Development (WID) to Women and Development (WAD) to Gender and Development (GAD) is often noted in feminist literature. However, in terms of the women's movement, the more significant switch is from integration to empowerment

(defined by feminists' networks like DAWN as distinct from the way the movement has been co-opted by international agencies).

9. The linking of local to global, as well as the working relationships and trust between women that had developed during the Decade.

10. Through the 1980s until the late 1990s, the Washington Consensus was the approach to structural reforms, economic liberalization, and privatization agreed to by the World Bank, the International Monetary Fund, and the US Treasury Department. It formed the basis of structural adjustment programs in many countries of the South.

11. It received little attention in the Plan of Action drawn up by the first World Conference on Women held in Mexico City in 1975.

12. Charlotte Bunch and N. Reilly, *Demanding Accountability: The Global Campaign and Vienna Tribunal for Women's Human Rights* (New Brunswick, NJ: Center for Women's Global Leadership, 1994).

13. The linkages between identity politics and the creation of a social project are complex, and we do not discuss them in detail in this chapter.

14. Development Alternatives with Women for a New Era (DAWN), a network of Southern feminist researchers and advocates, has given this priority in recent times through its "linkages" project See DAWN www.dawn.org.fj.

15. In many countries, feminists have been part of labor and other progressive movements and even of women's church groups, influencing their agendas and politics.

16. Marianne Braic and S. Wolte, eds., *Common Ground or Mutual Exclusion? Women's Movements and International Relations* (London: Zed Books, 2002). See especially the chapter by Nighat Said Khan, 35–45.

17. It is possible that those Third World women who have come out of the anticolonial struggles of the 1950s and 1960s have had a different experience of the State, particularly in countries like those of the English-speaking Caribbean, where the first political parties evolved from the labor movement.

18. DAWN, *Markers on the Way: The DAWN Debates on Alternative Development* (Barbados: Caribbean Graphics Productions, 1995), 38–41. Also available online at DAWN, www.dawn.org.fj.

CHAPTER NINE

Bridging Borders
for Human Rights

Alison Brysk
and Céline Jacquemin

Introduction

Human rights bridges many kinds of borders: the borders between countries, between State and individual, and the borders of our mutual responsibility for private suffering. In a world of diverse and constantly evolving human experience, human rights represents what poet Adrienne Rich called "the dream of a common language"[1] — from the anguished cry of mothers around the world mourning children shattered by violence, to the international discourse of scientists struggling to define our common heritage and map who controls it.

What are these principles of human rights that some die defending and others perish lacking? Human rights is a universal principle affirming the inalienable dignity and equality of all people. The founding principles of human rights limit the exercise of authority to bounded, legitimate forms of coercion and deprivation: governments may deprive citizens of jobs, but not of food, identity, or the exercise of freedom; socially harmful behavior must be penalized after a publicly accountable process; and torture, the deliberate infliction of pain for dominance, is absolutely prohibited. Human rights has philosophical roots in the powerful ideas of liberalism, which originated during the Enlightenment and evolved as the basis for a common, international system of exchange and governance following World War II. The fundamental tenets of liberalism then included the dignity of the individual, the desirability of political freedom, the superiority of reason over belief, and the possibility of progress through exchange.[2] But as we shall see, human rights has grown beyond its parent philosophy — and even come to challenge it.

Origin and Growth

Since the recognition of the horrors of the genocide perpetrated on the European Jews during World War II, the world community has struggled to define the full range of protections needed to safeguard universal human dignity and survival under diverse and changing conditions. In the early years, human rights expanded the circle of concern from war crimes to civilian victims of crimes against humanity, and eventually to all forms of "death by government."[3] The "first generation" of rights inscribed in international treaties and institutions thus protected an individual's life, liberty, and bodily integrity from persecution and discrimination.

Although the right to liberation from oppressive governments was an important and necessary first step, it did not address other kinds of threats to survival for a number of people. Therefore, the developing countries introduced a "second generation" of rights, focusing on social and economic rights, to international debate. While this debate foundered on East-West differences during the Cold War, the realization that social and economic rights in many parts of the world are intertwined with freedom and security has resulted in the increasing recognition of these rights.[4] The Human Rights Watch organization increased its emphasis on this connection when campaigns for the survival of indigenous peoples showed that physical attacks and political persecution were often linked to land rights and struggles by outsiders for control of tribal economic resources such as gold or oil. (See Box 9.1: Monitoring Violations around the World.) At another level, discussions on these social

BOX 9.1
Monitoring Violations around the World

Human Rights Watch (HRW) was founded in 1978 to address human rights violations in the USSR in accordance with the provisions spelled out in the Helsinki Accords of 1975. Major human rights violations in Central America in the 1980s led to the birth of Americas Watch, a new monitoring agency for this region. By the late 1980s, all the regional watch programs were integrated into HRW. With a total of only 150 lawyers, journalists, academics, and country experts, HRW is able to track human rights developments in seventy countries. The organization has two principal ways of fighting for universal rights: The first is based on factual accuracy, which entails fact-finding missions and a detailed collection of the accounts of victims, refugees, and other witnesses to piece together a complete picture of the violations. The second strategy involves lobbying government officials, prominent actors, and others in public life to speak up against human rights violations in different parts of the world. HRW is reputed for its evenhanded and accurate reporting and cooperates with States and intergovernmental organizations to bring violators to justice.

- HRW successfully led an international coalition to press for the adoption of a treaty in 2000 banning the practice of employing children as soldiers. (As many as three hundred thousand children are serving in armies and rebel forces around the world.) The treaty raises to eighteen the minimum age for participation in armed conflict.

- With partner organizations in the International Campaign to Ban Landmines, HRW won the 1997 Nobel Peace Prize for bringing about a treaty in the same year to ban the use of land mines in warfare. This victory was significant for human rights activists, as large numbers of civilians have been the innocent victims of this indiscriminately used weapon of destruction.

- HRW worked extensively with investigators for the International Criminal Tribunal for the former Yugoslavia. Six of the seven counts on which the tribunal finally indicted the late Serbian president Slobodan Milosevic in 1999 were cases that HRW had documented in Kosovo.

- HRW has provided extensive evidence of human rights abuses to the war crimes tribunal instituted for Rwanda, where the genocide in 1994 killed more than half a million people.

- HRW played an active role in the legal action against former Chilean dictator Augusto Pinochet in London, and helped to buttress the important principle that even former heads of State can be held accountable for the human rights crimes perpetrated by their regimes.[5]

---

rights have also led to reformed trade agreements allowing less affluent countries free access to patented pharmaceuticals in health emergencies such as the AIDS epidemic, thereby granting an emerging basis for the right to health.

In the last decade of the twentieth century, new challenges like environmental devastation and new movements such as indigenous peoples' campaigns auger a "third generation" of collective and cultural rights, which may be necessary to counter the fundamental threats to survival and self-determination that were not encompassed by individual civil liberties or even State-sponsored social rights.[6] Death by the degradation of a physical or social environment may be just as harmful as political persecution for distinctive ethnic groups such as the Ogoni in Nigeria. Like economic struggles, environmental conflicts often generate other kinds of violations: Ogoni leader Ken Saro-wiwa was executed by the Nigerian government in 1995 for seeking to defend his people from dislocation, pollution, and abuse by local and multinational security forces.

The Problem of Definition

Yet another issue that human rights proponents must negotiate is the indistinct border between public and private. In the last forty years, human rights activists have recognized that half the world's population — women — experience a complex and distinctive pattern of abuses that emanate from a combination of public and private sources (see Box 9.2). The illegitimate denial of women's life and liberty may come from families committing domestic violence, religious communities denying access to public functions, and governments that empower the private abuse of half their citizenry through discriminatory family law codes and the inadequate protection of women from acts such as "honor killings" by their families for perceived cultural "misconduct." Furthermore, some violations by public actors are still considered private rather than political crimes when they happen to women, such as rape by the police. The international campaign for "women's rights as human rights" has made great progress in promoting the recognition of domestic violence as a State responsibility, and rape in wartime as a crime against humanity — in international standards and legal accountability, if not yet in practice.[7]

BOX 9.2
A Crime Against Women

One of the most striking conflicts between cultural traditions and universal human rights norms centers on female genital mutilation (FGM).[8] This practice stems from the need for young women to be seen as virginal and desirable and therefore with a better opportunity to marry. FGM is a common phenomenon in countries like Senegal, Sudan, Guinea, Nigeria, and Algeria, but it also occurs in France, Germany, and Canada, where large immigrant communities favor FGM to control women's sexual and reproductive behavior. Girls and women who survive FGM regularly suffer incessant urinary tract infections, painful menstruation, recurrent blood in their urine, and other complications including sterility, and often die in childbirth. Many do not survive the surgery, dying from infections from the procedure itself.

When this practice is conducted under coercion and the implicit threat that without it women would be denied their right to a normal life, and the knowledge that after the procedure they are left with a lifelong legacy of infections, pain, and danger to their lives, FGM is an abrogation of their rights as human beings. The fact that in some African countries the surgeries take place without the benefit of painkillers and antibiotics can also be viewed as a clear case of threat to the lives of the victims. The international community has been fighting against FGM to support the right of young girls and women to life and dignity. While many young girls who have to undergo FGM are terrified by the procedure, many more succumb to it, driven by the fear that they will never be seen as desirable enough without it to be able to marry. It is estimated that to date over 135 million women have undergone FGM and an average of six thousand face this fate every day.[9] However, as is the case with many other challenges to universal human rights, education can decrease the likelihood of these violations. Mothers who are aware of the dangers of FGM and know of alternatives to it are less likely to force their daughters to suffer the surgery. Education must target women to provide them with options, and men to alter patriarchal norms of female subjugation. If an independent adult woman chooses to undergo FGM under safe, controlled conditions, her actions would not violate the provisions in the Vienna Declaration. However, when other group members forcefully hold down a girl or woman to be operated upon, under conditions that are unsafe and, more usually, unsanitary, their action becomes a clear violation of that girl or woman's human rights.[10]

At a time when globalization is increasing cultural exchange and homogenization, many groups, whose primary source of identity comes from unique cultural traditions, are resisting any change that is suggested in the name of universal human rights. They argue that cultural relativism or equal respect for all cultural practices should come before universal rights. While the Universal Declaration clearly intends the respect of diversity and cultural distinctiveness, cultural practices are only legal as long as they do not infringe on the human rights of both men and women. In an age when the diversity of the globe has paradoxically also highlighted the commonality that all human beings share, cultures can express their distinctiveness without the need to resort to violating their groups' or others' fundamental rights.

The culminating meeting of the global human rights community in the twentieth century — the 1993 United Nations Conference on Human Rights in Vienna — affirmed that human rights are universal standards that all members of the international community must strive to meet, although the mechanisms for enacting a specific standard in a particular society may vary. An inescapable aspect of the history of human rights, however, is an ongoing controversy over whether the concept is a Western invention, and therefore inappropriate for non-Western cultures. In this regard, human rights as enunciated today is just as Western in its origins but universal in its diffusion as many other international laws and organizations; that is to say, the leading vision was created by the then-dominant European powers, although there were, from the outset, critical inputs from some non-Western representatives. Furthermore, in the years since, activists and visionaries across the globe have *made* human rights universal, just like other Western inventions that have been adopted and adapted by diverse societies in different parts of the world. Human rights movements in every region, religious tradition, and social group tell us that people everywhere seek basic means of survival and respect, as well as the right to participate in important decisions that affect their rights.[11] Claims by national or religious leaders that the universally acknowledged rights of human beings are not appropriate for their people usually do not consult the people affected, and often reflect an inaccurate, frozen concept of an unchanging culture. For example, former political prisoner and later South Korean president Kim Dae Jung responded to Singapore's prime minister Lee Kuan Yew's claim that "Asian values" did not prioritize political freedom with the assertion that the millions of Asians Kim Dae Jung now represents were indeed very interested in the civil liberties that saved his life.[12]

Codifying Protection

The international response to the Holocaust after World War II resulted in the establishment of certain key elements of the human rights regime as we know it today: global standards through UN treaties, legal account-ability, monitoring commissions at all levels, and new understandings of transnational issues that transcend State sovereignty. Human rights are codified in a widely endorsed set of international undertakings: the Inter-national Bill of Human Rights (Universal Declaration of Human Rights, International Covenant on Civil and Political Rights, and International Covenant on Social and Economic Rights); phenomenon-specific treaties on war crimes (Geneva Conventions), genocide, and torture; and protec-tion for vulnerable groups in the form of the UN Convention on the Rights of the Child and the Convention on the Elimination of Discrimi-nation Against Women (CEDAW) (see Box 9.3: International Human Rights Documents).

Legal accountability for human rights violations is now possible in the International Court for Criminal Justice (extending the scope of the special International Criminal tribunals for Rwanda and the former Yugoslavia) as well as in the regional human rights courts in Europe and the Americas. Apart from countless national legal processes, there is also a growing acceptance of the principle of universal jurisdiction for certain abuses actionable in the United States and many European countries. Humanitarian intervention by the United Nations has super-vised human rights reform in El Salvador, Cambodia, Bosnia, and Haiti, among others. Major multilateral monitoring and prevention programs are implemented by the UN's High Commissioner for Human Rights; the Human Rights commissions of the European Union and the Orga-nization of American States (OAS); the UN Human Rights Committee and associated special committees on specific types of abuse, such as forced disappearance; the UN Human Rights Commission and associ-ated special rapporteurs on countries deemed at risk; and international organizations dedicated to the rights and needs of labor, women, chil-dren, and indigenous peoples (the ILO, CEDAW, UNICEF, and the Indigenous Peoples Forum, respectively).

These mechanisms were the result of a conscious effort by nongovern-mental organizations (NGO), grassroots campaigners, concerned experts, and visionary leaders, who worked together to raise consciousness, draft standards, staff committees, and gather information. They lobbied their own governments and leveraged international ties. The NGOs drafted many provisions of the UN Convention on the Rights of the Child, while indigenous movements played an important role in creating the UN Work-ing Group on Indigenous Peoples (which later became the Indigenous Peoples Forum). Similarly, the International Court for Criminal Justice is the result of a steadfast campaign by a coalition of dozens of movements advocating human rights, the rule of law, and global governance.

Box 9.3   International Human Rights Documents

Document Name	Entry Into Force	Members
Universal Declaration of Human Rights	5/1/1905	*
Charter of the United Nations	10/24/1945	50 original members
Convention on the Prevention and Punishment of the Crime of Genocide	1/12/1951	130
Geneva Convention relative to the Treatment of Prisoners of War	10/21/1950	191
Geneva Convention relative to the Protection of Civilian Persons in Time of War	10/21/1950	191
European Convention on Human Rights	9/3/1953	Members of the Council of Europe
Convention relating to the Status of Refugees	4/22/1954	*
Convention on the Non-Applicability of Statutory Limitations to War Crimes and Crimes Against Humanity	11/11/1970	45
International Covenant on Economic, Social and Cultural Rights (ICESCR or CESCR)	1/3/1976	148
International Covenant on Civil and Political Rights (ICCPR or CCPR)	3/23/1976	151
Optional Protocol to the International Covenant on Civil and Political Rights (CCPR-OP1 & CCPR-OP2-DP)	3/23/1976	104 & 50, respectively
Convention on the Elimination of All Forms of Discrimination against Women (CEDAW)	9/3/1981	174
Convention against Torture and Other Cruel, Inhuman or Degrading Treatment or Punishment (CAT)	6/26/1987	133
Convention on the Rights of the Child (CRC)	9/2/1990	192

The different documents parallel major developments in the fight to recognize international h
II. The tension between the two superpowers of the Cold War (the United States and the USSI
ICCPR). The 1980s brought a new era of protection for women. In the 1990s, children's rights

Adoption Date	Major Rights
GA 217 A (III) 12/10/48	Includes both negative rights preventing states or rights to education, health care, leisure, etc.
6/26/1945	Equal rights of men and women and of nations large and small.
12/9/1948	Forbids killing or any acts committed with intent to destroy, in whole or in part, a national, ethnic, racial, or religious group.
8/12/1949	Humane treatment of prisoners of war includes adequate food and medical treatment.
8/12/1949	All civilians and combatants who surrender shall in all circumstances be treated humanely. The wounded and sick shall be collected and cared for.
11/4/1950	Includes all rights in the Universal Declaration and more.
7/28/1951	Affords protection to person outside of own country who cannot return due to well-founded fear of persecution.
N/A	Covers war crimes, protection of war victims, and crimes against humanity even if such acts do not constitute a violation of the domestic law.
12/16/1966	Covers fair wages, safe and healthy work conditions, right to unions, to strike, to education, equal opportunity, and to take part in cultural life.
12/16/1966	Freedom of thought, conscience and religion, and of movement, plus equality before the law.
2/19/1999	Human Rights Committee and abolition of death penalty.
12/18/1979	To abolish all discriminatory laws and adopt appropriate ones prohibiting discrimination against women and to eliminate all acts of discrimination against women by persons, organizations, or enterprises.
12/10/1984	To prevent all forms of torture and of inhuman and degrading treatment.
11/12/1989	Sets standards in health care, education, and legal, civil and social services and by preventing the involvment of children in armed conflict, the sale of children, child prostitution, and child pornography.

tandards. The Charter of the United Nations came as a response to the horrors of World War
tification of two separate documents that emphasize different sets of rights (ICESCR and
spelled out.[13]

Millions of human rights activists around the world have thus crafted a new way of bringing principle into practice. It works by using global communications to capture the hearts and minds of the global public, who then pressure governments in their own constituencies. Human rights campaigns not only provide information and moving visuals on global suffering but also aid in the formation of solidarity networks and fact-finding efforts that trace international connections.[14] Advocates of human dignity are instrumental in the construction of cosmopolitan institutions at multiple levels, as, for example, the International Court for Criminal Justice, the OAS's Human Rights Commission, and the World Medical Association. Above all, human rights organizations actively promote the rule of national and international law. Their strategies of mobilization and global governance can pressure governments "from above and below" to change repressive practices or better protect overlooked, vulnerable citizens.[15] (See Box 9.4: South Africa — A Transnational Campaign against Racial Apartheid.)

BOX 9.4
South Africa — A Transnational Campaign against Racial Apartheid

Like many of the challenges faced by the global South, the South African struggle had its roots in colonialism. In the course of their conquest of the southern part of Africa, the British waged lengthy wars over land and cattle against the native Africans. In 1910, the British granted independence to South Africa and handed over control of its territories to the white settlers, who formed a government that solely acknowledged and protected the rights of white elites.

South Africa's Afrikaner government over the years completely disenfranchised the country's black and colored population. They were denied adequate education and barred from holding a wide array of jobs. Their movement within the country was restricted, and a number of humiliating laws governing their personal lives were passed. White settlers were given the freedom to force people off their land, and to confiscate diamond-rich areas. Depriving the Africans of the land they had tilled for centuries resulted in famines; those Africans who did not end up as low-wage laborers on white-owned farms drifted to the cities and established shantytowns characterized by overcrowding and poverty.

On January 8, 1912, chiefs of clans, community representatives, and other politically active Africans joined together to form the African National Congress (ANC). They hoped that by putting aside the differences between their groups and tribes, they could fight for their rights to land and self-determination. In the beginning the ANC favored a pacific course of action, which involved Gandhian techniques of resistance, and repeated petitions to the government of the UK for recognition of the rights of Africans. In 1944, Nelson Mandela founded the ANC Youth League, which demanded and initiated a more active agenda than the leadership's till-now polite petitions to foreign governments.

In 1960, the police responded to a peaceful demonstration in Sharpeville by killing 69 and wounding 186 people. This event marked the end of peaceful protests and started decades of armed struggle. On August 5, 1962, Nelson Mandela was arrested and imprisoned. Police brutality and government repression drastically increased. Yet by the 1980s, resistance organizations of youth, women, and students were growing around South Africa, and they were joined by solidarity movements in the United States and Europe.[16]

Neighboring countries too joined in the struggle. They provided refuge for ANC leaders evading arrest and developed support organizations. By the mid-1980s, as resistance mounted, the governing regime became more brutal. In 1985, the government declared a state of emergency that enabled it to detain hundreds of thousands of men, women, and children; to raid areas of ANC strongholds; to ban all organizations inimical to it; and to terrorize Africans in their everyday life.

Despite the increasing danger to its adherents, the struggle continued. Grassroots movements in South Africa joined with transnational student organizations around the world. They were aided by countless boycotts of corporations who did business there, including giants like PepsiCo Inc. South Africa was excluded from international sporting events, and was subjected to great diplomatic pressure.[17] The decades of tenacious, internal struggle coupled with international sanctions finally brought about a peaceful transition to democracy. In 1990, the government lifted the ban on the ANC. On May 10, 1994, in a fitting turn of events, Nelson Mandela became the first African president of South Africa. While South Africa continues to suffer underdevelopment as a legacy of apartheid, its people today no longer suffer daily human rights violations by the government.

Transnational Activism

Human rights campaigns simultaneously grow out of and build transnational movements. Thousands of NGOs from Tibet to East Timor monitor and defend various kinds of human rights. In terms of function and origin, they can be roughly categorized as civil libertarians, solidarity movements, victim and family organizations, and religious groups (and many overlap). Alongside principled proponents such as Amnesty International, globalization has generated new forms of transnational professional networks (such as the writers' organization PEN and Doctors Without Borders), global groups for conflict monitoring, and coalitions to address specific transnational issues. New forms of communication allow victims to videotape their plight, advocates to flood governments with faxes, and Web sites to mobilize urgent action alerts. (See Box 9.5: The "Fax" about Tiananmen Square.) In the final analysis, however, the effectiveness of global consciousness and pressure on the States, paramilitaries, and insurgents responsible for traditional human rights violations varies tremendously. Despite the giant strides in global connectivity, access to communications mechanisms, whether conventional or new, is still uneven, so that some of the neediest victims, like the illiterate rural poor or refugee women, are the least likely to receive domestic, let alone global, redress.

BOX 9.5
The "Fax" about Tiananmen Square

The information and communication technologies revolution of the late 1980s and 1990s has been a major advantage to human rights activists and resistance movements around the world by enabling them to cross well-guarded borders unnoticed. Activists transmit dramatic images of violations via the World Wide Web, send important information by faxes for mobilization in their struggles, and communicate on cell phones with areas of the world that still do not have land lines. One of the most dramatic examples of the use of such technology was in 1989, when the Chinese government eliminated thousands of peaceful pro-democracy protestors and jailed thousands more.

The Chinese government had long resisted upgrading its telecommunications systems and continues to very tightly control radio and TV broadcasts and the printed press within its borders. However, the fax machine became increasingly essential to the conduct of business by the booming Chinese manufacturing sector. In 1989, dissidents and exiled Chinese citizens began to flood fax machines in China with objective reports of events, foreign government messages of support for Chinese democratization, and information and strategies for organizing grassroots movements within China. The most effective use of the fax machines came after the Tiananmen Square massacre, when Chinese activists from around the world faxed a fake version of the *People's Daily* into government and party offices, disseminating in this way a true account of the event.

In response, the government attempted to control the influx of information by posting guards at every known fax machine location. Once again, the activists evaded the net by faxing page after page of Chinese government propaganda and approved communist newspapers, slipping in between a few important paragraphs of dissident information. The guards were easily fooled into allowing these faxes to be copied and distributed, unaware of their hidden content.

Over a decade later, the Chinese government still restricts access to "subversive Web sites" and e-mail. However, this is a battle that the government is slowly losing. The technology of international cell phones, fast and cheap computers, and Internet access have rendered the borders of China porous to human rights denunciations and democratization campaigns.

The Internet has increased accessibility to information and the possibilities of exchange for many previously isolated groups. Indigenous groups link up with NGOs around the world to expose the global public to remote cultures and conditions. Worldwide networks, such as EcoNet and PeaceNet, bring together environmentalists, supporters of peace, proponents of women's rights, and promoters of tolerance. These transnational networks bring together NGOs and individuals to form powerful coalitions that can have an impact by raising awareness and coordinating strategies on specific issues. Web sites regularly post reports and call for action. Today, the easy accessibility to information has meant that violations, of any kind and anywhere in the world, cannot be hidden for long.

The oldest tradition of humanitarian advocacy speaks for those victims across the globe who cannot speak for themselves. One of the oldest existing human rights organizations is the Anti-Slavery Society, founded in Britain more than a century ago. Along the same lines, members of the Witness for Peace and the Peace Brigades International in the 1980s demonstrated their solidarity by serving as unarmed bodyguards for local populations at risk of human rights abuse in El Salvador, Colombia, and Haiti.

A second kind of international protective association is one that unites people within common sectors — co-religionists, for example, or professional groups. The New York–based Committee to Protect Journalists, in this model, monitors and protests the harassment, persecution, and murder of journalists worldwide. They have recently been quite active in Colombia, where many journalists are killed each year.

Another growing form of international assistance consists of nonhierarchical coalitions of human rights organizations for specific purposes. One of the first such coalitions was the Federation of Families of the Disappeared (FEDEFAM), founded in Argentina in the 1980s to unite national human rights organizations comprising relatives of those who vanished after being taken into government custody. In Africa, one of the few NGOs credited with making some progress on the regionwide and culturally sensitive issue of female genital mutilation is a regional NGO network, the Inter-African Committee.[18]

Common concerns have resulted in informal human rights partnerships between Northern NGOs, including those that are not traditional human rights organizations, and grassroots groups in other parts of the world. The Amazon Alliance, for example, unites environmentalists from the North with indigenous peoples' organizations in Latin America. The Sierra Club has banded together with Amnesty International to provide for the protection of environmental activists worldwide and a special focus on the responsibility of multinational corporations to the environment. In one of their most celebrated cases, the jailed antilogging activist Rodolfo Montiel — winner of the Goldman Environmental Prize for the year 2000 — was declared a prisoner of conscience, and as a result of the pressure brought to bear on the Mexican government, was eventually released. Shared concerns often unite an eclectic mix of labor, religious, and human rights groups in the North. The Texas-based Coalition for Justice in the Maquiladoras, for example, comprises the Interfaith Center for Corporate Responsibility, the American Friends Service Committee, Human Rights Watch, and the United Auto Workers.

Challenges

While the growth of regional, issue-based, and sectoral networks has brought about an increasing participation by the South, the global human rights movement is still struggling for ways to better reflect a wider constituency. The South, with problems and issues particular to the region, has introduced new faces, challenges, and venues to the human rights struggle. International movements and institutions now try to include participants from as many societies as possible, but the barriers of affordability, communication, and freedom of movement is often a constraining factor for these representatives. Moreover, delegates appointed to these forums who can overcome these barriers are sometimes thus exceptional and *unrepresentative* of their own nation's diversity of identity and opinion.

The wide divergence between the Northern-generated structures of international law and the urgent issues of survival and interconnected dilemmas of development is another handicap to North-South efforts at human rights cooperation. Many human rights organizations in the North start with the relative advantage of the basic rights of the individual being recognized in their region. Time-honored institutions have been established and accepted as the guardians of an individual's rights. This is not the case in some areas in the South, where the concept of equality for all under the law is new, startling, and disturbing. Moreover, these concepts often do not address threats to collective self-determination, still a major issue in most of the developing world, nor enable the resources needed to access these rights. Ultimately, a mechanism for the enforcement of legal rights moves slowly, and still usually depends on a functional State authority to enforce it.

Organizations in the global South would also benefit from interaction with other movements and organizations, not necessarily labeled human rights movements, that are central to the defense of human dignity during development struggles. For instance, the building of a dam for "development" purposes may affect the rights to livelihood and even physical security of a larger number of people than the total number of political prisoners in a given society, or the large number of poor killed by paramilitary gangs that will not show up in the monitoring of official police and prison abuses. The perils and promise of globalization, an evolving locus of human rights threats, may impinge on the labor rights and even civil liberties of hundreds of millions as trade organizations, multinational corporations, and international financial institutions reshape to their advantage the rules and resources of developing countries.

The Pitfalls of Globalization . . .

By the end of the Cold War, most international interactions — from negotiations to lower trade tariffs to appeals against torture — shared the common elements of a globalizing, liberal worldview. The liberal vision of democracy and free markets promises freedom, development, and progress through open societies. But by the end of the twentieth century, the relationship between globalization and human rights had become more complicated — and, at times, even contradictory. Human rights promise the first half of the liberal vision — freedom and the development of human potential through principle and law — but some kinds of rights are also threatened by globalization's promise of progress through exchange. The phenomenon of globalization has resulted in the spread of impersonal giant corporations that take advantage of lax labor laws in Third World countries to establish sweatshops; epidemic diseases like AIDS; and new forms of conflict with their attendant legacies, such as land mines (which kill about seventy people each day). Increasingly porous borders have made it possible for new groups of rebels, terrorists, paramilitaries, and organized crime to spread beyond their earlier, geographical limits. With every new threat, human rights proponents have had to devise new countermeasures to bolster or supplement those already in existence. Human rights activists also concurrently participate in global civic initiatives that bypass governments — such as codes of conduct for multinational corporations — to enforce these standards on global and private actors.[19] (See Box 9.6: The "Swoosh" Loses the Case.)

BOX 9.6
The "Swoosh" Loses the Case

In the past decade, many human rights watch organizations, students' organizations, and rock stars have denounced corporate giants like Nike for committing human rights violations abroad. Reports from several NGOs, international journalists, and news agencies of worker abuse, unsafe working conditions, below-minimum-wage salary, impossible quotas, and exposure to dangerous chemicals tarnished Nike's image in the late 1990s. In 1999, Nike's shareholders received letters from sweatshop activists and fellow shareholders detailing these conditions in the companies' factories abroad, and a boycott campaign spread to Canada and Europe, hijacking the Nike slogan to urge consumers to "Just Do It, Boycott Nike!"

In response to this and similar challenges, Nike launched a public relations campaign that painted the giant as a leader in improving factory conditions abroad. Nike declared that it had mended its ways, that physical and sexual abuse were not tolerated, and that it had established fair quota systems with fair pay. Mark Kasky, a longtime environmental activist, brought a lawsuit against Nike, seeking monetary and injunctive relief under California laws designed to curb false advertising and unfair competition. Kasky alleged that Nike had made false statements of fact about its labor practices and working conditions in its overseas factories in order to induce consumers to continue to buy its products.

Nike tried to claim that the company was exercising its First Amendment right of free speech. After the California Supreme Court clearly labeled Nike's statements as commercial speech, Nike decided to settle. This time Nike paid a higher price for violating the rights of its employees: the settlement included a USD 1.5 million contribution to the Fair Labor Association for monitoring human rights violations in factories, and a micro-loans program to provide seed money for Vietnamese workers at a minimum of USD 500,000 over the next two years. Although this sum makes only a tiny dent in the corporation's bottom line, the judgment has served to publicize Nike's labor practices, which will affect the company more directly. This judgment has also served as a warning to other corporations who do business in California and elsewhere in the world.

While the California court cannot regulate how Nike treats its workers in Vietnam, it can prevent Nike from making false claims about improved working conditions in its factories. Human rights activists hope that the publicity engendered by the case and the resulting awareness of a hitherto unknown facet of many multinationals' commercial practices abroad will eventually lead to more humane working conditions in their factories overseas.

The disparate effects of globalization help to explain why it is a double-edged sword for human rights.[20] Increasing traffic across borders brings human rights monitors to Chiapas, but it also brings sex tourists to Thailand. The growth of global governance creates a UN Human Rights Commission and countless NGOs to condemn China's abuse of political dissidents and religious minorities, yet the growth of global commerce has made China an increasingly indispensable trade partner to the United States, and thus relatively immune to human rights pressures.

. . . and Its Advantages

One of the most positive aspects of globalization is the growth of transnational legal accountability. Spain's attempt to extradite former Chilean dictator Augusto Pinochet from Britain to face human rights charges was a major step representative of larger trends. (See Box 9.7: The Pinochet Case.) Spain's Baltasar Garzón, the judge prosecuting Pinochet, also issued arrest warrants for ninety-eight Argentine military officers from the same era. Within the United States, the Alien Torts Act has been used by victims to bring civil action against torturers when both are resident in the United States, resulting in judgments against several Latin American generals and the estate of former Philippines dictator Ferdinand Marcos. In 1999, an OAS Human Rights Court ruling forced Honduras to acknowledge responsibility for its death-squad activities in the 1980s and pay USD 2.1 million in compensation to the victims' families.

BOX 9.7
The Pinochet Case

Former Chilean dictator Augusto Pinochet was arrested in London in October 1998, following an extradition request from Spanish judge Baltasar Garzón. As Chile's next president, Ricardo Lagos, expressed it, "Pinochet's detention in London has shown that globalization has now expanded from economic affairs to the institutions of politics and justice. Chile enjoys the unique status of having been buffeted by both forms of global contagion — with diametrically opposite results."[21]

After numerous delays and appeals through every level of the British legal system, Britain's High Court eventually ruled that Pinochet was unfit to stand trial for health reasons. However, subsidiary rulings along the way established important principles and precedents for transnational accountability. First, the Pinochet proceedings affirmed that Britain — and implicitly its partners in the European Union — was bound by international convention to extradite suspected torturers. Second, Spain's request contributed to the doctrine of indirect chain-of-command responsibility for human rights violations established after

World War II at Nuremberg. Finally, Britain's courts clarified the potential culpability of former heads of State for human rights abuse.

In addition, this transnational activity catalyzed a new wave of human rights accountability within Chile. Pinochet himself has been stripped of his parliamentary immunity by Chilean courts, allowing the possibility of domestic prosecution for the disappearances authorized by his military regime. Following the Pinochet case, Chilean courts have partially withdrawn the clause of self-amnesty promulgated by his regime in 1978, which has resulted in the arrests of several dozen military officers. The charges they face are the result of an evolving legal doctrine that forced disappearance — kidnapping — is an ongoing crime not subject to the statute of limitations.

Current and Future Challenges

In an ironic paradox, human rights today suffer most in the places where globalization has gone too far — and the places where globalization has not gone far enough. In the least developed corners of the globe, rogue States and cultural relativists resist universal human rights standards and international law even as they seek global trade and global security support. States like Sudan, Burma, and North Korea have murdered, tortured, imprisoned, starved, and even enslaved millions of their own citizens in the name of national ideologies — even as they seek foreign investment to bankroll repressive dictatorships. Furthermore, the crimes against humanity wrought by terrorist networks are more common and overall more costly in failed or weak States that lack strong national government or powerful regional and global overseeing organizations, such as Afghanistan. Terrorism also flourishes in societies experiencing an unhealthy and unsustainable imbalance in some aspects of globalization, such as in Pakistan.

On the one hand, globalization has not gone far enough in the world's strongest State, as the Bush administration has sought to substitute US hegemony for global participation in a way that has damaged international human rights treaties, programs, and institutions. For example, US objections and ultimate withdrawal from the International Court for Criminal Justice have complicated a goal the United States claims to share: bringing war criminals and dictators guilty of genocide to justice. US policymakers have manipulated aid and trade agreements to impose special clauses exempting US personnel from international legal accountability on States that had agreed to participate in the Court. This rejection of a uniform international law by the United States has also diminished its respect for human rights in the conduct of its military interventions; the treatment of immigrants, prisoners, and terrorist suspects; and even, increasingly, the everyday civil liberties of ordinary US citizens. The World Court recently ruled that the United States' treatment of foreign nationals in death penalty cases, a longstanding irritant in its relations with its closest allies and trade partners, violates international law.

On the other hand, globalization has gone too far where the neoliberal policies and pressures of today's world have resulted in an inequality in international commerce and global governance that has generated impoverishment, destabilizing discontent, and decaying democracy in Latin America and parts of Africa and Asia. The victims of repression in contemporary Latin America or the post-Soviet republics are now less often political dissidents; they are increasingly economic protesters, journalists who control information flows, street children and shantytown dwellers marginalized by economic adjustment, and defenders of the environment. Many residents of these regions are migrants, refugees, or "second-class citizens," whose rights are determined anonymously from beyond their borders. No one elects multinational corporations, and States are not accountable to the UN High Commission on Refugees. Who does the migrant maid call when she is assaulted or exploited?

Conclusion

Yet while the overall trend of oppression remains discouraging, hope lies in the fact that human rights resistance has already inspired some changes in globalization itself. Debt relief has begun to recognize the plight of the poorest nations in response to transnational campaigns, and even US foreign aid has been increased — with an enhanced focus on the human rights conditions in recipient States. Also, continuing pressure and a growing awareness of the interconnectedness of economic and political development have recently resulted in the World Bank and the International Monetary Fund instituting some human rights–related programs.

The challenge for human rights in the new millennium will be to reach across barriers and keep building connections. We must strengthen the transnational bridges over the gulf of national sovereignty, and continue to link global responsibility to local oppression. But we must also reach out in new directions: across public and private, upwards to global processes and institutions, and below to the grassroots and the global South. In the defense of human dignity, these are bridges worth building.

Notes

1. Adrienne Rich, *The Dream of a Common Language: Poems 1974–1977* (New York: W. W. Norton, 1993).

2. Biran Orend, *Human Rights: Concept and Context* (Ontario: Broadview Press, 2002).

3. R. J. Rummel, *Death by Government* (Somerset, NJ: Transaction Publishers, 1994).

4. William Felice, *The Global New Deal: Economic and Social Human Rights in World Politics* (Lanham, MD: Rowman and Littlefield, 2003).

5. Human Rights Watch, www.hrw.org/home.html (accessed September 14, 2003).

6. Alison Brysk, *From Tribal Village to Global Village: Indian Rights and International Relations in Latin America* (Stanford, CA: Stanford University Press, 2000).

7. Julie Peters and Andrea Wolper, eds., *Women's Rights, Human Rights* (New York: Routledge, 1995).

8. FGM refers to cutting off part of the genitals of a young, virginal girl or woman and often sewing her shut to different degrees.

9. Amnesty International, www.amnesty.org/ailib/intcam/femgen/fgm1.htm#a3 (accessed October 23, 2003).

10. United Nations Foundation, "Africa: Some Progress Fighting FGM," WIN News, UN Wire (Spring 2000), www.unfoundation.org (accessed March 26, 2004). In an effort to lessen social pressure for the practice to continue, the World Bank supports micro-credit for former practitioners in order to help them reestablish themselves in other businesses.

11. Mahmood Monshipouri, Neil Englehart, Andrew J. Nathan, and Kavita Philip, eds., *Constructing Human Rights in the Age of Globalization* (New York: M. E. Sharpe, 2003).

12. Kim Dae Jung, "Is Culture Destiny?" *Foreign Affairs* 73, no. 6 (1994): 189.

13. See United Nations High Commissioner for Human Rights, www.unhchr.ch/pdf/report.pdf (accessed September 9, 2003).

14. Margaret E. Keck and Kathryn Sikkink, *Activists beyond Borders* (Ithaca, NY: Cornell University Press, 1999).

15. Alison Brysk, "From Above and Below: Social Movements, the International System and Human Rights in Argentina," *Comparative Political Studies* 26 (October 1993): 259–85.

16. African National Congress, "A History of the African National Congress," www.anc.org.za/ancdocs/about/umzabalazo.html (accessed September 14, 2003).

17. Audie Klotz, *Norms in International Relations: The Struggle against Apartheid* (Ithaca, NY: Cornell University Press, 1995).

18. Claude Welch, *Protecting Human Rights in Africa* (Philadelphia: University of Pennsylvania Press, 1995).

19. Alison Brysk, ed., *Globalization and Human Rights* (Berkeley: University of California Press, 2002).

20. Alison Brysk, "Globalization: The Double-edged Sword," *NACLA Report on the Americas* 34, no. 1 (2000): 29–33.

21. Ricardo Lagos and Heraldo Munoz, "The Pinochet Dilemma," *Foreign Policy* 114 (Spring 1999): 26–39.

CHAPTER TEN

Waging Peace:
Transnational Peace Activism

Motoko Mekata

Introduction

A peace movement, in its broadest sense, can be defined as a series of activities to protest against a case for war and the use of force, and to encourage the exploration of alternative avenues. It involves street demonstrations and other forms of direct action as well as advocating its cause in various forums, influencing election campaign issues, and submitting petitions to governments as a means of influencing policy decisions. Although the aims and methods of peace movements are complex and have become highly diversified over time, peace movements have constituted an integral part of civic movements throughout the post–World War II period. The antinuclear/disarmament movements in particular have been the most sustained of these movements, reflecting the ever-present public fear of nuclear annihilation during the last half-century.

The end of the Cold War in 1989 dramatically decreased the potential danger of an all-out nuclear war and changed the terms of the nuclear predicament. A new opportunity was created to "end the forced cohabitation with horror" and to "annul the suicide pact dictated by the doctrine of deterrence."[1] As a consequence, activists seized the chance to reframe the concept of peace, including a wide range of humanitarian issues on their agenda. Rather than merely reacting to political exigencies and policy outcomes, activists today structure their efforts as proponents and advocates of specific issues, focusing on those that were often concealed and/or inadequately addressed during the Cold War. They often do so by engaging in close partnership with governments and international organizations that share similar concerns and means to achieve their goal.

More recently, however, globalization, which has intensified the mobility of people, money, commodities, and information, has added a significant variable, changing the landscape of international security once again. Nuclear tests conducted by India and Pakistan, the longstanding conflict in the Korean peninsula (with the suspicion of the People's Republic of Korea developing nuclear capacity), and continuing instability in the Middle East has intensified apprehensions about nuclear proliferation on a global scale. The terrorist attack on the World Trade Center in September 2001 symbolized the new form of threat posed by faceless, non-State actors, awakening the world to the fact that traditional State security frameworks may no longer guarantee public safety. The changing global environment is therefore bringing about new challenges to the peace movement.

The history of the major peace movements since the end of World War II is outlined in this chapter, followed by an overview of the characteristics and outcomes of these initiatives. What are the changes that activists have had to reckon with in this age of globalization, and what are the challenges that they will have to overcome? An attempt will also be made to answer these questions.

History

The history of the peace movement falls into two broad categories, which closely follow the two most significant world events since World War II: the Cold War, and the period following the breakup of the Soviet Union.

The Cold War Era

Over two hundred armed conflicts can be counted between 1946 and 1999, often predicated on the ideological, religious, and political independence that effectively split the world into two main camps during this period.[2] Throughout these years, numerous peace movements emerged in an attempt to deter armed attacks or escalations of conflict. The most notable one, and indeed the one that left the most indelible impression on the world psyche, was the peace movement against the Vietnam War in the 1960s and early 1970s, which, intentionally or not, also had a significant social impact. Nevertheless, it is not too much to say that the prime focus of the peace movements during the Cold War was on the reduction and ultimate disarmament of nuclear weapons by nuclear arms-bearing States, principally the United States and the Soviet Union. Their efforts often reflected the ebb and flow of contemporary hostile currents, and therefore rarely maintained a continuous pitch in force and action.

1945–1947: Inspired by the fear that Germany under Adolf Hitler might be the first to develop atomic bombs, the United States initiated its own nuclear initiative, the Manhattan Project, in 1942. This project, conceived and carried out in top secret, was an ambitious quest by distinguished scientists and engineers to create nuclear explosives. The nuclear bombs they manufactured and used in Hiroshima and Nagasaki that left over two hundred thousand dead, and the shock and devastation, galvanized a "movement against nuclear weapons, led by atomic scientists, pacifists, and political internationalists . . . overnight."[3]

In 1945, several former members of the Manhattan Project, appalled by the destructive magnitude of the bomb they had created, founded the Federation of Atomic Scientists (FAS) (later changed to the Federation of American Scientists) to express a deep concern for the implications of the nuclear age on the future of humankind. Many, like Robert Oppenheimer, a prominent physicist and the director of the Manhattan Project, were racked by doubt and guilt. On meeting President Truman he said, "I feel we have blood on our hands."[4] Although Oppenheimer did not join the FAS, he too made initiatives toward nuclear arms control by proposing the establishment of an international agency, the Atomic Development Authority, to be vested with a worldwide monopoly of control over dangerous elements in the whole field of atomic energy, from mining to manufacturing, and all forms of nuclear research and development.[5] Partly influenced by Oppenheimer's proposal, the US government tabled a plan for an international agency to control atomic power and weapons at the UN Security Council in 1946.

Although this plan was vetoed by the Soviet Union, Oppenheimer's efforts inspired the first of many waves for nuclear disarmament. Many civic groups joined the scientists in promoting Oppenheimer's idea. In the United States, the most notable one was the National Committee on Atomic Information, in which leaders of influential organizations like the National Farmers' Union, the American Federation of Labor, and the League of Women Voters became engaged. After the failure of the US proposal at the United Nations, however, the first wave of antinuclear protest declined.

The characteristic of the peace movement in this period was that it was articulated and led mainly by professional scientists and experts like the FAS, while other nongovernmental organizations (NGO) simply supported them. Although the overwhelming shadow of the Cold War and the intense rivalry between the two blocs led by the United States and the Soviet Union soon blocked off the concerns of the antinuclear movement, the coming together of knowledgeable scientists and civic organizations was a significant step forward in the fledgling field of movements for peace.

1954–1963: On 1 March 1954, the United States undertook its first hydrogen bomb (thermonuclear bomb) test at Bikini Atoll in the Marshall Islands. The hydrogen bomb had an explosive power a thousand times greater than those that had decimated Hiroshima and Nagasaki. As it was an atmospheric test, heavy doses of radioactive ash fell on the Marshall Islands, and on a Japanese fishing boat, the *Lucky Dragon*, that was sailing 100 miles (160 km) east of the epicenter. As a consequence, twenty-three crewmembers suffered from radiation sickness, and one died six months later. It now dawned on citizens around the world that "a hydrogen bomb could kill people not only nearby, but hundreds of miles distant."[6]

Once more, the potential of atomic bombs as an uncontrollable and hugely destructive force revived movements against them the world over. Two large NGOs that focused specifically on nuclear disarmament and had much impact were the Committee for a Sane Nuclear Policy (SANE) established in 1957 in New York and the Campaign for Nuclear Disarmament (CND), which held its inaugural public meeting in London in February 1958 to protest the British testing of the hydrogen bomb. SANE's aim was primarily to stimulate public opinion with a view to a multilateral ban on atomic testing. It initiated a number of public education and advertising projects, including full-page advertisements in *The New York Times* and other papers, warning the public that "we are facing a danger unlike any danger that has ever existed."[7] These advertisements brought home the case for nuclear disarmament to millions of ordinary Americans. The CND, which brought together scientists, pacifists, environmentalists, and prominent writers and musicians, was a mass political protest movement to advocate unilateral British nuclear disarmament. The now-famous peace symbol, designed by artist Gerald Holtom, first appeared on placards on a march organized by them in the same year.

In a parallel to the civic movement, professionals and scientists also embarked on new initiatives. In 1955, Bertrand Russell and Albert Einstein issued the so-called Russell–Einstein Manifesto, which called upon scientists to expose the threat posed to civilization by the development of hydrogen bombs. Influential scientists and scholars, stimulated by the Manifesto, concerned by the danger of nuclear annihilation, convened the Pugwash Conference in 1957. Twenty-two eminent scientists from all over the world participated in the conference.[8] In the United States, the FAS renewed its activities as well. It advocated a worldwide ban on further tests at its testimony before the Senate Subcommittee on Disarmament in

June 1956.[9] The Physicians for Social Responsibility, founded in 1961, also joined the campaign to end atmospheric nuclear tests by "documenting the presence of Strontium 90, a byproduct of atomic tests, in children's teeth."[10]

Such was the momentum generated by these disarmament movements that the president of the United States, Dwight Eisenhower, could no longer ignore public antinuclear sentiment, and especially a call for a nuclear test ban. However, the United States and the Soviet Union were locked in a nuclear arms race due to the intensifying Cold War rivalry between the East and the West; moreover, US military strategy had come to be highly dependent on its nuclear arsenal by then, making it nearly impossible to abandon the nuclear option. Thus, on 22 August 1958, the president in conjunction with the Soviet Union announced a moratorium on nuclear weapons tests, which continued until 15 September 1961, when the United States resumed nuclear weapons testing in response to the Soviet Union breaking their nuclear test moratorium.[11]

During this hiatus, the United States initiated test ban treaty negotiations with the Soviet Union and the United Kingdom. However, none of the parties could reach an agreement on the mechanisms for the verification of underground nuclear testing. Eventually, on 5 August 1963, the United States, the United Kingdom, and the Soviet Union signed the Partial Test Ban Treaty (PTBT), which prohibited underwater, atmospheric, and outer space nuclear tests, but allowed for underground nuclear testing to continue. Although peace activists and scientists asserted that even underground nuclear testing was verifiable, the governments of nuclear weapon states did not share this view.[12]

The vision of a comprehensive ban on nuclear tests thus ended as a mirage for peace activists. Although pushed by heightened public sentiment in the West to reexamine their nuclear arms policies, the United States, the United Kingdom, and the Soviet Union nevertheless managed to foil the aspirations of antinuclear and peace activists by exempting underground nuclear tests from the PTBT. However, compared to the first wave of antinuclear movements in 1945–47, the activities of the NGOs in this period played a remarkable role in formulating public opinion: the NGOs set the tone, and the scientists reinforced the NGOs' standpoint with scientific knowledge and expertise. The pressure of public opinion was so influential that it was necessary for the US government to modify its nuclear test programs and seek a way to conclude a legally binding instrument with other nuclear weapon States. But, as with all movements motivated by fear, the fact that nuclear tests continued underground, where it was invisible and usually did not spread radioactive fallout, meant that awareness and public concern about nuclear tests declined rapidly after the PTBT was signed.

1968–1972: In early 1965, the United States began air raids and combat operations against communist-controlled North Vietnam in keeping with their avowed intention of containing communism and preventing its further expansion into other countries in Southeast Asia. By April of that year, more than twenty thousand US troops were deployed in Vietnam, and many more were poured in during the next seven years. American fatalities in Vietnam during the entire US military involvement (1961–72) reached more than fifty thousand. The South Vietnamese dead were estimated at more than four hundred thousand, and the Viet Cong (insurgents aided by North Vietnam) and the North Vietnamese fatalities totaled over nine hundred thousand.[13]

The early phase of the anti–Vietnam War movement utilized several pre-existing institutions, including the civil rights movement, and these provided an entry into several fairly distinct, broader constituencies as the antiwar movement began to articulate a comprehensive critique of US policy in Vietnam. These movements were somewhat random, dispersed, and divided, but as time went on they began to take a more structured form. In November 1966, a national coalition was created to arrange the largest-yet national demonstration in April 1967. The coalition, called the Spring Mobilization Committee to End the War in Vietnam, was joined by other coalitions and welcomed any organization opposed to the Vietnam War, regardless of political or social background.[14] Millions of Americans participated in demonstrations and other forms of protests over the next few years. The protests brought together ordinary Americans, Vietnam veterans, political figures, and academics. Their spontaneous and sustained campaign illustrated the breadth and depth of antiwar sentiment in the country. Although ostensibly a movement against US military engagement in Vietnam, the movement had the unprecedented impact of affecting every sphere of life, overturning heretofore stable, conventional perceptions of social mores, individual rights, and the moral certitude of governments. This counterculture had a tremendous impact on other movements that were sweeping through Europe and Asia.

Although subsumed for a while by the greater urgency of protest against the Vietnam War, the focus on disarmament had not entirely disappeared. In the first half of the 1960s, France and China joined the nuclear club; to avoid a further proliferation of nuclear weapons, several countries put forward the idea of a Non-Proliferation Treaty (NPT), and it was finally signed on 1 July 1968. The critical point in the treaty was the concession made by the nonnuclear weapons States to refrain from acquiring nuclear weapons, and in exchange the nuclear weapons States agreed to make progress towards nuclear disarmament. An unpopular war in Vietnam and the rise of social demonstrations across the world facilitated the NPT, and nudged the United States and the Soviet Union towards strategic arms limitation talks aimed at limiting missile systems and bombs that carried strategic nuclear warheads. The talks were held from 1969 to 1972, and the first Strategic Arms Limitation Treaty (SALT I) and an Anti-Ballistic Missile Systems (ABM) Treaty were signed in May 1972.

In contrast to the popular involvement in protests against the Vietnam War, nuclear disarmament concerns were limited to being voiced by scientists and other experts in the field. Although SANE carried out advertisement campaigns attacking ABMs and held national conferences on ABMs in Washington in 1969, public opinion did not seem sensitive to nuclear weapons issues. This was partly due to public preoccupation with the Vietnam War in the United States and to student protests and riots in Europe and Japan, as well as, ironically, to nuclear arms control efforts and the détente between the two superpowers.[15] That people were inclined to think that the world had become safer was exemplified by the Doomsday Clock, first printed on the cover of the June 1947 issue of the *Bulletin of Atomic Scientists*, a magazine providing information and analyses on the continuing dangers posed by nuclear weapons. In 1953, the hands of the clock were shown at two minutes to midnight (doomsday), but by 1972, they had been moved back to twelve minutes to midnight.[16] From the mid-1960s, "nuclear issues were increasingly replaced as the subject of mass popular protest by anger over the United States' part in the Vietnam War."[17]

Overshadowed by the emotive issues of the Vietnam War and the social upheavals that ensued, scientists nevertheless continued to plough a lonely furrow, periodically bringing to the notice of the public, and the legislative and the executive arms of Western governments, the dangers inherent in uncontrolled and unmonitored growth of nuclear weapons. As in the previous decades, however, mass involvement and the role of professional groups in the context of antinuclear movements and disarmament were limited in efficacy.

The 1970s were devoted to various negotiations between the United States and the Soviet Union. The Nixon and subsequently Carter administrations negotiated the SALT I (1972) and SALT II (1979) treaties, but neither was comprehensive. The Soviet Union's invasion of Afghanistan in December 1979 brought negotiations to an end, and in fact led to the US Senate refusing to ratify SALT II.

1981–1987: By 1981, heightened tensions between the East and the West and a consequent buildup of arsenals in both camps led to the Doomsday Clock being set to four minutes to midnight. In December of that year, an NBC/Associated Press survey showed that 76 percent of the US public felt that nuclear war was "likely" within a few years.[18] Increased fear of nuclear war, as a matter of course, reignited public concern once again. The accidents in the nuclear power plants at Three Mile Island in 1979 and Chernobyl in 1986 also reanimated public sensitivity to nuclear issues.

The Nuclear Weapons Freeze Campaign, based on a grassroots movement in the United States, called for both superpowers to accept a mutual freeze on the testing, production, and deployment of nuclear weapons and missiles. Although the national office coordinated overall activities, the Freeze Campaign had a decentralized structure that allowed a degree of flexibility to local groups to formulate and execute their plans.[19] The petitions of the Freeze Campaign were signed by more than 2.3 million Americans and delivered to the United States and Soviet missions of the United Nations in New York City. By November 1983, more than 370 city councils, 71 county councils, and one or both houses of 23 state legislatures had adopted the endorsement resolutions.[20] SANE also actively engaged in this movement and eventually merged with the Freeze Campaign. This merger proved to be very effective, since the Freeze Campaign had a vigorous grassroots network of over eighteen hundred local organizations throughout the country, while SANE had a strong presence in Washington and a membership base of 150,000.[21]

In Europe, the disarmament movement was focused on the deployment of the Intermediate Nuclear Force (INF), namely, the Cruise and Pershing missiles. In 1979, the North Atlantic Treaty Organization (NATO) proposed deploying the new INFs in Western Europe as the Soviet Union had already started to deploy its new INFs, the SS-20 missiles, in East European countries.

Judging from their flight range, it was presumed that the INFs would be used principally in the European theater, which created an uproar across Europe. In the United Kingdom, huge protest marches were arranged by the CND, and the movement blossomed as "thousands of new members were joining every month." Among the many other movements that grew out of the protests was the Greenham Common Women's Peace Camp. In September 1981, a mainly women's march arrived at Greenham Common US Air Force base, where the first cruise missiles were supposedly deployed. Then, "a temporary camp soon became both a permanent peace camp and a women-only camp," and it "quickly became a focus and a symbol of women's resistance to the male-dominated world of nuclear weapons."[22]

Fear of nuclear war had become a defining feature of the peace movement in Germany as well. Leading West German peace groups organized a demonstration in the fall of 1981, which drew some 250,000 to 300,000 protesters, making it the largest demonstration in German history. The Easter March, modeled on the CND's annual march to the British nuclear weapons site at Aldermaston, had been held in Germany since 1960; the movement had been quiescent during much of the seventies, but was brought back to life in the eighties. While 200,000 people participated in the Easter March of 1982, the number grew to 400,000–500,000 in 1986.[23] At the same time, high-ranking ex-NATO officers formed the Ex-NATO Generals for Peace and Disarmament movement, and issued a memorandum to the foreign and defense ministers and senior military officers of the NATO member States, calling for a political rather than a military settlement to the East-West conflict and a move toward a nonnuclear Europe. Scientists in various fields also embarked on a sharp criticism of the nuclear arms race. In the United States, the Union of Concerned Scientists (UCS) and dozens of other NGOs held teach-ins on nuclear war at 151 campuses in 41 states in November 1981.[24] The International Physicians for the Prevention of Nuclear War (IPPNW), established in 1980, played an important teaching role on the hazardous fallout of a war fought with nuclear weapons.[25]

Notwithstanding the huge outcry against the buildup of arsenals in general and nuclear weapons in particular, the martial brinkmanship of the time empowered President Reagan to unleash a new dimension to warfare called the Strategic Defense Initiative (SDI). The SDI was a futuristic vision of a shield, using systems on land and in space, against incoming nuclear missiles.[26] Amid fears that this initiative would lead to a new escalation in weapons one-upmanship, the UCS mobilized opposition in the scientific community and published its analyses of SDI's technical weak points and strategic disadvantages. In 1985, more than seven hundred members of the National Academy of Sciences, including fifty-seven Nobel laureates, signed UCS's "Appeal to Ban Space Weapons" and urged the two superpowers "to ban testing and deployment of weapons in space."[27] In a similar vein, the FAS contended that the SDI "would accelerate the arms race, undermine the ABM treaty, and provide an unreliable defense for the United States."[28] These interventions by scientists contributed a sobering counterweight to the optimistic promises of the SDI's proponents.

In a reflection of the groundswell of social and political awareness, the debate on nuclear arms control entered a new stage in 1985. In the Soviet Union, a crumbling political edifice and the accident at the Chernobyl nuclear power plant provided an impetus for the Soviet premier, Mikhail Gorbachev, to seek a disarmament agreement on nuclear forces. In the

United States, the Reagan administration faced strong congressional opposition to the SDI, after senators and representatives echoed the criticisms presented by the scientists. Finally in 1987, the United States and the Soviet Union concluded the INF treaty.

Although antinuclear/disarmament movements in this period did not necessarily achieve all their goals, the impact of these movements was never negligible. A study on the Freeze Campaign, for instance, concluded that the movements "had a major impact with respect to arms control's place on the national agenda." [29] And although the overwhelming number of antinuclear/antiwar activities had initiated in the West, their influence was not lost in the Soviet Union, particularly in the latter half of the 1980s. After the conclusion of the INF talks, Gorbachev said that, "without [the IPPNW] and other powerful antinuclear initiatives, it is unlikely that the INF treaty would have come about." [30] Indeed, the "INF treaty led directly to the relaxation of superpower tensions, the fall of the Berlin Wall, and the collapse of state socialism in Eastern Europe and the former Soviet Union," and "the disarmament agreement was the central catalyst for the end of the Cold War." [31]

In retrospect, the antinuclear/disarmament movements during the Cold War "change[d] the political climate in which decision makers operate[d]," [32] but in most cases the movements "did not succeed in altering the arms control agenda itself in the way its organizers had hoped." [33] The difficulty in sustaining a movement through to its desired outcome was shown up time and again: the protests against nuclear testing forced the nuclear weapons States to sign a treaty, but public opinion declined sharply once the PTBT was concluded, despite the fact that nuclear tests continued underground. Similarly, the Freeze Campaign contributed to sensitizing the US government on nuclear policies, but a complete halt to the production of nuclear weapons did not become a policy agenda, and waning public interest after the INF treaty was signed ensured that the issue was buried till the next alarm. In other words, much of the peace movement during the Cold War was a reaction to a particular State's policy, and was thus subject to the changing dynamics of domestic and international political environments, which also meant that movements were unable to maintain persistent public interest on nuclear issues. Early efforts at nuclear control were of an elitist nature, confined to scientists and other experts who tried to guide government policy in containment rather than a total suspension of nuclear weapons. In some ways, this was a more pragmatic approach than that of the later calls for complete disarmament, given that the Soviet Union and the Eastern bloc were almost completely immune to the kind of pressures of public opinion that drove policy in the West. In the later years, notwithstanding the attempts by scientists and grassroots organizations to join their efforts, these were not quite enough to formulate a strong base from which to force through their ultimate goals. Although NGOs and scientists attempted international collaborations by holding conferences, conducting joint projects, and exchanging strategies and tactics for mass demonstrations, the movements were basically focused on domestic campaigns. The meeting between Gorbachev and some NGOs in 1985 may be a good example of international dialogue, but, in the main, NGOs and professional groups exerted their influence mainly through domestic decision-making processes, and their basic battlefields were confined by national boundaries. Thus, although the nuclear age had a global implication from its very beginning, the world still lacked transnational linkages among civil society activists.

Peace Initiatives after the Cold War

The post–Cold War era witnessed two fundamental changes in peace movements. The first was an opportunity to widen the spectrum of agendas within this genre. As the risk of nuclear annihilation retreated, the concept of what really constituted a threat to human survival shifted from an all-out war to concerns such as poverty, political and economic refugees, discrimination of various kinds, environmental degradation, infectious diseases, and other humanitarian issues often neglected during the Cold War period. As these issues gained ground in the perceptions of political leaders and NGOs, the antinuclear/disarmament movements also began to view their campaign from a similar perspective; just as these other threats to human survival had to be eradicated, so also disarmament activists needed to alter their approach to the issue from short-term containment to a total abolition of nuclear arsenals. The second fundamental change was the means by which peace proponents pursued their agenda. In addition to demonstrations and direct public mobilizations, activists along with experts and professional groups increasingly engaged in advocating specific goals in policy by directly influencing governments and intergovernmental negotiations. Such actions were directly facilitated by building strong transnational linkages between civil societies, harmonizing on strategies and tactics, and engaging in partnerships with nation-states sharing the same goals.

These changes were brought about by many factors, of which two are especially noteworthy. The first was the transformation of the former socialist states of Eastern Europe and the Soviet Union, and of the military dictatorships and authoritarian regimes in South America, Asia, and Africa into democratic countries.[34] Increasingly democratic systems led to the rise and flowering of civil societies and "associational revolution[s]" in many countries.[35] The rights to freedom of speech and association inherent in democratic systems were prime tools used by peace activists to advocate global issues through cross-border partnerships. The other factor was the revolution in information technology, which allowed civil society actors to communicate with each other, exchange information, and facilitate coordination much faster and at less cost than ever before. The imperatives of globalization had a felicitous effect in that declining airfares also enabled physically dispersed groups and individuals to come together. Although the exchange of information and ideas through email and the Internet was essential to their activities, face-to-face communication was indispensable in getting to know one another and building trust among the activists. This not only meant that the peace movements became more transnational but also that they began to have more participation from countries that were often left out during the Cold War.

BOX 10.1
The World Court Project

The moral grounds for the use of, or the threat to use, nuclear weapons had exercised peace activists for a long time. With the end of a bipolar world after the breakup of the Soviet Union, and therefore, ostensibly, no further requirement of nuclear arsenals as weapons of deterrence, attempts were made to obtain an advisory opinion from the International Court for Criminal Justice (ICCJ) on the legality of the threat or use of nuclear weapons. The World Court Project (WCP) was officially launched in 1992 by three prominent NGOs: the International Physicians for the Prevention of Nuclear War (IPPNW), the International Peace Bureau (IPB), and the International Association of Lawyers Against Nuclear Arms (IALANA). Under Article 96 of the UN Charter, requests for an advisory opinion could be made to the ICCJ only by the Security Council, the UN General Assembly (UNGA), or other organs and specialized agencies of the United Nations when so authorized by the General Assembly. Consequently, the strategy of the WCP was to influence member States at the World Health Organization (WHO) and the UNGA to sponsor resolutions asking the Court for an advisory opinion on this issue.

In pursuance of its aims, the WCP extensively lobbied non-aligned countries and organized mass mobilizing campaigns across the world. One of its most notable achievements was a drive begun in 1992 to gather individual "Declaration[s] of Public Conscience," tailored to the Martens Clause of the 1899 Hague convention.[36] In 1993, 170,000 declarations were presented to the registrar of the ICCJ, which "was the first time that the Court had received such 'evidence' from the public."[37]

The nuclear weapons States, especially the United States, United Kingdom, and France, put up a stiff opposition to the WCP, but eventually, in December 1994, with most of the non-aligned countries throwing their weight behind the WCP, the UNGA adopted a resolution asking the Court for an advisory opinion on the following question: "Is the threat or use of nuclear weapons in any circumstance permitted under international law?" During the oral hearings at the Court in 1995, the WCP provided legal assistance, and observed the proceedings and reported to the world. Forty-three governments and the WHO made written submissions, and twenty-two governments and the WHO made oral statements — the greatest participation of States in any ICCJ case. In several cases, the NGOs were said to have been "largely responsible for the wording of many national statements."[38]

On July 8, 1996, the Court issued a judgment that said that the use of or threat to use nuclear weapons is generally unacceptable, and would be contrary to the rules of international law in just about any imaginable circumstance. The Court also unanimously stressed that States had a legal obligation not only to pursue "negotiations leading to nuclear disarmament in all its aspects," in accordance with Article 6 of the NPT, but also to "bring to a conclusion" such negotiations.[39]

The Court's opinion was a significant victory for the WCP in particular and the peace movement in general in that it mandated a clear obligation by nuclear weapons States to pursue meaningful nuclear disarmament and bring these negotiations to a finite conclusion. Based on this judgment, activists, organizations, and countries in favor of nuclear disarmament launched new initiatives against the nuclear weapons States.

This remarkable effort by the WCP demonstrated how civil society organizations, working with governments, could play an effective role in influencing decision making at the very apex of international governing bodies: the United Nations.

BOX 10.2
The International Campaign
to Ban Landmines

Although the threat of war of Armageddonic proportions had receded after the end of the Cold War, the world was still plagued by several low-intensity conflicts that were nevertheless claiming fatalities on a worrisomely large scale. These concerns led to the launch of a new campaign that aimed at banning antipersonnel land mines (AP mines) by six NGOs in 1992. In the early 1990s, it was estimated that around two thousand people, mainly civilians in some sixty countries around the world, were the victims of land mines every month. Cheap, easy to make or procure, and devastatingly effective, AP mines inflicted "more death and injury than nuclear and chemical weapons combined" over the past fifty years.[40] To make matters worse, while the cost of production of a simple AP mine was only between USD 3 and USD 20, the average cost of disarming and removing it ranged anywhere from USD 300 to USD 1,000 per mine.

The six organizations that initiated the International Campaign to Ban Landmines (ICBL) were all involved in one way or another in clearing land mines and helping mine victims. It was clear to them that the only solution to this scourge was to eradicate AP mines through a total ban, like the bans imposed on biological and chemical weapons, by prohibiting their production, transaction, storage, and usage.

One of the key figures to quickly and positively respond to the land mine issue was the Canadian foreign minister, Lloyd Axworthy. Convening a strategic conference in Ottawa in October 1996, Axworthy proposed the establishment of a new comprehensive ban treaty, and urged that a treaty-signing conference be held there in December 1997. Axworthy stated that "there is momentum, there is political commitment, and most importantly, the peoples of the world support what we are trying to do." Speaking of the ICBL, he said, "the challenge is also to the International Campaign to ensure that governments around the world are prepared to work with us to ensure that a treaty is developed and signed next year. This is not far-fetched. You are largely responsible for our being here today. The same effective arguments you used to get us here must now be put to work to get foreign ministers here to sign the treaty."[41]

The fourteen months that followed after the strategic conference came to be known as the Ottawa Process, and the ICBL members collaborated closely with pro-ban countries, including Austria, Canada, Ireland, Norway, and South Africa. The treaty was signed in Ottawa on December 2, 1997, and entered into force on March 1, 1999. Today, over 140 countries are party to the treaty.[42] The ICBL was awarded the Nobel Peace Prize in 1997 for its efforts. The Nobel Committee noted that the Ottawa Process could be "a model for similar processes in the future," and that "it could prove of decisive importance to the international effort for disarmament and peace."[43] The secretary-general of the United Nations, Kofi Annan, also celebrated the conclusion of the Ottawa Treaty by stating that the "union of governments, civil society and international organizations" was the "international community of the future," and praised the Ottawa Process as "a remarkable expression of the new diplomacy."[44]

The land mines case had a spillover effect on NGOs working in other fields related to peace and security. While some banded together to establish the International Court for Criminal Justice, others worked to contain the devastation caused by small arms and formed the International Action Network on Small Arms.

Action groups such as these and many others have benefited hugely from the interest shown by more and more governments to work in close collaboration with civil society. Two common features can be identified in the activities of transnational civil societies in the post–Cold War era. First, strong cross-border linkages among civil societies became a driving force in mobilizing world public opinion. Although the WCP and the ICBL were loose coalitions and adopted nonbinding and nonobligatory policies toward their supporters, they succeeded in creating a global momentum through close collaboration among individuals and organizations that shared a common goal. Setting a very simple and clear objective enabled groups like the WCP and the ICBL to unite civil society actors for the achievement of a concrete goal. Second, both the WCP and the ICBL strove to establish a working relationship with those governments who were in favor of transnational civil society objectives. This simple but clear deviation from the past, in which civil society and governments were almost always perceived to be by nature at odds with each other, changed the way diplomatic negotiations could be conducted. In the case of the land mines campaign, the negotiations process became increasingly transparent; the ICBL was allowed to participate at virtually every level of negotiation, including informal bilateral talks and lobbying forums organized by governments. The WCP achieved a similar rapport between NGOs and political entities by "help[ing to] empower many non-nuclear weapons states to speak up at the World Court," and providing a voice to those States that are usually less powerful in influencing the UN decision-making processes.[45] The success of the ICBL showed that the absence of big powers did not automatically undermine the initiatives of middle-power States like Canada to establish global rules and new norms; on the contrary, it clearly demonstrated that if cohesiveness of strategy and goal was maintained, and if these were backed up by the force of an active transnational civil society, no power on Earth could prevent their formulation.

Organizations such as those mentioned above are being supplemented by other emerging initiatives in the quest for peace. Many of these are ongoing processes, and expectations of a concrete outcome would thus be premature. However, the potential of their impact is huge, and they are worthy of a special mention.

BOX 10.3
Track II Diplomacy

Track I, or conventional, diplomacy is conducted by decision makers such as politicians, bureaucrats, and diplomats. Track II diplomacy usually attempts to bring together people who are experts in their various fields but are unfettered by ideological differences and bureaucratic caution. This platform allows NGOs, professionals, academics, and experts from both sides a chance to exchange views and information. Their outcomes often add fresh input to decision-making processes and serve as confidence-building measures as well. Since the mid-1990s, various kinds of Track II diplomacy have been initiated or are still under way.

In the Asia-Pacific region, the Council for Security Cooperation in the Asia-Pacific was established in 1993 to "contribute to the efforts towards regional confidence building and enhancing regional security through dialogues, consultation and cooperation."[46] The legacy of the Cold War is still present in the Korean peninsula; the territorial disputes over Takeshima and Spratly Islands continue; ethnic conflicts are alive in Sri Lanka, Nepal, and Indonesia; and military dictatorship continues in Myanmar.

In South Asia, several channels of Track II diplomacy have been established to bring about a *rapprochment* between the two traditional antagonists, India and Pakistan. The Neemrana dialogue in 1991 served as a forum at which former diplomats, military personnel, and academics had a chance to meet, many of them for the first time, and discuss contentious issues. Their agenda ranged from the fundamental point of contention, Kashmir, to confidence-building measures and trade. Other efforts to keep the door open have been made by the India-Pakistan Friendship Society, the Peoples of Asia Forum, the Pakistan-India Forum for Peace and Democracy, the Women's Initiative for Peace in South Asia, and the Pakistan-India Peoples' Solidarity Conference.[47] Similar Track II initiatives are also being made in the Middle East to further dialogue on security in the region, and to build trust between the two deeply adversarial parties of Israel and Palestine.

It is too much to expect Track II diplomacy to lead to a swift policy shift in official negotiations. Its aim has primarily been to further a greater understanding of the issues and imperatives that have driven official policies on both sides, and to explore the possibilities of alternative policy options. Its efficacy is hampered by the very nature of its composition, as its participants do not have direct access to decision-making processes. But by enduring efforts, they can bring influence to bear in the right quarters. If people evaluate the outcome of Track II initiatives "based on what the process itself produces, both in terms of changing regional perceptions among its participants and impacting regional security policy in an incremental fashion,"[48] its value will be recognized.

BOX 10.4
Geneva Call

Around the world, close to two hundred armed entities, many with lands and populations under their sway, stand outside the international system. This figure is higher than the current number of States recognized by the United Nations.[49] Many of these armed opposition groups, called non-State actors (NSA),[50] are directly involved in the manufacturing, trading, and use of land mines. Some States justify their continued use or stockpile of land mines on the basis of the NSAs' presence, or even the mere threat of such presence, within their territories.

In March 2000, about 120 people from over thirty countries gathered in Geneva to discuss ways of engaging the NSAs in an effort to eradicate land mines. Participants included not only NGO representatives and academics but also representatives of governments and NSA members. It was felt that the overwhelming onus in global relations and treaties was on nation-states, but, pragmatically, the Ottawa Treaty could not be completely binding on governments if the NSAs continued to use land mines to further their cause. A new NGO called Geneva Call eventually evolved from this meeting in 2000. Geneva Call proposed that the NSAs sign a Deed of Commitment for Adherence to a Total Ban on Anti-Personnel Mines and for Cooperation in Mine Action, or deposit its own declaration eschewing the use of land mines. The Government of the Republic and Canton of Geneva would act as the guardian of these deeds. Remarkably, more than twenty NSAs have signed a Deed of Commitment so far, including the Sudan People's Liberation Movement/Army, the Moro Islamic Liberation Front from the Philippines, and the National Socialist Council of Nagalim (Nagaland), the largest armed group in the Indian subcontinent.[51]

In the aftermath of September 11, 2001, it has become increasingly difficult for NSAs to secure armaments and financial resources to continue fighting. On the other hand, governments prefer to avoid the internationalization of domestic conflicts and the ensuing, unnecessary, foreign interventions. This has renewed the impetus for both NSAs and governments to reach agreements on ceasefires and peace processes, which development has allowed Geneva Call to approach NSAs in several countries, including Nepal and Sri Lanka, to sign the Deed of Commitment.

The endeavor to bring NSAs into the international system of accountability is by no means a simple task. The outcome of the initiative by Geneva Call remains to be seen, but, like Track II diplomacy, it demands patience, endurance, and infinite optimism. Above all, it should be recognized that no actors other than civil society organizations could have undertaken such a task.

Conclusion

Interstate wars have been mainly responsible for destabilizing peace for most of the past two centuries. The end of the Cold War, however, brought to a close an era in which territorial and ideological imperatives were the source of global conflict. Since then, there has been a willingness to end wars through negotiated peace agreements rather than by victories in the field. Contrary to general perception, "There has been a decline in the number of conflicts between and within states, in the number of terrorist incidents and in the number of people killed in battle," in the period between the end of the Cold War and 2003.[52] Today, resorting to war is universally proscribed except in self-defense or with the authorization of the UN Security Council.

However, the September 11, 2001, terrorist attacks have changed global perspectives on the issue of security. Terrorism is now seen to be the new threat, and fighting it has become a vital component of the foreign policy for the United States. The George W. Bush administration initiated war first in Afghanistan and then in Iraq without UN Security Council approval, and in the face of widespread public condemnation, on the grounds that these nations posed an imminent threat to the security of the United States, and, by extension, to the rest of the world. In both cases, large-scale antiwar movements were organized, reminiscent of the anti–Vietnam War protests of the 1960s. Yet what distinguished these new demonstrations from the Vietnam days was that they were held simultaneously on a global scale. Organizers called for a "Global Day of Action," and on March 15, 2003, just a few days before the US bombings began in Iraq, demonstrations were held in more than two thousand cities in over ninety-eight countries, including countries like Spain and Italy, whose governments supported the US policy of invasion.[53] Hundreds of thousands of people in Washington and San Francisco, Montreal, Paris, Berlin, São Paulo, London, Seoul, Beirut, New Delhi, Moscow, Bangkok, Amman, and other cities filled the streets calling for a peaceful solution instead of the use of force. Activists the world over mounted a strong opposition to the preemptive war of aggression waged by the Bush administration as a means of combating terrorism. Their contention that aggression would beget aggression and that, as Mahatma Gandhi said, "An eye for an eye would make the whole world blind"[54] has, sadly, been borne out in US-occupied Iraq.

Peace movements, by their very nature, cannot be divorced from the reality of world politics. In that sense, it is clear from the history of peace movements that they are inevitably influenced and limited by the conduct of nation-states. Notwithstanding such constraints, the achievements of peace activists should not be underestimated; citizens around the globe have managed, if not comprehensively to deter nation-states from their courses of action, to at least nudge them towards safer channels. By mobilizing public opinion, advocating specific goals, and promoting transparency and accountability in negotiations, transnational civil society has become a major arbiter of peace in the last half-century.

Notes

1. Jonathan Schell, *The Gift of Time: The Case for Abolishing Nuclear Weapons Now* (New York: Metropolitan Books, 1998), 10–11.

2. "Armed conflict" here means "a contested incompatibility that concerns government or territory or both where the use of armed force between two parties results in at least 25 battle-related deaths. Of these two parties, at least one is the government of a state." Nils Petter Gleditsch, Harard Strand, Mikael Erikkson, Margareta Sollenberg, and Peter Wallensteen, "Armed Conflict 1946–99: A New Dataset," paper presented at the 42nd Annual Convention of the International Studies Association, Chicago, IL, February 20–24, 2001.

3. Davis S. Meyer, "Peace Protests and Policy: Explaining the Rise and Decline of Antinuclear Movements in Postwar America," *Policy Studies Journal* 21 (1993): 35.

4. Richard Rhodes, *Dark Sun: The Making of the Hydrogen Bomb* (London: Simon and Schuster, 1996), 205.

5. McGeorge Bundy, *Danger and Survival: Choices about the Bomb in the First Fifty Years* (New York: Vintage Books, 1988), 159.

6. Spencer Weart, *Nuclear Fear: A History of Images* (Cambridge, MA: Harvard University Press, 1988), 184.

7. Charles Chatfield, *The American Peace Movement: Ideals and Activism* (New York: Twayne Publishers, 1992), 105.

8. The Pugwash Conference was named after the location of its first meeting in the village of Pugwash in Nova Scotia, Canada. See www.pugwash.org (accessed June 20, 2004).

9. Lawrence Wittner, *Resisting the Bomb* (Stanford, CA: Stanford University Press, 1997), 11.

10. Physicians for Social Responsibility, www.psr.org/home.cfm?id=about (accessed June 20, 2004).

11. For the history of US policy, see History Division of the Department of Energy, http:/ma.mbe.doe.gov/me70/history/1951-1970.html (accessed June 20, 2004).

12. Hans A. Bethe, *The Road from Los Alamos* (New York: Simon and Schuster, 1991), 37–53.

13. *The Columbia Encyclopedia,* 6th ed., s.v. "Vietnam War."

14. George R. Vickers, "The Vietnam Antiwar Movement in Perspective," *Bulletin of Concerned Asian Scholars* 21, no. 2–4 (1989): 100–110.

15. During the late 1950s and early 1960s, tensions eased between the Western and Eastern blocs, enabling the two superpowers to explore new avenues for dialogue. This period, with a less rabid tone of international rivalry, was one of détente.

16. For background on Doomsday Clock, see Bulletin of Atomic Scientists, www.thebulletin.org/clock/html (accessed June 20, 2004).

17. On the historical background of the Campaign for Nuclear Disarmament, see www.cnduk.org/INFORM~1/cndcuban.html (accessed June 20, 2004).

18. Coalition to Reduce Nuclear Danger, www.clw.org/coalition/ctch7080.html (accessed June 20, 2004).

19. National Nuclear Weapons Freeze Campaign, www.ratical.org/co-globalize/whm0454.html (accessed June 30, 2004).

20. Lawrence Wittner, *Toward Nuclear Abolition: History of the World Nuclear Disarmament Movement, 1971 to the Present* (Stanford, CA: Stanford University Press, 2003), 176.

21. Miton S. Katz, *Ban the Bomb: A History of SANE — The Committee for a Sane Nuclear Policy* (New York: Praeger, 1987), 173.

22. CND, www.cnduk.org/INFORM~1/greenham.html (accessed June 20, 2004).

23. Steve Breyman, *Why Movements Matter: The West German Peace Movement and US Arms Control Policy* (Albany: State University of New York Press, 2001), 94–95.

24. Coalition to Reduce Nuclear Danger.

25. Founded at the height of the Cold War by a group of Soviet and American doctors to educate health professionals, political leaders, and the public on the health consequences of nuclear war, the IPPNW was awarded the Nobel Peace Prize in 1985.

26. For details on the SDI, see Frances FitzGerald, *Way Out There in the Blue* (New York: Simon and Schuster, 2000).

27. Union of Concerned Scientists, www.ucsusa.org/ucs/about/page.cfm?pageID=767 (accessed June 21, 2004).

28. Wittner, *Toward Nuclear Abolition,* 173.

29. Jeffrey W. Knopf, "The Nuclear Freeze Movement's Effect on Policy," in *Coalitions and Political Movements: The Lessons of the Nuclear Freeze,* ed. Thomas R. Rochon and Davis S. Meyer, 127–62 (Boulder, CO: L. Rienner, 1997), 154.

30. Wittner, *Toward Nuclear Abolition,* 404.

31. Breyman, *Why Movements Matter,* 261.

32. Meyer, "Peace Protests and Policy," 13, 18.

33. Knopf, "Nuclear Freeze," 154.

34. According to Freedom House, a nonprofit and nonpartisan organization founded over sixty years ago to pursue democratic values and freedom, the number of electoral democracies increased from 70 countries in 1989 to 120 by the late 1990s. See www.freedomhouse.org (accessed June 21, 2004).

35. Lester M. Salamon, "The Rise of the Non-Profit Sector," *Foreign Affairs* 73, no. 4 (1994): 112.

36. The Martens Clause is named after Fyodor Fyodorovich Martens, a leading member of the Russian delegation to the 1899 and 1907 Hague peace conferences. He sought to prevent nation-states from attempting to justify barbaric new methods of slaughter that were not explicitly prohibited at that time. The clause was later relied on in the post–World War II war crimes trials. See Rupert Ticehurst, "The Martens Clause and the Laws of Armed Conflict," *International Review of the Red Cross* 317 (1997): 125–34.

37. Ved P. Nanda and David Krieger, *Nuclear Weapons and the World Court* (New York: Transnational Publishers, 1998), 89.

38. Maurice Bleicher, "The Ottawa Process: Nine-Day Wonder or a New Model for Disarmament Negotiations?" *Disarmament Forum* 2 (2000): 73.

39. Article 6 of the NPT states "[e]ach of the Parties to the Treaty undertakes to pursue negotiations in good faith on effective measures relating to cessation of the nuclear arms race at an early date and to nuclear disarmament, and on a treaty on general and complete disarmament under strict and effective international control."

40. International Committee of the Red Cross, *Anti-Personnel Landmines — Friend or Foe? A Study of the Military Use and Effectiveness of Anti-Personnel Mines* (Geneva: ICCR, 1996), 9.

41. Speech given by the then Canadian foreign minister Lloyd Axworthy on the occasion of the International Strategy Conference toward a Global Ban on Antipersonnel Mines, Ottawa, Canada, October 5, 1996.

42. International Campaign to Ban Landmines, www.icbl.org (accessed June 20, 2004).

43. Nobel Peace Prize for 1997, Norwegian Nobel Institute, October 10, 1997.

44. Speech to the Ottawa Convention Signing Ceremony on December 3, 1997. See UN Press Office, "Secretary-General Welcomes Convention Banning Landmines as 'Landmark Step in History of Disarmament,'" www.atimes.com/atimes/South_Asia/EG16Df03.html (accessed June 23, 2004).

45. Nanda and Krieger, *Nuclear Weapons and the World Court*, 86.

46. For details on Council for Security Cooperation in the Asia Pacific, see www.cscap.org (accessed June 26, 2004).

47. Navnita Chadha Behera, "Need to Expand Track-Two Diplomacy," Asia Time Online, www.atimes.com/atimes/South_Asia/EG16Df03.html (accessed June 30, 2004).

48. Salia Dassa Kaye, "Track Two Diplomacy and Regional Security in the Middle East," *International Negotiation* 6, no. 1 (2001): 50.

49. See non-State actors homepage at www.genevacall.org (accessed June 26, 2004). The official UN member countries presently stand at 191.

50. NSA, more commonly known as "rebel groups," "liberation movements," "terrorist organizations," and "authorities" are defined as "organizations which do not accept the authority of a recognized government over them and do not have full international recognition as governments themselves." Geneva Call, *Engaging Non-State Actors in a Landmine Ban,* full conference proceedings, International Conference Centre of Geneva, Geneva, March 24–25, 2000, 3.

51. Geneva Call, www.genevacall.org (accessed June 26, 2004).

52. The World Economic Forum, "Peace and Security," *Global Governance Initiative 2004,* 2. See www.weforum.org/site/homepublic.nsf/Content/Global+Governance+Initiative (accessed June 26, 2004).

53. For details on number of participants and location of worldwide demonstrations, see www.internationalanswer.org (accessed June 22, 2004).

54. M. K. Gandhi, attributed.

Shaping the Global Human Project: The Nature and Impact of Transnational Civil Activism

Srilatha Batliwala and L. David Brown

The rich fund of information and analysis in the preceding chapters of this volume demonstrates that transnational civil society (TCS) presents us with two choices: We could view it quite pragmatically as a new realm of cross-border civil society formations, the globalization of civil society itself, and as a response to the broader processes of globalization. Or, we could set it in a deeper historical context and see it as a manifestation of an older, complex, and deeply contentious historical process of creating a more just, equitable, and democratic world.[1] We take the latter view, and encourage our readers to do so as well, to consider TCS as part of a long-term effort to achieve visions of a more just, tolerant, and civil society for all people and for the planet we inhabit.

This transnational human project, as Kumi Naidoo points out, has been going on for a long time. The struggles against slavery were transnational. The struggles against colonialism were also linked, intellectually and politically, across borders. Therefore, the many transnational coalitions, networks, and movements described in this book are far greater than the sum of their parts. Taken together, they are facets of a complex historical process that is attempting to reconstruct human relationships, social norms, cultural practices, economic arrangements, political power, and relationships between the human and natural worlds. At the global level, they are "restructuring world politics."[2] In doing so, they are helping reshape the relationship of power among governments, politicians, business interests, and the interests of ordinary people. In some cases — such as the human rights, economic justice, or peace struggles — they are also trying to protect or promote the interests of people who have been particularly impoverished, marginalized, displaced, violated, or exploited.

Marsha Darling shows us that these relationships have been deeply unequal and problematic for a long time; some peoples, regions, and nations have been exploited, oppressed, and politically and economically dominated by others for many centuries. To correct this imbalance, civil society actors have played major roles in many of the big struggles of the twentieth century for equality, democratic participation, and human rights. On the other hand, Sanjeev Khagram reminds us that such progressive transnational action is but one part of a wider range of transnational organizing — such as terror networks — which includes actors espousing goals and values that they believe in just as passionately. This approach helps us locate progressive transnational formations within a broader spectrum of non-State actors that attempt to influence global processes.

The significance of these dynamics can be grasped more readily when we step back and take a broader look at the current historic period. We are clearly living in a time of great change and complexity, when many different forces are acting on the world and its peoples. Figure 1 attempts to depict this.

Figure 1: Forces Acting on the World Today

We see on one side a set of broadly positive forces, operating to promote equity, peace, sustainability, and tolerance, and on the other, a set of negative forces that tend to reduce or diminish these values. In the center are a cluster of factors that both sets of actors can utilize, for both positive and negative effects on the world.

Some of these forces and trends support the civil society project. The "third wave" of democratization has set the stage for the growth of civil societies in many countries, and those civil society actors have contributed to and benefited from the activities of TCS.[3] The push for decentralization of governance that has often accompanied this third wave has created greater possibilities for grassroots people to influence local resource allocation and decision making. The rise of global norm structures — on human rights, women's rights, labor rights, and so forth — has created a value base against which both governments and transnational activity can be assessed. Those norms have been framed, debated, and ratified by many nations, often with major inputs from, as well as benefits to, civil society groups.[4] The rise of civil society organizations around the world has created momentum for transnational activity; this emergence in many countries and regions has been characterized as a "global associational revolution" that is as important to the twenty-first century as the rise of nation-states was to the last.[5] One product of this ferment is a serious search for more equitable and sustainable alternative models of development at both micro and macro levels, such as small producers bypassing middlemen to link directly with global markets, the creation of ecologically sound and renewable energy and cropping systems for villages, and frameworks for fair regulation of international trade and financial flows. Globalization has also increased attention to cultural identities and cross-cultural sharing, and such processes can lead to mutual understanding and enrichment.

Other forces and trends challenge or undermine the long-term project. The emergence of a unipolar world, where power is highly concentrated in the United States after the decline of the Soviet Union, potentially undermines the roles of TCS. When the United States unilaterally abrogates the Anti-Ballistic Missile System Treaty or the Kyoto Protocol on climate change, refuses to ratify international agreements like the Convention on Elimination of All Forms of Discrimination against Women, and acts on preemptive war doctrines, civil society's value- and norm-based influence on transnational issues is greatly eroded. The failure of the massive and unprecedented protests all over the world to stop the US invasion of Iraq is an example of this. Similarly a global economic architecture that is tilted to the financial and trade advantage of the industrialized countries systematically excludes much of the world's population from the fruits of global markets, and contributes to the runaway concentration of wealth within and across countries. While the level of inter-State conflict appears to have declined since the Cold War, militarization and intra-State conflict continue to be major concerns, particularly in weak States and those with entrenched ethnic differences.[6] The lack of civic rights and security in militarized and conflict-ridden situations undercuts the capacity of civil society actors to pursue their goals or even to intervene. Finally, the rise of militant fundamentalisms of various kinds — religious, racial/ethnic, and economic — that are willing to use force to achieve their aims challenges the capacity of civil society actors to exist and act. Though fundamentalist actors, like civil society organizations, are grounded in the concept of shared values and ideologies, they are often highly intolerant of other perspectives. Religious fundamentalists sometimes reject other religions or even nonfundamentalist co-religionists, and so make civil engagement and problem solving difficult or impossible. It is also important to note that these negative forces are usually well resourced and powerful.

The third set of global forces can be exploited by either side, though resources make a difference in access to and control over them. These forces may either support or undermine TCS, depending on the particular circumstances. The information and communications revolution, for example, has made possible information sharing and joint learning by TCS actors — but it provides the same opportunities to transnational corporations or intergovernmental organizations, many of whom may be better able to take full advantage of the new tools than civil society actors. The enormous reach and influence of the mass — particularly electronic — media has similarly enabled the immediacy of issues to grab the attention of people around the world. This helps spur transnational citizen action, but also allows powerful actors to spin information in their own favor. Globalization has brought dramatic increases in travel and transport across national boundaries: increasingly, young leaders from both Southern and Northern countries can build on transnational experience, education, and contacts to work for or against civil society initiatives (though these opportunities are more available to Northern than Southern citizens, both because of resource availability and because of growing restrictions on travel to the North due to the war on terror). The current knowledge explosion, along with information and communication technologies, has ironically helped level the playing field between the positive and negative global forces. On the one hand, there is the privately owned and controlled knowledge economy, where knowledge is commodified, patented, privatized, and sold for profit, so that patents on AIDS drugs, for example, make them unaffordable to the developing world. Private sector–funded research in human and plant genetics and biotechnology, linked to the international property rights regime, can foster advances in service and productivity, but can also enable profiteering from the traditional knowledge of small, relatively powerless indigenous communities. But this knowledge economy is being increasingly countered by the dramatic growth of the knowledge democracy, supported by information and communication technologies, that makes it possible for people to freely share information across all kinds of barriers and boundaries. Open-source software and the hundreds of thousands of Web sites maintained by transnational and national civil society networks to share information and knowledge are examples of how knowledge democracy works. All these trends have helped spur the formation of transnational associations and action to democratize access to new knowledge, and particularly to the fruits of new research and technology.

It is against this global background that we have to assess the role and work of progressive TCS and examine what we have learned about it from the preceding: how it is structured and organized, the roles it has played, the work it has done, and the impact it has had.

We suggested in the introduction that we might understand transnational civil society from three different perspectives. First, we can look at TCS as transnational associations that enable widespread expression and participation, often by otherwise excluded populations, in transnational activities and decisions. Second, we can assess TCS as a source of aspirations for a civil global society. In this perspective the focus is on the creation of values, aspirations, and alliances that build a society characterized by peace, tolerance, equity, and inclusiveness. Third, we can examine TCS as a catalyst for public discourse across national boundaries. This perspective emphasizes its role as a purveyor of new ideas and alternatives. In the rest of this chapter we explore how the analysis presented by our various authors contributes to these three perspectives. Then we briefly discuss the effects of TCS on the world so far, and the challenges and opportunities it may face in the coming years.

Transnational Civil Society as Associations

The most common definition of TCS focuses on associations that are mobilized around shared values and visions. Those associations may be organizations, networks, coalitions, or movements. Transnational organizations are relatively integrated and centralized formations that have governance and operational structures in more than one country, and usually share assumptions about mission, strategy, and the division of organizational authority and work. Networks, coalitions, and movements are combinations of organizations and individuals, with varying degrees of cohesion and capacity; as pointed out in the introduction, transnational networks are loosely linked assemblages of organizations and individuals that hold common values, exchange information, and engage in a common discourse about critical issues. Transnational coalitions and campaigns share values, information, and discourses, and are also committed to shared strategies and tactics. Transnational movements have common values; share information, discourses, strategies, and tactics; and are also able to sustain social mobilization and active challenges to the status quo in multiple countries.[7] Using these distinctions, the majority of the TCS formations we have encountered in this book seem to be networks and coalitions rather than transnational movements.[8]

The choice of associational form seems to be related to several factors. As the diversity of association membership increases, it may be easier to contain it in a relatively loose structure like a network. The economic justice campaign, for example, includes a very wide range of actors: unions, churches, Southern grassroots groups, development nongovernmental organizations (NGO), policy think tanks, environmentalists, anarchists, and so on. More tightly organized coalitions or movements, such as Greenpeace in the environmental arena or the International Confederation of Free Trade Unions, are composed of members with quite similar values and commitments to the campaign. The choice of association form may also be related to the degree of mission and strategy focus. Associations that seek to foster a broad range of interests of large constituencies (such as expanding the roles of women or conserving the environment) may be more loosely constructed than those that have specific and time-bound goals (such as stopping the Iraq War or influencing the UN Conference on Population and Development). A third dimension that can influence the choice of organizational form is the intensity of member commitment. Transnational movements that challenge existing authority (such as human rights demonstrations in the Soviet Union or workers' strikes in many countries) require more commitment than membership in loosely organized networks that share information and values (such as most environmental conservation groups or economic justice alliances). A fourth influential factor may be the prevalence of existing models of organizing. The organization of labor unions into federations that speak on behalf of their members now has a long history that informs the creation of new associations, for example, while the participants in the economic justice movement have little shared history of collective action and are often inventing their associational forms as they go along.

The challenges of leadership and internal politics discussed in the chapter on economic justice activism are in fact also applicable to most of the formations described in the other chapters. Most progressive transnational formations have attempted to some extent to build relatively decentralized and democratic leadership structures with elected leaders, or collective leadership, or limited terms for formal leaders. Some have no formal leadership structures, and thus must contend with the hidden hierarchies and power patterns that arise under those circumstances. Many of these transnational initiatives struggle to build internally the participatory, democratic, transparent, equitable, and inclusive structures and decision-making processes that they seek to enable in the external world. To the extent that these associations aim to bring the voices and views of ordinary people, and particularly marginalized and disempowered groups, into global policy making, remedying their internal democracy deficits may be essential to their legitimacy as proponents of a more democratic transnational order.

The chapters also suggest that TCS associations evolve over time, and that their influence may depend on their ability to survive and adapt over significant periods. It seems clear that the long history of the labor movement has developed some well-understood organizational forms — and also that those forms are less flexible and responsive to changing conditions than might be desired. The ability of formations like SANE to survive and adapt over three decades of peace activism, eventually allying with the Nuclear Weapons Freeze Campaign to significantly shape the course of nuclear disarmament discussions, illustrates the importance of long-term engagement and creative response to changing circumstances.

The organization of TCS also reflects the ability to expand alliances to include other civil society actors and key participants from other sectors as well. The campaign for women's rights built links among women's organizations around the globe and alliances with human rights networks, and then expanded to include sympathetic governments with a view to influencing the outcomes of the UN conferences in Cairo and Beijing. Environmental associations mobilized thousands of civil society organizations in the global "green web" to "close the circle" from local to global in discussions at the Earth Summit in Rio de Janeiro.[9] Human rights organizations are increasingly exploring how they can expand their success with civil and political rights campaigns to foster more attention to economic, social, and cultural rights, and build common cause with networks of poverty alleviation organizations experimenting with rights-based development. More generally, the long-term success of many of these initiatives requires building alliances with other sectors — government agencies and business interests — that can mobilize political power and economic resources to implement new visions of transnational action.

Transnational Civil Society
and Visions of Global Society

Transnational civil society may also refer to a kind of transnational society that promotes civil engagement to solve problems, operating on the basis of norms of tolerance, trust, cooperation, nonviolence, inclusion, and democratic participation. Imagining such a civil global society requires articulating aspirations for the society as a whole, including relations among sectors (for example, business, governments, and civil society organizations) and across levels (i.e., local, national, regional, and global) to deal with global challenges and dilemmas.

Many of the chapters described the importance of articulating aspirations and visions of a good society. The women's movement, for example, voiced a desire for the future of women and for the future of societies that is unencumbered by gender discrimination. Similarly, the labor movement sought to improve the conditions of its worker members, but also articulated visions of societies that would value all their citizens rather than exploit some on behalf of others. The human rights movement articulated a set of universal human rights for societies around the world as well as challenged particular perpetrations of human rights violations.

Several chapters also indicate tensions between long- and short-term aspirations, between societal visions and the needs of their members. Thus, the women's movement struggled to balance advocacy to advance the immediate interests of women with campaigns for long-term social projects that would benefit society as a whole. Labor leaders were often compelled to prioritize short-term wage and working condition benefits for their members over long-term campaigns for more egalitarian societies. The strength of the peace movement was often greatest in response to immediate threats of war or nuclear devastation, yet tended to decline when decreased tensions increased the opportunities for long-term gains in membership. Often immediate threats to member interests are more powerful mobilizing tools than aspirations for long-term social change and justice, but successful social movements make clear the links between short-term mobilization and long-term commitment to social change.

Many chapters also reflect the interaction of national and transnational campaigns. Some chapters describe civil society campaigns whose initial aspirations focused on national rather than transnational issues. The labor, women's, and human rights movements all focused initially on national and local concerns. The articulation of the aspirations and visions of a civil global society are more central to initiatives focused on inherently transnational problems, such as peace and nuclear war, environmental degradation, and global economic justice. Thus, the peace movement has worked with governments and other allies to implement mechanisms and action plans for regulating the proliferation and use of nuclear weapons. The environmental movement has worked with scientists, governments, and corporations to craft policies and market mechanisms to deal with ozone losses, toxic rain, and climate change. The economic justice movement seeks to influence transnational institutions to offer Third World countries more development opportunities, to remedy the democracy deficits in global policy making, and to regulate runaway concentrations of wealth and power in the hands of the already rich and powerful nations and corporations.

Articulating aspirations and visions for a better world is one thing; creating and implementing new institutions is something else again. Designing new arrangements, mobilizing resources, implementing action plans, and revising systems and structures in response to actual experience demands creativity, sophisticated knowledge, and political will. Few if any civil society actors can mobilize the resources, expertise, or legitimacy necessary to create sustainable global governance mechanisms by themselves. So the creation of civil global society institutions and systems demands that civil society actors work with other key stakeholders to implement shared aspirations and visions: governments, intergovernmental organizations, transnational corporations, international media, scientific experts, and many others.

Alliances with technical experts have been critical for analyzing problems and defining solutions in many campaigns. As the complexity of global politics, structures, and problems increases, TCS formations have often emerged from partnerships between technical experts and social activists. The early stages of transnational peace, environment, and human rights activism show deep linkages with nuclear scientists, biologists, and legal experts committed to peace, sustainability, and social justice. More recently, many economic justice coalitions have been strengthened by partnerships with economists who are critical of neoliberal economic policies. Partnerships with the environment and peace networks were often launched by technical experts whose research was already linked across borders. The scientific establishment had been sharing ideas across borders for centuries, and so had created transnational identities and linkages grounded in shared aspirations for developing knowledge long before terms like "transnational civil society" were coined.

Creating and implementing systems for solving transnational problems and aspirations for a civil global society have often required that civil society actors engage, influence, and eventually work with from other sectors and institutions, including governments, ir ernmental agencies, and business interests. While the human rig.... .... peace movements often began with criticism and campaigns against governments, their long-term success depended on getting governments to cooperate in implementing human rights protections or reducing risks of war. While the environmental civil society coalitions began by sounding the alarm on environmental abuses by corporations and governments, long-term environmental risk management required a variety of new initiatives by governments and businesses, often in cooperation with civil society actors.

The cooperation of other sectors is often central to constructing effective and sustainable solutions to complex problems, since those sectors have access to information and resources (such as capital, technology, formal authority) that can complement or extend the resources civil society brings (such as creative ideas, popular support, moral authority). In short, the creation of aspirations and visions of a better world is a project that often requires participation by stakeholders beyond TCS organizations. Civil society organizations may be able to identify critical problems or to articulate initial visions of a better way, but creating sustainable solutions requires expanding participation and building institutional arrangements with other sectors and stakeholders.

Transnational Civil Society as a Catalyst for Public Discourse

In every chapter on issue-based initiatives in part 2 of this book, we have seen that TCS actors have catalyzed debate and discussion of issues otherwise left unexamined. The labor movement fostered discussion of a vision of a society that provided better lives for workers; the women's movement enabled debate and exploration of the gendered nature of economies, cultures, and social structures, and showed that less discriminatory social relations were possible; the environmental movement identified threats to what had been widely seen as an unlimited natural resource base, and encouraged exploration of how those risks could be better managed. The creation, discussion, evolution, and dissemination of critical ideas lie at the heart of these TCS initiatives.

One aspect of the transnational discourse has been the use of compelling ideas and social visions to mobilize people and resources across wide differences in interest and experience. The labor movement, for example, articulated a social vision that appealed to workers across many different countries and contexts, and its organizers recognized very early that workers were interdependent across national boundaries. Emigrants, travelers, and written materials were active ingredients in spreading ideas across boundaries even before the organization of the early workers' internationals. The human rights movement has capitalized on ideas in the Universal Declaration and associated documents to mobilize people and resources to challenge failures to live up to those principles, often at very significant risk to their own lives. The visions and ideas described in these transnational campaigns are often centrally important to those who become active in them — important enough to justify great risks and costs.

Maintaining the momentum generated by discussions of ideas is not always easy. Many chapters speak of the likelihood of diversions or loss of momentum. The labor movement has had difficulty maintaining its social vision, particularly as it became more successful in gaining wage and legal benefits for its members. The women's movement has an ongoing internal debate about the extent to which it is focused on women's rights rather than on working towards a larger social project. The peace movement has been subject to large ebbs and flows in tides of public opinion that favor or undermine its ability to mobilize concerted action. In some cases, discourses have been subject to tugs of war between other forces: the struggle over communist control of the labor movement and the ongoing pulls among different wings of the economic justice movement are examples of this. While catalyzing discourses and new ideas can be a powerful way of mobilizing people and resources, many forces can undermine the focus and power of those discourses.

An important common theme across many chapters is the importance of international forums for framing and acting on emerging discourses. The new spaces for engagement opened up by the UN conferences of the 1990s provided opportunities for civil society to participate in influencing global agreements and policy documents on the environment, human rights, women's rights, and economic development. Those conferences probably did more to spawn, foster, and expand progressive transnational civic formations than any other single factor in recent history. The Earth Summit in Rio was ostensibly for governments but in fact also served as a gathering point for thousands of civil society organizations, and hence became a watershed for advocacy and activism on the environment and the concept of sustainable development. The UN conferences in Cairo and Beijing were critical events in the evolution and impact of the transnational women's movement, as they provided opportunities for transnational networking and joint learning as well as forums for influencing global and national policies.

The Battle of Seattle[10] is generally recognized as a major organizing event as well as a public voicing of concerns about globalization and international trade, where the meetings of the WTO were eclipsed by the TCS activities in the streets outside. Without such forums it would be much more difficult for many decentralized TCS actors to develop common positions, focus action on common targets, or build the social capital required to make loosely organized networks function across transnational spaces.

Our chapters also suggest some common patterns of transnational discourse across issues and organizations. The first phase identifies and frames the issue, and builds wider awareness of its impacts. The custom of female genital mutilation was identified and framed as a violation of women's rights; the problem of ozone depletion was identified as a risky degradation of the environment; and the nuclear arms race was identified as a threat to peace and the future of the planet. This framing process is the basis for mobilizing public support, so capturing the problem in terms that resonate with the target audience is central to future success. In most cases, TCS frames, analyzes, and defines issues very differently from mainstream institutions' and actors' definitions. They have, for instance, redefined the notions of peace and security as not just the absence of war but the presence of social and economic well-being; broadened the definition of human rights to include social, economic, and cultural rights; called attention to the unrecognized crisis of climate change and its causes; demonstrated the negative effects of global economic integration on the poor and on developing countries; redefined "work" to include biological and social reproduction work of women; and promoted a different view of a good society for workers.

The next phase involves mobilizing support, increasing understanding, and amplifying recognition of the problem and the alternative discourse. The targets include the communities or constituencies most directly affected by the issue (such as marginal farmers, indigenous people, grassroots women, or citizens facing the threat of nuclear attack). This process often includes deepening and diversifying the discourse across levels (including local, national, and transnational), and across audiences (such as researchers, social activists, community or mass organizations, legal experts, government representatives, business leaders, and others). In many cases it may also involve research and an enhanced understanding of the issues (such as the investigation of the causes and consequences of climate change, further work on the consequences of gender discrimination, or more analysis of the implications of nuclear warfare).

In the advocacy phase, participation in the discourse is extended to engage transnational policy- and decision-making processes to influence them in a particular direction. The economic justice campaigners, for example, have tried to influence discussions of the World Trade Organization (WTO), the World Economic Forum, and the World Bank/International Monetary Fund (IMF) meetings. Greenpeace and the World Wide Fund for Nature have organized campaigns to shape discussion of conservation and environmental pollution issues. The transnational women's movement has engaged in debates to influence programs of action emerging from UN meetings on Population and Development in Cairo and on Women in Beijing. These events offer opportunities to shape the discourse on key issues as it moves to the world stage and potentially influences global and national public policies.

When advocacy campaigns are successful, the discourse may enter into an institutionalization or mainstreaming phase as it becomes incorporated into national and transnational policies and practices. Ironically, success in mainstreaming and institutionalizing discourses may undermine recognition for the movement's contributions to that discourse. The labor movement's contribution to widespread acceptance of the eight-hour workday or the right to strike, for example, may be less widely recognized than it deserves. In some countries, the women's movement has been sufficiently successful so that young potential activists no longer recognize the need for it.

In summary, TCS is often a catalyst for launching new public discourses and debates of previously unnoticed issues and problems. The organizations and networks described in this book are particularly likely to catalyze discussion of issues facing disempowered populations with relatively little political voice: workers, women, economically marginal groups, victims of wars, and targets of human rights violations. Compelling visions and ideas are central to launching this discourse, as are efforts to maintain momentum and avoid capture. International forums have been critical arenas for developing the ideas and mobilizing allies as well as articulating possible solutions. The patterns of discourse evolution, from initial formulation to mobilization to advocacy to institutionalization, appear to be quite common across issues and constituencies.

Achievements and Impacts

What has TCS achieved through the engagements described in this book? First and foremost, these initiatives have created widespread recognition that TCS formations can have a credible voice in transnational governance. Transnational civic activism and advocacy have demonstrated that even democratically elected governments do not always represent the interests and perspectives of all their citizens — particularly marginalized and disempowered citizens — when they participate in multilateral decision making. The right of independent representation of such groups and viewpoints has gained gradual purchase and acceptance in international arenas, though not without opposition and contestation. In this process, millions of ordinary but committed people have created what has been called a "power shift" or a "third force" in international decision making.[11] TCS has therefore established a niche for itself as a critical actor in global politics and policy.[12] This is by no means a small achievement, given that just twenty years ago such a scenario seemed a pipedream.

Second, progressive TCS has influenced the framing, analyses, priorities, and outcomes of many international agreements, commitments, and normative guidelines. These substantive impacts include human rights conventions and campaigns, environmental standards, peace accords and weapons treaties, women's empowerment and gender-equality commitments, labor rights and standards, and economic and trade policies. These policy results have changed the institutional context that governs debate and decision making in many regions and countries as well as in the global arena, making them relatively more democratic and accountable.

Even more important, though less visible, is how progressive transnational activism and advocacy have changed discourses that shape the way we think about important international issues. TCS has indelibly shaped the nature of global discourse and debate on issues that affect the lives and well-being of the world's peoples, and the world's poor and vulnerable people in particular. On many issues, values articulated by civil society actors have become widely accepted in principle, if not always implemented in practice. For example, most public actors today would hesitate to contest the idea that all people should have equal rights, regardless of race, religion, ethnicity, gender, caste, nationality, sexual orientation, ability, or age; most would also pay at least lip service to the importance of safeguarding the earth's natural resources and environment. Many people believe in the dignity of labor, equal pay for equal work, and the right of workers to challenge exploitative or unsafe working conditions. Few of us would advocate the commodification and patenting of human or plant genes so that a handful of private multinational companies could profit from them. Even fewer subscribe to the idea that the poor in heavily indebted nations should starve while their governments spend the bulk of public revenue on servicing their national debt. Yet a few decades ago such ideas were new, strange, and not widely accepted. We rarely recognize that the energy, insight, and commitment to egalitarian values of TCS have made these ideas a part of our normative worldview.

Finally, TCS has opened up great new possibilities for action and engagement at the global level by people who never believed they could influence world events. The campaigns of the last several decades have illustrated that activists can make a difference even without access to governmental power or great wealth. In doing so they have demonstrated how to be heard at national and transnational forums. The campaigns have built social and intellectual capital that can be used in future campaigns — the legacy of organizations and networks and the knowledge of strategies and tactics created by earlier initiatives are available to future campaigns. A third product of early campaigns has been the creation of institutions and attitudes among other actors that make them more willing to engage with TCS in the future. Intergovernmental organizations like the World Bank, for example, have created departments and programs to engage more effectively with civil society actors,[13] and many transnational corporations are increasingly interested in concepts of corporate social responsibility that encourage them to engage constructively with civil society initiatives.[14]

Future Challenges

While TCS has clearly achieved much, many aspects of the international arena pose significant challenges to their future work. How much such initiatives achieve in the future will depend on how factors within and outside civil society evolve.

The future role of TCS will be influenced, for example, by trends toward more autocratic global governance. Good governance, according to the World Bank, includes (a) the rule of law, so that the wealthy and powerful must follow the same rules as others; (b) transparency, so that information about decisions and resource use is widely available; (c) accountability, so that officials can be held to account for their actions; and (d) citizen voices, so that people affected can make their views heard.[15] As we saw earlier, some forces in the changing global political environment — US unilateralism, war and militarization, concentration of wealth, and militant fundamentalisms — tend to undermine these trends in international governance. The United States has long claimed that it seeks to promote a pluralistic international society governed by the rule of law. But in recent years, spurred in part by the fear of terrorism, the United States has acted more to maintain its military and economic dominance in the world, and to restrict dissent and activism domestically.

Those actions are seen by many to have contributed as much or more to undermining progress towards a civil global society as the acts of the terrorists themselves.

The war on terror has in fact led to the restriction of civil liberties, and hence of space, for the democratic expression of dissent in many other parts of the world as well. Many regimes now police their citizens and deny them some of their rights under the pretext of fighting terrorism. The war on terror has affected TCS by restricting the entry of citizens from Southern countries to North America and Europe for international meetings and advocacy work. The rise of fundamentalism and terrorism has made local and transnational action not only more difficult but also politically more risky. In India and Pakistan, strong antiterrorism legislation has been used to silence activists critical of their governments' policies.[16] Pakistan's Anti-Terrorism Ordinance includes "causing civil commotion" in its definition of terrorism and so enables that government to treat civic activists staging peaceful protests as terrorists.[17] So in both national and international contexts, the war on terrorism has often been used to reduce the transparency of government actions, their democratic accountability, their adherence to the rule of law, and their attention to citizen voices. These trends bode ill for the future of advocacy and expression by TCS as well as for good governance at the global level.

A second set of challenges involves questions about the legitimacy and accountability of civil society. These challenges are being raised from both within and outside civil society. In part these issues are being raised more vociferously as civil society influence and visibility have increased in international policy arenas. The massive protests staged at World Bank, IMF, and WTO meetings have captured unprecedented media attention. At UN conferences on the environment, population, human rights, women's rights, and habitat, TCS alliances have played critical roles in gathering data, analyzing issues, highlighting shortcomings, and influencing the resulting conventions and platforms of action. TCS initiatives have also monitored and exposed multinational corporations that violate environment, labor, or human rights standards. It is not surprising that there should be a strong backlash against these initiatives, and many targets of civil society campaigns have asked questions about their legitimacy and accountability: Who elected them? How are they accountable to those they claim to represent? Where do they get their resources? Conservative think tanks like the American Enterprise Institute in the United States have set up special units, such as NGO Watch, to monitor NGO behavior and provide information on their policy advocacy campaigns.[18]

These issues are also raised by voices sympathetic to civil society, who are concerned about the need for greater transparency and accountability among civil society organizations, particularly at the transnational level. Some civil society organizations have not been clear about their own basis for legitimacy or the stakeholders to whom they are accountable. Others have transgressed their own claims for legitimacy: Greenpeace's flawed analysis of the costs of sinking the *Brent Spar* oil rig in the North Sea, for example, has been frequently cited as an illustration of questionable conduct.[19] Many organized grassroots networks are beginning to challenge the right of international civil society advocacy groups to represent their issues, and are now doing their own global advocacy.[20] Many transnational advocacy agencies are based in and led from the North, causing tensions with and challenges from their Southern members and independent Southern networks. Transnational networks like Third World Network, Focus on the Global South, and Development Alternatives for Women in a New Era (DAWN) were formed to create Southern platforms independent of Northern groups and perspectives.

For transnational associations, these accountability and legitimacy questions are complex and challenging, since many are loose networks of individuals and organizations, often without formal membership or decision-making systems. Transnational entities often have at best indirect contacts with poor or marginalized constituents, and they often lack ways to consult with these stakeholders. Many reflective and responsible individuals and organizations within TCS are attempting to address these questions and to build better systems for representation,[21] but the challenge of legitimacy and accountability will continue to be an important issue for TCS in the immediate future.

A third set of challenges, related to these issues, revolve around the internal governance and leadership of TCS associations and organizations. Balancing the different perspectives of diverse members is an ongoing challenge for transnational entities. Many of our chapters commented on the difficulties of coordinating the interests of Northern and Southern members. The issue of enabling mutual influence rather than the widespread domination of Northern members (who often bring greater resources and influence to the network or campaign) is being increasingly accepted. Another facet of this dominance is the use of English as a lingua franca, in spite of the fact that it is not the birth language of the vast majority of the world's peoples. Recognizing and responding to the concerns of transnational members calls for a better understanding of contentious issues, and the sensitive negotiation of competing concerns.

Another aspect of this challenge is balancing the influence of alliance members from different levels: the interests of actors from local, national, and international organizations may be very different, and it is all too easy for international members to misunderstand or ignore the concerns of local actors. Yet another issue is the problem of balancing long-term social visions with the immediate interests of association members: both the labor and women's movements found it difficult to manage the tensions between long- and short-term goals. Creating and institutionalizing democratic and efficient arrangements for decision making is a major challenge for transnational groups, especially when the issues they work on are being rapidly affected by external forces. Economic justice groups, for instance, may have to respond very quickly to the internal machinations in the WTO, leaving little time for consultation with their entire membership. Local grassroots members, who may consider these decisions very remote from their concerns, often have little capacity or inclination to contribute to them, which makes achieving the ideal of democratic and participatory decision making a daunting challenge.

A final set of challenges revolves around the difficulty of developing new institutional arrangements to solve complex global problems. Even as transnational associations have learned to intervene in complex global policy processes, these processes themselves are increasing in intricacy. Multilateral deliberative mechanisms like the WTO are evolving and changing, and making up new policy rules as they go along. Our understanding of the dynamics of globalization, and its impacts on global markets, politics, and cultures, is incomplete at best. There is, therefore, a growing need for "social learning" that provides new understanding and practices to deal with emerging problems.[22] While transnational civil society actors are often in the lead in identifying the effects of emerging transnational forces on grassroots and marginalized populations, they seldom have easy access to the expertise needed to develop the technical solutions or large-scale institutional innovations needed for effective long-term action. At a minimum, such institutional innovations will require partnerships with technical experts, and creating new institutional arrangements will require work with governments and business interests as well. Thus, innovations like the World Commission on Dams, created to assess the socioeconomic and ecological impacts of large dams as well as to create criteria for evaluating future dam proposals, required an institutional space in which governments, business interests, technical experts, and civil society actors could engage with one another to answer critical questions. Such forums and other innovative structures may be required for effective social learning on many transnational issues.

Future Opportunities

These challenges are serious, and it is not clear that TCS and its allies will easily solve them. We do know that many of the initiatives described in this volume faced many daunting challenges in the past. Overcoming them is important for taking advantage of the opportunities that are also visible on the horizon. At least four trends indicate significant opportunities for future TCS initiatives.

First, experience over the last two decades has created expanding political clout and leverage for TCS. In part this leverage has emerged from increased capacity among civil society actors. The campaigns of the last twenty years have built social and intellectual capital within civil society, so that it has become easier to create networks, coalitions, and movements that represent broad constituencies, and the access to expertise needed to make convincing cases and effective advocacy strategies. In part the leverage grows from increased recognition and respect for civil society actors among those who have been the targets of their advocacy, such as the World Bank, the WTO, and transnational corporations. Experience has taught many corporations and intergovernmental organizations that TCS campaigns are worthy of attention, so future engagements will benefit from the capacities and relationships created by past campaigns.

Second, the failures of dominant economic paradigms are creating space for conceptual and practical innovation. The Washington Consensus on neoliberal economic strategies for fostering development has produced disastrous results in many developing countries, with more concentration of wealth rather than sustainable economic development being created. That failure has opened the door to important innovations in economic theory and ground-level experiments, with many possibilities for expanded civil society roles.[23] Increasing questions about the utility of leaving important decisions to technical experts without involving many other stakeholders have fostered a variety of efforts to enable broader participation in critical decisions.[24] People have become increasingly disaffected with democracy deficits in both the developing and the industrialized world, while the Information Revolution makes increased citizen participation in deliberative democracy possible.[25] After growing public censure on many counts, transnational corporations are beginning to ask whether they have a responsibility beyond maximizing profits to their shareholders; many are actively exploring whether corporate social responsibility suggests they should work with civil society to contribute to social problem solving.[26] Questions about these paradigms are creating opportunities for civil society organizations to propose alternative theories and innovative practices that respond to widely held values.

Finally, the emergence of transnational problems has often demonstrated the inadequacy of existing transnational institutions. Many of the chapters in this book have documented the importance of TCS actors in responding to otherwise intractable problems, like cross-border environmental degradation, human rights abuses, or nuclear proliferation. The phenomena of globalization have created new and unmanageable burdens on many old institutional arrangements.[27] TCS organizations and associations are positioned to play a key role in the creation of new institutions for handling these emergent problems. They are particularly well suited to campaigning for institutions that contribute to good global governance by emphasizing the importance of accountability, transparency, the rule of law, and citizen voice in their deliberations and decisions. TCS actors potentially have a critical role to play in creating the institutions that will shape both national and global societies of the next century.

Conclusion

The chapters in this book demonstrate that many of the world's greatest problems are inherently international challenges: poverty, polluted air, wars, unfair terms of international trade, and so on. These problems must be tackled through transnational as well as national action. Other problems — unfair labor practices, oppression of women, violations of human rights — appear at first glance to be internal to specific countries, but cannot be resolved in the longer term without international action. The transnational labor movement, for example, recognized early the need for transnational alliances, since the industrial revolution in Europe and North America resulted in workers being exploited in very similar ways. It became clear that introducing and enforcing labor protections in one country would just drive businesses to other countries where workers were less expensive. The great gathering of workers' organizations and labor activists formed in the late nineteenth and early twentieth centuries were therefore called "internationals."

Progressive TCS organizations and associations have become pivotal to identifying transnational problems, to articulating alternatives, and to campaigning for reforms or creating transnational problem-solving institutions. The creation of the International Court for Criminal Justice is an outstanding example of this vital role of TCS. Globalization is creating more transnational problems and facilitating recognition of the need for transnational answers. The complexity of these problems is leading to widespread acceptance that governments alone do not have the requisite information, resources, support, or creativity required to develop sustainable solutions, and that much of governance in the twenty-first century will require multisectoral approaches involving business and civil society as well as governments.[28]

In conclusion, we think it is important to return to the theme with which this chapter began: there is a great human project at work — a search for a world in which all people get a fair share of the world's prosperity and a fair share of its burdens. This project, whether we recognize it or not, is moving us toward a more equitable, sustainable, and peaceful future, toward better governance and greater accountability. The path is complex, even tortuous, and there are times when we appear to be moving away from rather than toward these goals. But even the setbacks and losses can become part of our collective learning, equipping us to move ahead once again. The objective of this volume has been to demonstrate the central roles that TCS organizations and associations have played, and will continue to play, in this great human project of creating a more just, equitable, and democratic world.

Notes

1. See, for example, John D. Clark, *Worlds Apart: Civil Society and the Battle for Ethical Globalization* (Bloomfield, CT: Kumarian Press, 2003); Michael Edwards, *Civil Society* (Cambridge: Polity Press, 2004); Michael Edwards and John Gaventa, eds., *Global Citizen Action* (Boulder, CO: Lynne Rienner, 2001); Ann Florini, ed., *The Third Force: The Rise of Transnational Civil Society* (New York: Carnegie Endowment for International Peace; Tokyo: Japan Center for International Exchange, 2000); John Keane, *Transnational Civil Society* (Cambridge: Cambridge University Press, 2003); and Mary Kaldor, *Global Civil Society: An Answer to War* (Cambridge: Polity Press, 2003).

2. See Kathryn Sikkink, "Restructuring World Politics: The Limits and Asymmetries of Soft Power," in *Restructuring World Politics: Transnational Social Movements, Networks and Norms*, ed. Sanjeev Khagram, James V. Riker, and Kathryn Sikkink, 301–17 (Minneapolis: University of Minnesota Press, 2002), 302.

3. The third wave of democratization of States began in 1974, when 39 democracies (27 percent of all countries) existed. By 1997, 117 countries (61 percent) were formally democratic. See Larry Diamond, *Developing Democracy: Toward Consolidation* (Baltimore: Johns Hopkins University Press, 1999), 24–25. Thomas Risse, "The Power of Norms versus the Norms of Power: Transnational Civil Society and Human Rights," in *The Third Force: The Rise of Transnational Civil Society*, ed. Ann Florini, 177–210 (Washington, DC: Carnegie Endowment for International Peace; Tokyo: Japan Center for International Exchange, 2000).

4. Sikkink, "Restructuring World Politics."

5. Lester M. Salamon, "The Rise of the Non-Profit Sector," *Foreign Affairs* 73, no. 4 (1994): 109–22.

6. See Robert Rotberg, ed., *When States Fail: Causes and Consequences* (Princeton, NJ: Princeton University Press, 2004).

7. These definitions are drawn from Khagram, Riker and Sikkink, eds., *Restructuring World Politics,* 6–10.

8. These actors commonly describe themselves as transnational movements, implying that they are struggling for similar kinds of changes or transformations in the relations of power and the distribution of resources. However, few of them are sufficiently integrated to be able to mobilize coordinated challenges to established institutions across multiple countries, as the definition of movement requires.

9. These phrases are taken, respectively, from International Union for the Conservation of Nature, "Welcome to IUCN — World Conservation Union," www.iucn.org/about/index.htm (accessed September 1, 2004); and B. Rich, *Mortgaging the Earth: The World Bank, Environmental Impoverishment, and the Crisis of Development* (Boston: Beacon Press, 1994), 132.

10. A phrase attributed to Paul Reynolds, "Eyewitness: The Battle of Seattle," BBC News, December 2, 1999, http://news.bbc.co.uk/1/hi/world/americas/547581.stm (accessed February 18, 2005).

11. For a discussion on the shifting power of civil society in international affairs, see Jessica Mathews, "Power Shift," *Foreign Affairs* 76, no. 1 (1997): 50–67. For the description of civil society as a third force, see Florini, ed., *Third Force,* 1–15.

12. See Keane, *Transnational Civil Society;* Wolfgang Reinicke and Francis Deng, *Critical Choices: The United Nations, Networks and the Future of Global Governance* (Ottawa: International Development Research Centre, 2000); and Oran Young, ed., *Global Governance* (Cambridge, MA: MIT Press, 1997).

13. Jane G. Covey, "Is Critical Cooperation Possible?" in *The Struggle for Accountability,* ed. Jonathan A. Fox and L. David Brown, 81–119 (Cambridge, MA: MIT Press, 1998).

14. See J. E. Austin, "Strategic Collaboration between Nonprofits and Businesses," *Nonprofit and Voluntary Sector Quarterly* 29, no. 1 (2000): 69–97; Darcy Ashman, "Civil Society Collaboration with Business: Bringing Empowerment Back In," *World Development* 29, no. 7 (2001): 1097–1113; and Simon Zadek, "The Path to Corporate Responsibility," *Harvard Business Review* 82, no. 12 (2004): 125–32.

15. See World Bank, *Governance and Development* (Washington, DC: World Bank, 1992); and Clark, *Worlds Apart*, 191–92.

16. The Indian parliament passed the Prevention of Terrorism Act (POTA) in 2002, which greatly enhanced the provisions of the earlier Prevention of Terrorism Ordinance, considered by it as too weak. Many of the features of POTA (such as sweeping powers of surveillance granted to government agencies) strongly resemble the Patriot Act of the United States. See www.satp.org/satporgtp/countries/india/document/index.html (accessed November 24, 2004).

17. See Section 6, Pakistan Anti-Terrorism (Amendment) Ordinance, 1999, available at www.satp.org/satporgtp/countries/pakistan/document/actsandordinences/anti_terrorism.htm (accessed November 24, 2004).

18. See, "Holding Civic Groups Accountable," *New York Times* editorial, July 21, 2003; and Naomi Klein, "Bush to NGOs: Watch Your Mouths," *Globe and Mail* (Canada), June 20, 2003.

19. See Clark, *Worlds Apart*, 102.

20. See Srilatha Batliwala, "Grassroots Movements as Transnational Actors: Implications for Global Civil Society," *Voluntas* 13, no. 4 (2002): 397.

21. See, for instance, Clark, *Worlds Apart:* 169–85; Michael Edwards, *NGO Rights and Responsibilities: A New Deal for Global Governance* (London: The Foreign Policy Centre, 2000); and Hetty Kovach, Caroline Neligan, and Simon Burall, *Power without Accountability?* (London: One World Trust, 2003). For other examples, see "NGO Accountability and Performance," *AccountAbility Forum*, no. 2 (Winter 2004).

22. See The Social Learning Group, *Learning to Manage Global Environmental Risks*, vol. 2 (Cambridge, MA: MIT Press, 2001); and Lester Milbrath, *Envisioning a Sustainable Society: Learning Our Way Out* (Albany: State University of New York Press, 1989).

23. See Joseph Stiglitz, *Globalization and Its Discontents* (New York: W. W. Norton, 2002); and Amartya Sen, *Development as Freedom* (New York: Random House, 1999).

24. James C. Scott, *Seeing Like a State: How Certain Schemes to Improve the Human Condition Have Failed* (New Haven, CT: Yale University Press, 1998).

25. For examples, see Archon Fung and E. O. Wright, eds., *Deepening Democracy: Institutional Innovations in Empowered Participatory Governance* (London: Verso, 2003).

26. See Zadek, "Path to Corporate Responsibility"; J. E. Austin, *The Collaboration Challenge: How Nonprofits and Business Succeed through Strategic Alliances* (San Francisco: Jossey-Bass, 2000).

27. J. F. Rischard, *High Noon: 20 Global Problems; 20 Years to Solve Them* (London: Basic Books, 2002).

28. Joseph S. Nye Jr. and John D. Donohue, eds., *Governance in a Globalizing World* (Washington, DC: Brookings Institution Press, 2000).

Glossary

Bretton Woods Institutions   Composed of the World Bank, the International Monetary Fund, and the International Gold Standard. These were established at a conference held in July 1944 in Bretton Woods, New Hampshire.

Deliberative democracy   The system of political decision-making that emphasizes public deliberations among citizens to reach consensus, in contrast to the emphasis on electing representatives to make decisions, as in representative democracies.

Democratic deficits   Attributes of public decision-making that fall significantly short of the democratic ideal of responsiveness to citizens, as in the failure of many international institutions like the IMF or the World Bank to create mechanisms by which citizens affected by their policies and projects can hold them accountable.

Earth Summit   The UN Conference on Environment and Development held in Rio de Janeiro in 1992, bringing representatives of 172 governments as well as more than 2,400 NGOs at the parallel NGO Forum. The conference achieved agreement on Agenda 21 and the Rio Declaration and led to legally binding conventions on Biological Diversity and Climate Change.

GATT — General Agreement on Tariffs and Trade   Initiated in 1948 to develop trade regulations, GATT is a predecessor to the World Trade Organization and is now the element of the WTO that regulates international trade in goods.

G8 — Group of Eight   A group of nations formed in 1975, presently including Japan, the United States, Germany, the United Kingdom, Canada, Russia, and France. At annual summits organized in the country of each year's president, country leaders seek to reach informal agreements on cooperative measures on key issues of the day.

Global Governance   Efforts to identify, understand, and address worldwide problems that go beyond the capacity of individual nation-states to solve, often involving states, markets, citizens, and organizations in articulating interests, establishing rights and obligations, and mediating differences.

Globalization   A descriptive and contested term initially connoting the increasing integration of national economies into the global market, but now also applied to the growing planetwide awareness and interdependence resulting from exchanges of knowledge and information, and expanding political, economic, and social activity across national borders.

Identity Politics   The politics of movements that represent the interests and identity of a particular social group, rather than society as a whole. The group identity ("my people") provides a political basis for collective action.

IMF — International Monetary Fund   Conceived at Bretton Woods at the end of World War II to support economic cooperation that would prevent repetition of the Great Depression. Today, the IMF has 184 member countries and claims to foster global monetary cooperation, secure financial stability, facilitate international trade, promote high employment and sustainable economic growth, and reduce poverty. The IMF's lending policies particularly in Third World countries have been highly controversial.

Jubilee 2000   A campaign to cancel Third World debt at the millennium organized coalitions in more than 40 countries, drawing on the tradition in many religions of forgiving debt at special periods of time. The campaign built wide support for debt relief for poor countries whose ability to invest in their own development is severely undermined by the repayment of international debt often incurred by corrupt and irresponsible leaders.

Multilateralism   International policy-making and problem-solving that builds consensus across many nations and constituents for collective action to deal with issues. The creation of the EU or the coalition in the first Iraq War are examples of multilateralism.

Neoliberalism   An economic theory that emphasizes deregulating markets and trade and opposes state intervention in the economy. Neoliberalism calls for freeing markets from regulation, reducing public expenditure for social services, privatizing public enterprises, and emphasizing individualism and individual responsibility.

NGO — nongovernmental organization   In the broadest sense, any organization that is independent from the government. More commonly it refers to organizations that emphasize serving the public interest, such as promoting the interests of the poor, protecting the environment, providing basic social services, or addressing community development.

OECD — the Organization for Economic Cooperation and Development
A group of thirty member countries that share a commitment to democratic government and the market economy. It is best known for its publications and its statistics on economic and social issues and for fostering good governance in the public service and in corporate activity.

Social Capital The existence of social relationships and norms of trust and reciprocity that enable cooperative problem solving within a group or society.

State A sovereign political entity that occupies a territory and has an organized government. The term is often confused with "country" (a geographical area) and "nation" (usually referring to people who share a political identity).

TNC (MNC) — transnational (multinational) corporation A for-profit entity that has production, distribution, and research operations in more than one country.

UN Conference Decade During the 1990s a series of UN Conferences, including the Earth Summit in Rio de Janeiro, the Population Conference in Cairo, the World Summit on Sustainable Development, and the Women's Conference in Beijing, which created opportunities for large parallel conferences of civil society organizations that helped build many transnational movements.

Unilateralism International policy making and problem solving that is initiated by one nation with little or no consultation with or agreement from other affected countries. The second Iraq War or the US rejection of the Kyoto Agreement on climate change are frequently cited as examples of a "go-it-alone" unilateral approach.

Washington Consensus Widely held agreements by major government and intergovernmental organizations (e.g., the World Bank, the IMF, etc.) about the superiority of neoliberal or market-driven policies for promoting development.

WEF — World Economic Forum A gathering that brings together leaders from the world's largest companies with leaders from academia, government, religion, the media, nongovernmental organizations, and the arts. Annual meetings, held in Davos, Switzerland, convene people from more than one hundred countries for economic and social initiatives that will improve the state of the world.

World Bank   Headquartered in Washington, DC, a lending institution and a consortium of financial development institutions that is governed by 184 member countries. In 2004, the World Bank provided $20.1 billion for 245 projects in developing countries. Its lending policies and projects in many Third World countries have been controversial.

World Trade Organization (WTO)   Established in 1995 in Geneva, Switzerland, to create rules to regulate trade between nations. It has 148 member countries and regulates trade through agreements negotiated and signed by the bulk of the world's trading countries with the aim of helping producers of goods and services, exporters, and importers conduct their business on a level playing field. The power exercised by developed countries in WTO decision making has made it a controversial body.

WSF — World Social Forum   An open meeting place where social movements, networks, NGOs, and other civil society organizations come together to debate ideas, formulate proposals, share their experiences, and network for effective action. Its primary goal is to enable civil society actors to evolve alternative development paradigms based on equity, sustainability, and peace. It was launched in 1999 and has been held in Porto Alegre, Brazil, and Mumbai, India, and usually meets at the same time as the World Economic Forum.

List of Abbreviations

ABM	Anti-Ballistic Missile Systems
AFofL	American Federation of Labor
APEC	Asia Pacific Economic Cooperation
ANC	African National Congress
AU	Africa Union, originally Organization of African Unity
BP	British Petroleum
CAN	Climate Action Network
CBO	community based organization
CEDAW	Convention on the Elimination of Discrimination Against Women
CIO	Congress of Industrial Organizations
CND	Campaign for Nuclear Disarmament
CSO	civil society organization
CTA	clandestine transnational actors
DAWN	Development Alternatives with Women for a New Era
EJM	economic justice movement(s)
ETUC	European Trade Union Confederation
ETUF	European Trade Union Federation
EU	European Union
EWC	European works councils
FAS	Federation of Atomic (American) Scientists
FEDEFAM	Federation of Families of the Disappeared
FGM	female genital mutilation
FOE	Friends of the Earth

GATT	General Agreement on Tariffs and Trade
GCC	Global Climate Coalition
G8	Group of Eight nations
GNP	gross national product
GONGO	government-organized nongovernmental organizations
GUF	global union federation
HIPC	Heavily Indebted Poor Countries Initiative
HRW	Human Rights Watch
IALANA	International Association of Lawyers Against Nuclear Arms
ICBL	International Campaign to Ban Landmines
ICFTU	International Confederation of Free Trade Unions
ICCJ	International Court for Criminal Justice
ICPD	International Conference on Population and Development
ICSU	International Conference of Scientific Unions (International Council for Science)
ICT	information and communication technologies
IFA	international framework agreement
IFCTU	International Federation of Christian Trade Unions
IFI	international financial institutions
IFTU	International Federation of Trade Unions
IGO	intergovernmental organization
IGTN	International Gender and Trade Network

IGY	International Geophysical Year
ILO	International Labor Organization
IMF	International Monetary Fund
INF	Intermediate Nuclear Force
IPB	International Peace Bureau
IPCC	Intergovernmental Panel on Climate Change
IPPNW	International Physicians for the Prevention of Nuclear War
ISA	inter-State actors
ITS	international trade secretariats
IUCN	International Union for the Conservation of Nature and Natural Resources
IUF	International Food Workers
IWW	Industrial Workers of the World
MAI	Multilateral Agreement on Investment
MERCOSUR	Mercada Comun del Sur, or Common Market of Argentina, Brazil, Paraguay and Uruguay
MPI	Middle Powers Initiative
NATO	North Atlantic Treaty Organization
NGO	nongovernmental organization
NPT	Non-Proliferation Treaty
NSA	non-State actors
OAS	Organization of American States
OATUU	Organization of African Trade Union Unity
OECD	Organization for Economic Cooperation and Development
OPEC	Organization of Petroleum Exporting Countries

OSCE	Organization for Security and Cooperation in Europe
POTA	Prevention of Terrorism Act (India)
PSR	Physicians for Social Responsibility
PTBT	Partial Test Ban Treaty
RILU	Red International of Labor Unions
SA	(nation)-State actors
SALT	Strategic Arms Limitation Treaty
SANE	Committee for a Sane Nuclear Policy
SAP	structural adjustment policies
SCOPE	Scientific Committee on Problems of the Environment
SDI	Strategic Defense Initiative
SEWA	Self-Employed Women's Association
SM	social movements
TCS	transnational civil society
TCSO	transnational civil society organization
TNC	transnational corporation
TPCA	transnational progressive civic advocacy actors
TRAFFIC	Trade Records Analysis of Fauna and Flora in Commerce
UCS	Union of Concerned Scientists
UK	United Kingdom
UN	United Nations
UNEP	United Nations Environment Programme
UNGA	United Nations General Assembly
UNICEF	United Nations international
US	United States
WCL	World Confederation of Labor

WCP	World Court Project
WFTU	World Federation of Trade Unions
WSF	World Social Forum
WEF	World Economic Forum
WTO	World Trade Organization
WWF	World Wide Fund for Nature

Bibliography

Books

Al-Ali, Nadje, and Khalid Moser, eds. *New Approaches to Migration: Transnational Communities and the Transformation of Home.* London: Routledge, 2001.

Amin, Samir. *Accumulation on a World Scale: A Critique of the Theory of Underdevelopment.* 2 vols. New York: Monthly Review Press, 1974.

Anderson, Benedict. *Imagined Communities: Reflections on the Origin and Spread of Nationalism.* London and New York: Verso, 1991.

Anderson, Sarah, John Cavanagh, Thea Lee, and the Institute for Policy Studies. *Field Guide to the Global Economy.* New York: New Press, 2000.

Appadurai, Arjun. "The Capacity to Aspire: Culture and the Terms of Recognition." In *Culture and Public Action,* ed. V. Rao and M. Walton. Stanford, CA: Stanford University Press, 2004.

Ashworth, William. *A Short History of the International Economy since 1850.* London: Longmans, Green, 1962.

Austin, J. E. *The Collaboration Challenge: How Nonprofits and Business Succeed Through Strategic Alliances.* San Francisco: Jossey-Bass, 2000.

Barrett, Scott. *Environment and Statecraft: The Strategy of Environmental Treaty-Making.* Oxford: Oxford University Press, 2003.

Benedick, Richard. *Ozone Diplomacy: New Directions in Safeguarding the Planet.* Cambridge, MA: Harvard University Press, 1991.

Bethe, Hans A. *The Road from Los Alamos.* New York: Simon and Schuster, 1991.

Bigelow, Bill, and Bob Peterson. "Colonialism: The Building Blocks." In *Rethinking Globalization: Teaching for Justice in an Unjust World,* ed. Bill Bigelow and Bob Peterson, 35–37. Milwaukee: Rethinking Schools, 2002.

Boli, John, and George M. Thomas, eds. *Constructing World Culture: International Organizations Since 1875.* Stanford, CA: Stanford University Press, 1999.

Braic, Marianne, and S. Wolte, eds. *Common Ground or Mutual Exclusion? Women's Movements and International Relations.* London: Zed Books, 2002.

Breyman, Steve. *Why Movements Matter: The West German Peace Movement and US Arms Control Policy.* Albany: State University of New York Press, 2001.

Brundtland, G., ed. *Our Common Future: The World Commission on Environment and Development.* Oxford: Oxford University Press, 1987.

Bruyn, Severyn T. *A Civil Economy: Transforming the Market in the Twenty-first Century.* Ann Arbor: University of Michigan Press, 2000.

Brysk, Alison. *From Tribal Village to Global Village: Indian Rights and International Relations in Latin America.* Stanford, CA: Stanford University Press, 2000.

————, ed. *Globalization and Human Rights.* Berkeley: University of California Press, 2002.

Bunch, Charlotte, and N. Reilly. *Demanding Accountability: The Global Campaign and Vienna Tribunal for Women's Human Rights.* New Brunswick: Center for Women's Global Leadership, 1994.

Bundy, McGeorge. *Danger and Survival: Choices about the Bomb in the First Fifty Years.* New York: Vintage Books, 1988.

Buss, Doris, and Didi Herman. *Globalizing Family Values: The Christian Right in International Politics.* Minneapolis: University of Minnesota Press, 2003.

Chatfield, Charles. *The American Peace Movement: Ideals and Activism.* New York: Twayne Publishers, 1992.

Civicus. *Civil Society at the Millennium.* West Hartford, CT: Kumarian Press, 1999.

Clark, John D. *Worlds Apart: Civil Society and the Battle for Ethical Globalization.* Bloomfield, CT: Kumarian Press; London: Earthscan, 2002.

Covey, Jane G. "Is Critical Cooperation Possible?" In *The Struggle for Accountability,* ed. Jonathan A. Fox and L. David Brown, 81–119. Cambridge, MA: MIT Press, 1998.

Croly, H. *The Promise of American Life.* New York: Macmillan, 1909.

DAWN, *Markers on the Way: The DAWN Debates on Alternative Development.* Barbados: Caribbean Graphics Productions, 1995. Also available online at DAWN, www.dawn.org.fj.

De Soto, Hernando. *Mystery of Capital.* New York: Basic Books, 2000.

Diamond, Larry. *Developing Democracy: Toward Consolidation.* Baltimore: Johns Hopkins University Press, 1999.

Doherty, A. "The Role of Nongovernmental Organizations in UNCED." In *Negotiating International Regimes: Lessons Learned from the United Nations Conference on Environment and Development,* ed. Bertram I. Spector, Gunnar Sjostedt, and I. William Zartman, 199–218. London: Graham and Trotman, 1994.

Edwards, Michael. *Civil Society.* Cambridge: Polity, 2004.

————. *NGO Rights and Responsibilities: A New Deal for Global Governance.* London: The Foreign Policy Centre, 2000.

Edwards, Michael, and John Gaventa, eds. *Global Citizen Action.* Boulder, CO: Lynne Rienner, 2001.

Evans, Peter, Dietrich Rueschemeyer, and Theda Skocpol, eds. *Bringing the State Back In: New Perspectives on the State as Institution and Social Actor.* Cambridge: Cambridge University Press, 1985.

Felice, William. *The Global New Deal: Economic and Social Human Rights in World Politics.* Lanham, MD: Rowman and Littlefield, 2003.

Finger, M. "The Ivory Trade Ban: NGOs and International Conservation." In *Environmental NGOs in World Politics: Linking the Local and the Global,* ed. T. Princen and M. Finger, 121–59. London: Routledge, 1994.

FitzGerald, Frances. *Way Out There in the Blue.* New York: Simon and Schuster, 2000.

Florini, Ann, ed. *The Third Force: The Rise of Transnational Civil Society.* Washington, DC: Carnegie Endowment for International Peace; Tokyo: Japan Center for International Exchange, 2000.

Fung, Archon, and E. O. Wright, eds. *Deepening Democracy: Institutional Innovations in Empowered Participatory Governance.* London: Verso, 2003.

Galambos, L. "The Emerging Organizational Synthesis in American History." In *Men and Organizations: The American Economy in the Twentieth Century,* ed. E. J. Perkins, 1–15. New York: G. P. Putnam, 1977.

Gobin, Corinne. *L'Europe Syndicale.* Brussels: Editions Labor, 1997.

Grubb, Michael, Matthias Koch, Abby Munson, Francis Sullivan, and Koy Thomson. *The Earth Summit Agreements: A Guide and Assessment.* London: Earthscan, 1993.

Haas, Peter. *Saving the Mediterranean.* New York: Columbia University Press, 1990.

Hall, Peter Dobkin. *The Organization of American Culture, 1700–1900: Institutions, Elites, and the Origins of American Nationality.* New York: New York University Press, 1982.

Hart, Keith. *The Memory Bank: Money in an Unequal World.* London: Profile Books, 2000.

Hannerz, Ulf. *Transnational Connections: Culture, People, Places.* London: Routledge, 1996.

Haynes, Jeff. "Power, Politics and Environmental Movements in the Third World." In *Environmental Movements: Local, National and Global,* ed. Christopher Rootes, 222–42. London and Portland, OR: Frank Cass, 1999.

Heijden, Hein-Anton van der. "Environmental Movements, Ecological Modernisation and Political Opportunity Structures." In *Environmental Movements: Local, National and Global*, ed. Christopher Rootes, 199–221. London and Portland, OR: Frank Cass, 1999.

Hirschmann, Albert. *Exit, Voice, and Loyalty.* Cambridge, MA: Harvard University Press, 1970.

Hoffman, Andrew. *From Heresy to Dogma: An Institutional History of Corporate Environmentalism.* San Francisco: New Lexington Press, 1997.

International Committee of the Red Cross. *Anti-Personnel Landmines — Friend or Foe? A Study of the Military Use and Effectiveness of Anti-Personnel Mines.* Geneva: ICRC, 1996.

Jaeger, J., and H. L. Ferguson, eds. *Climate Change: Science, Impacts and Policy: Proceedings of the Second World Climate Conference.* Cambridge: Cambridge University Press, 1990.

Johnson, Douglas A. "Confronting Corporate Power: Strategies and Phases of the Nestle Boycott." In *Research in Corporate Social Performance and Policy*, ed. Lee Preston and James Post, 8:323–44. Greenwich, CT: JAI Press, 1986.

Josselin, Daphne, and William Wallace, eds. *Non-State Actors in World Politics.* New York: Palgrave, 2001.

Kaldor, Mary. *Global Civil Society: An Answer to War.* Cambridge: Polity, 2003.

Katz, Miton S. *Ban the Bomb: A History of SANE — The Committee for a Sane Nuclear Policy.* New York: Praeger, 1987.

Keane, John. *Transnational Civil Society.* Cambridge: Cambridge University Press, 2003.

Keck, Margaret E., and Kathryn Sikkink. *Activists beyond Borders.* Ithaca, NY: Cornell University Press, 1998.

Khagram, Sanjeev, James V. Riker, and Kathryn Sikkink, eds. *Restructuring World Politics: Transnational Social Movements, Networks and Norms.* Minneapolis: University of Minnesota Press, 2002.

Klotz, Audie. *Norms in International Relations: The Struggle against Apartheid.* Ithaca, NY: Cornell University Press, 1995.

Knopf, Jeffrey W. "The Nuclear Freeze Movement's Effect on Policy." In *Coalitions and Political Movements: The Lessons of the Nuclear Freeze*, ed. Thomas R. Rochon and Davis S. Meyer, 127–62. Boulder, CO: L. Rienner, 1997.

Kohli, Atul, ed. *The State and Development in the Third World.* Princeton, NJ: Princeton University Press, 1986.

Kovach, Hetty, Caroline Neligan, and Simon Burall, *Power without Accountability?* London: One World Trust, 2003.

Lamb, Robert. *Promising the Earth*. London and New York: Routledge, 1996.

Lemann, Nicholas. *The Big Test: The Secret History of the American Meritocracy*. New York: Farrar, Straus, and Giroux, 2000.

Lindenberg, Marc, and Coralie Bryant. *Going Global: Transforming Relief and Development NGOs*. Bloomfield, CT: Kumarian Press, 2001.

Lorde, Audre. *Sister Outsider: Essays and Speeches by Audre Lorde*. 11th ed. Freedom, CA: The Crossing Press, 1996.

Lorwin, Lewis. *The International Labor Movement: History, Policies, Outlook*. New York: Harper, 1953.

MacEwan, A. "World Capitalism and the Current Economic Crisis." In *The Capitalist System*, ed. Richard C. Edwards, Michael Reich, and Thomas E. Weisskopf.Englewood Cliffs, NJ: Prentice-Hall, 1986.

Mander, Jerry, and Edward Goldsmith, eds. *The Case against the Global Economy*. San Francisco: Sierra Club Books, 1996.

Manno, J. P. "Advocacy and Diplomacy: NGOs and the Great Lakes H_2O Quality Agreement." In *Environmental NGOs in World Politics: Linking the Local and the Global*, ed. T. Princen and M. Finger, 69–120. London: Routledge, 1994.

Marx, Karl. *Das Kapital*. Washington, DC: Regnery Gateway, 2000.

McAdam, D., J. McCarthy, and M. Zald, eds. *Comparative Perspectives on Social Movements: Political Opportunities, Mobilizing Structures, and Cultural Framing*. New York: Cambridge University Press, 1996.

Mekata, Motoko. "Building Partnerships toward a Common Goal: Experiences of the International Campaign to Ban Landmines." In *The Third Force: The Rise of Transnational Civil Society*, ed. Ann Florini, 143–76. Washington, DC: Carnegie Endowment for International Peace, 2000.

Milbrath, Lester. *Envisioning a Sustainable Society: Learning Our Way Out*. Albany: State University of New York Press, 1989.

Monshipouri, Mahmood, Neil Englehart, Andrew J. Nathan, and Kavita Philip, eds. *Constructing Human Rights in the Age of Globalization*. New York: M. E. Sharpe, 2003.

Nanda, Ved P., and David Krieger. *Nuclear Weapons and the World Court*. New York: Transnational Publishers, 1998.

Nelson, Ralph L. *Merger Movements in American Industry, 1895–1956*. New Brunswick, NJ: Princeton University Press, 1959.

Nye, Joseph S., Jr., and John D. Donahue, eds. *Governance in a Globalizing World*. Washington, DC: Brookings Institution Press, 2000.

Orend, Biran. *Human Rights: Concept and Context*. Ontario: Broadview Press, 2002.

Passas, Nikos. *Transnational Crime*. Brookfield, VT: Ashgate, 1999.

Peters, Julie, and Andrea Wolper, eds. *Women's Rights, Human Rights*. New York: Routledge, 1995.

Peterson, Bob. "Burning Books and Destroying Peoples: How the World Became Divided between Rich and Poor Countries." In *Rethinking Globalization: Teaching for Justice in an Unjust World*, ed. Bill Bigelow and Bob Peterson, 38–43. Milwaukee: Rethinking Schools, 2002.

———. "Introduction to Inequality Activities." In *Rethinking Globalization: Teaching for Justice in an Unjust World*, ed. Bill Bigelow and Bob Peterson, 68. Milwaukee: Rethinking Schools, 2002.

Rahman, A., and A. Roncerel. "A View from the Ground Up." In *Negotiating Climate Change: The Inside Story of the Rio Convention*, ed. Irving M. Mintzer and J. Amber Leonard, 239–72. Cambridge: Cambridge University Press, 1994.

Reinicke, Wolfgang, and Francis Deng. *Critical Choices: The United Nations, Networks and the Future of Global Governance*. Ottawa: International Development Research Centre, 2000.

Rhodes, Richard. *Dark Sun: The Making of the Hydrogen Bomb*. London: Simon and Schuster, 1996.

Rich, Adrienne. *The Dream of a Common Language: Poems 1974–1977*. New York: W. W. Norton, 1993.

Rich, B. *Mortgaging the Earth: The World Bank, Environmental Impoverishment, and the Crisis of Development*. Boston: Beacon Press, 1994.

Rischard, J. F. *High Noon: 20 Global Problems; 20 Years to Solve Them*. London: Basic Books, 2002.

Risse, Thomas. "The Power of Norms versus the Norms of Power: Transnational Civil Society and Human Rights." In *The Third Force: The Rise of Transnational Civil Society*, ed. Ann Florini, 177–210. Washington, DC: Carnegie Endowment for International Peace; Tokyo: Japan Center for International Exchange, 2000.

Risse-Kappen, Thomas, ed. *Bringing Transnational Actors Back In: Non-State Actors, Domestic Structures, and International Institutions*. Cambridge: Cambridge University Press, 1995.

Roberts, J. M. *Twentieth Century: The History of the World, 1901–2000*. New York: Viking, 1999.

Rootes, Christopher. "Environmental Movements from the Local to the Global." In *Environmental Movements: Local, National and Global,* ed. Christopher Rootes, 1–12. London and Portland, OR: Frank Cass, 1999.

Rotberg, Robert, ed. *When States Fail: Causes and Consequences.* Princeton, NJ: Princeton University Press, 2004.

Rothchild, Donald, and Naomi Chazan. *State and Society in Africa.* Boulder, CO: Westview, 1988.

Rudolph, Susanne Hoeber. "Dehomogenizing Religious Formations." In *Transnational Religion and Fading States,* ed. Suzanne Hoeber Rudolph and James Piscatori, 243–61. Boulder, CO: Westview, 1997.

Rummel, R. J. *Death by Government.* Somerset, NJ: Transaction Publishers, 1994.

Schell, Jonathan. *The Gift of Time: The Case for Abolishing Nuclear Weapons Now.* New York: Metropolitan Books, 1998.

Schiller, Nina Glick. "Transmigrants and Nation-States: Something Old and Something New in the U.S. Immigrant Experience." In *The Handbook of International Migration,* ed. Charles Hirschman, Philip Kasinitz, and Josh DeWind. New York: Russell Sage Foundation, 1999.

Scott, James C. *Seeing Like a State: How Certain Schemes to Improve the Human Condition Have Failed.* New Haven, CT: Yale University Press, 1998.

Sen, Amartya. *Development as Freedom.* New York: Random House, 1999.

Sikkink, Kathryn. "Restructuring World Politics: The Limits and Asymmetries of Soft Power." In *Restructuring World Politics: Transnational Social Movements, Networks and Norms,* ed. Sanjeev Khagram, James V. Riker, and Kathryn Sikkink, 301–17. Minneapolis: University of Minnesota Press, 2002.

Silver, Beverly J. *Forces of Labor: Workers Movements and Globalization since 1870.* Cambridge: Cambridge University Press, 2003.

Singer, P. W. *Corporate Warriors: The Rise of the Privatized Military Industry.* Ithaca, NY: Cornell University Press, 2004.

Sklar, M. J. *The Corporate Reconstruction of American Capitalism, 1890–1916.* New York: Cambridge University Press, 1988.

Social Learning Group, The. *Learning to Manage Global Environmental Risks.* 2 vols. Cambridge, MA: MIT Press, 2001.

Sparke, Matthew. *Hyphen-Nation-States: Critical Geographies of Displacement and Disjuncture.* Minnesota: University of Minnesota Press, 2003.

Stepan, Alfred. *The State and Society: Peru in Comparative Perspective.* Princeton, NJ: Princeton University Press, 1978.

Stiglitz, Joseph. *Globalization and Its Discontents.* New York: W. W. Norton, 2002.

Tandon, Rajesh, and Kumi Naidoo. "Civil Society at the Millennium." In *Civil Society at the Millennium,* ed. Kumi Naidoo, 193–207. West Hartford, CT: Kumarian Press, 1999.

Wapner, P. *Environmental Activism and World Civic Politics.* Albany: State University of New York Press, 1996.

Warkentin, C. *Reshaping World Politics: NGOs, the Internet, and Global Civil Society.* Lanham, MD: Rowman and Littlefield, 2001.

Waters, B. *A Yale Book of Numbers, 1976–2000.* New Haven, CT: Yale University Office of Institutional Research, 2001. Also available online at www.yale.edu/oir/pierson_update.htm#D.

Weart, Spencer. *Nuclear Fear: A History of Images.* Cambridge, MA: Harvard University Press, 1988.

Welch, Claude. *Protecting Human Rights in Africa.* Philadelphia: University of Pennsylvania Press, 1995.

William, William A. *Americans in a Changing World.* New York: Harper and Row, 1978.

Wittner, Lawrence. *Resisting the Bomb.* Stanford: Stanford University Press, 1997.

———. *Toward Nuclear Abolition: History of the World Nuclear Disarmament Movement, 1971 to the Present.* Stanford, CA: Stanford University Press, 2003.

World Bank. *Governance and Development.* Washington, DC: World Bank, 1992.

Young, Oran, ed. *Global Governance.* Cambridge, MA: MIT Press, 1997.

Journals

Abugre, Charles. "Global Conferences and Global Civil Society in the 1990s: New Arenas of Social Struggle or New Illusions?" *Montreal International Forum: Forum 2001* 3, no. 1 (2002): 10–17.

Ashman, Darcy. "Civil Society Collaboration with Business: Bringing Empowerment Back In." *World Development* 29, no. 7 (2001): 1097–1113.

Austin, J. E. "Strategic Collaboration between Nonprofits and Businesses." *Nonprofit and Voluntary Sector Quarterly* 29, no. 1 (2000): 69–97.

Batliwala, Srilatha. "Grassroots Movements as Transnational Actors: Implications for Global Civil Society." *Voluntas* 13, no. 4 (2002): 393–410.

Baubock, Rainer. "Towards a Political Theory of Migrant Transnationalism." *International Migration Review* 37 (Fall 2003): 700–723.

Bleicher, Maurice. "The Ottawa Process: Nine-Day Wonder or a New Model for Disarmament Negotiations?" *Disarmament Forum* 2 (2000): 69–77.

Bonbright, David. "NGO Accountability and Performance: Introducing Access," *AccountAbility Forum,* no. 2 (Winter 2004): 4–13

Bratton, Michael. "Civil Society and Political Transition in Africa." *Institute for Development Research Reports* 11, no. 6 (1994): 1–21.

Brysk, Alison. "From Above and Below: Social Movements, the International System and Human Rights in Argentina." *Comparative Political Studies* 26 (October 1993): 259–85.

———. "Globalization: The Double-edged Sword." *NACLA Report on the Americas* 34, no. 1 (2000): 29–33.

Day, Jeremiah, and James L. Kingsley. "Original Papers in Relation to a Course of Liberal Education." *American Journal of Science* 15 (January 1829): 297–351.

Eliot, C. W. "The New Education." Pts. 1 and 2. *Atlantic Monthly* 23 (February 1869): 202–20; 23 (March 1869): 363–66.

Enders, Walter. "Is Transnational Terrorism Becoming More Threatening? A Time Series Investigation." *Journal of Conflict Resolution* 44, no. 3 (2000): 307–32.

Feraru, Anne Thompson. "Transnational Political Interests and the Global Environment." *International Organization* 28, no. 1 (1974): 31–60.

Galambos, L. "Technology, Political Economy, and Professionalization: Central Themes of the Organizational Synthesis." *Business History Review* 57 (Winter 1983): 471–93.

Haas, P., M. Levy, and T. Parson. "Appraising the Earth Summit: How Should We Judge UNCED's Success?" *Environment* 34, no. 8 (1992): 6–11, 26–33.

Jung, Kim Dae. "Is Culture Destiny?" *Foreign Affairs* 73, no. 6 (1994): 189–94.

Kaye, Salia Dassa. "Track Two Diplomacy and Regional Security in the Middle East." *International Negotiation* 6, no. 1 (2001): 49–77.

Kearney, Michael. "The Local and the Global: The Anthropology of Globalization and Transnationalism." *Annual Review of Anthropology* 24 (1995): 547–65.

Keohane, Robert O., and Joseph S. Nye Jr. "Transgovernmental Relations and International Organizations." *World Politics* 27, no. 1 (1972): 39–62.

Lagos, Ricardo, and Heraldo Munoz. "The Pinochet Dilemma." *Foreign Policy* 114 (Spring 1999): 26–39.

Mandhane, Renu, and Alison Symington. "Facts and Issues: Ten Principles for Challenging Neoliberal Globalization." *Association for Women's Rights in Development* 6 (December 2003): 1–7.

Mathews, Jessica. "Power Shift." *Foreign Affairs* 76 no. 1 (1997): 50–67.

Meyer, Davis S. "Peace Protests and Policy: Explaining the Rise and Decline of Antinuclear Movements in Postwar America." *Policy Studies Journal* 21 (1993): 35–55.

Mwangi, Wagaki. "A Report on Forum 2000." In *Montreal International Forum: Forum 2000* 2, no. 1 (2001): 6–10.

Peterson, M. J. "Whalers, Cetologists, Environmentalists, and the International Management of Whaling." *International Organization* 46, no. 1 (1992): 147–86.

Portes, Alejandro, Luis Guarnizo, and Patricia Landolt. "Introduction: Pitfalls and Promise of an Emergent Research Field." *Ethnic and Racial Studies* 22, no. 2 (1999): 217–37.

Price, Richard. "Transnational Civil Society and Advocacy in World Politics." *World Politics* 55, no. 4 (2003): 579–606.

Raustiala, K. "States, NGOs, and International Environmental Institutions." *International Studies Quarterly* 41, no. 4 (1997): 719–40.

Salamon, Lester M. "The Rise of the Non-Profit Sector." *Foreign Affairs* 73, no. 4 (1994): 109–22.

Seoane, Jose, and Emilio Taddei. "From Seattle to Porto Alegre: The Anti-Neoliberal Globalization Movement." *Current Sociology* 50, no. 1 (2002): 99–123.

Slaughter, Anne-Marie. "The Real New World Order." *Foreign Affairs* 76, no. 5 (1997): 183–98.

Smith, J. Eric. "The Role of Special Purpose and Nongovernmental Organizations in the Environmental Crisis." *International Organization* 26, no. 2 (1972): 302–26.

Ticehurst, Rupert. "The Martens Clause and the Laws of Armed Conflict." *International Review of the Red Cross* 317 (1997): 125–34.

Tuijl, Peter van, and Lisa Jordan. "Political Responsibility in Transnational NGO Advocacy." *World Development* 28, no. 12 (2000): 2051–65.

Vickers, George R. "The Vietnam Antiwar Movement in Perspective." *Bulletin of Concerned Asian Scholars* 21, no. 2–4 (1989): 100–110.

Waddell, Steve. "Global Action Networks: A Global Invention to Make Globalisation Work for All." *Journal of Corporate Citizenship* 12 (Winter 2003): 1–16.

Williams, Phil. "Transnational Criminal Organizations and International Security." *Survival* 36, no. 1 (1994): 96–113.

Zadek, Simon. "The Path to Corporate Responsibility." *Harvard Business Review* 82, no. 12 (2004): 125–32.

Newspapers, Magazines, Bulletins, and Interviews

The Economist. "Anti-Capitalist Protests: Angry and Effective." September 23, 2000.

———. "The Bubble-and-Squeak Summit." September 4, 2002.

Edwards, Michael. "Victims of Their Own Success." *Guardian Weekly,* July 6, 2000.

European Trade Union Information Bulletin, no. 4 (1994).

Hare, Bill (Greenpeace International policy director). Interview with W. E. Franz, February 1997, Bonn.

Kaldor, M. "'Civilizing' Globalization: The Implications of the 'Battle in Seattle.'" *Millennium,* January 29, 2000.

Klein, Naomi. "Bush to NGOs: Watch Your Mouths." *Globe and Mail* (Canada), June 20, 2003.

———. "Signs of the Times: Protests Aimed at Powerful Symbols of Capitalism Find Themselves in a Transformed Landscape." *The Nation,* October 22, 2001.

New York Times. "Holding Civic Groups Accountable." Editorial, July 21, 2003.

Tyler, Patrick E. "Threats and Responses: A New Power in the Streets." *New York Times,* February 17, 2003.

Witte, Jan Martin, Wolfgang H. Reinicke, and Thorsten Benner. "Beyond Multilateralism: Global Policy Networks." *International Politics and Society* 2 (2000). www.fes.de/IPG/ipg2_2000/artwitte.html.

Wolf, Martin. "Trade: Uncivil Society," *Financial Times,* September 1, 1999.

248   Transnational Civil Society: An Introduction

Websites

Act Now to Stop War & End Racism Coalition, www.international answer.org/.

African National Congress. "A History of the African National Congress." www.anc.org.za/ancdocs/about/umzabalazo.html.

Albert, Michael. "The Movements Against Neoliberal Globalization from Seattle to Porto Alegre." *Z Magazine*, www.zmag.org/albertgreecetalk.htm.

Amnesty International. www.amnesty.org/ailib/intcam/femgen/fgm1.htm#a3.

Anderson, Sarah, and John Cavanagh. "The Top 200: The Rise of Global Corporate Power." www.ips-dc.org/reports/top200text.htm.

Asia Times Online, www.atimes.com/atimes/South Asia/EG16Df03.

Behera, Navnita Chadha. "Need to Expand Track-Two Diplomacy." *Asia Time Online*, www.atimes.com/atimes/South_Asia/EG16Df03.html.

British Petroleum. "Environment and Society." www.bp.com.

Bulletin of Atomic Scientists. www.thebulletin.org/clock.

Campaign for Nuclear Disarmament. www.cnduk.org/INFORM~1/ cnd-cuban.htm.

———. www.cnduk.org/INFORM~1/cndreviv.htm.

———. www.cnduk.org/INFORM~1/greenham.htm.

Choudry, Aziz. "Neoliberal Globalization: Cancun and Beyond." *Action for Social and Ecological Action*. Green Paper no. 4. www.asej.org.

Climate Action Network. "What Does CAN Hope to Achieve." www.climatenework.org/pages/aboutCANInt.html

Coalition to Reduce Nuclear Danger. www.clw.org/coatlition/ctch7080.htm.

Council for Security Cooperation in the Asia Pacific. www.cscap.org.

DAWN (Development Alternatives with Women for a New Era). www.dawn.org.fj.

Electronic Mine Information Network, www.mineaction.org.

Executive Summary, "Global Transformations." www.polity.co.uk/global/executiv.htm.

Freedom House. www.freedomhouse.org.

Friends of the Earth, "Towards Sustainable Economies: Challenging Neoliberal Economic Globalization." Friends of the Earth, www.foe.co.uk/campaigns/sustainable_development/publications/trade.

Geneva Call. /www.genevacall.org.

George, Susan. "A Short History of Neoliberalism." Paper presented at the conference on Economic Sovereignty in a Globalising World, March 24–26, 1999. www.globalpolicy.org/globaliz/econ/histneol.htm.

GlobeScan, www.globescan.com/

History Division of the Department of Energy. http://ma.mbe.doe.gov/me70/history/1951-1970.htm.

Human Rights Watch. www.hrw.org/home.html.

Institute of International Education. "American Students Study Abroad in Growing Numbers." www.opendoors.iienetwork.org/?p=36524.

———. "International Student Enrollment." www.opendoors.iienetwork.org/?p=36523.

———. "Open Doors 2003: International Students in the United States," www.opendoors.iienetwork.org.

International Campaign to Ban Landmines. www.icbl.org.

International Union for the Conservation of Nature. "Welcome to IUCN — World Conservation Union." www.iucn.org/about/index.htm.

National Academy of Sciences. www.nas.edu/history/igy/.

National Center for Education Statistics, 1997, nces.ed.gov/das/library/tables_listing/show_nedrc.asp?rt=p&tableID=233.

National Nuclear Weapons Freeze Campaign. www.ratical.org/co-globalize/whm1454.html.

NGO Alternative Treaties, The. "People's Earth Declaration," article 23. http://habitat.igc.org/treaties/.

Pakistan Anti-Terrorism (Amendment) Ordinance, 1999. www.satp.org/satporgtp/countries/pakistan/document/actsand ordinences/anti_terrorism.htm.

Physicians for Social Responsibility. www.psr.org/home.cfm?id=about.

Prevention of Terrorism Act (India). www.satp.org/satporgtp/countries/india/document/index.html.

Program of the Center for International Earth Science Information Network (the Socioeconomic Data and Applications Center, database 1885–2004). www.ciesin.columbia.edu/.

Reynolds, Paul. "Eyewitness: The Battle of Seattle," BBC News, December 2, 1999. http://news.bbc.co.uk/1/hi/world/americas/547581.stm.

Tuijl, Peter van, and Lisa Jordan. "Political Responsibility in Transnational NGO Advocacy." Bank Information Center, www.bicusa.org/bicusa/issues/misc_resources/138.php.

Union of Concerned Scientists. www.ucsusa.org/ucs/about/apge.cfm?pageID=767.

United Nations Foundation. "Africa: Some Progress Fighting FGM." WIN News, UN Wire (Spring 2000). www.unfoundation.org.

United Nations High Commissioner for Human Rights. www.unhchr.ch/pdf/report.pdf.

United Nations Johannesburg Summit 2002. www.johannesburgsummit.org/html/basic_info/basicinfo.html.

United Nations Press Office. "Secretary-General Welcomes Convention Banning Landmines as 'Landmark Step in History of Disarmament.'" www.atimes.com/atimes/South_Asia/EG16Df03.html.

Waters, B. *A Yale Book of Numbers, 1976–2000.* www.yale.edu/oir/pierson_update.htm#D.

World Bank. www.worldbank.org/data/quickreference/quickref.html.

World Economic Forum. "Peace and Security." Global Governance Initiative 2004, www.weforum.org/site/homepublic.nsf/Content/Global+Governance+Initiative.

———. "Results on the Survey on Trust." www.weforum.org/site/homepublic.nsf/Content/Annual+Meeting+2003%5CResults+of+the+Survey+on+Trust#II.

World Wide Fund for Nature. www.panda.org/about_wwf/who_we_are/history/seventies.cfm.

Dissertations, Papers, Speeches, and Unpublished Monographs

Axworthy, Lloyd. Speech on the occasion of the International Strategy Conference toward a Global Ban on Antipersonnel Mines, Ottawa, Canada, October 5, 1996.

Cardoso Panel Report. *We the Peoples: Civil Society, the United Nations and Global Governance.* Report of the Panel of Eminent Persons on UN–Civil Society Relations. A/58/817, General Assembly, United Nations, 11 June 2004.

Climate Action Network Charter. Working document dated March 12, 1989. On file with Wendy E. and Andrew Torrance.

"Diaspora Philanthropy: Perspectives on India and China." Global Equity Initiative Workshop, Harvard University, Cambridge, MA, May 7–8, 2003.

Fowler, Alan, "Social Economy in the South: A Civil Society Perspective." Unpublished monograph, May 2001. Obtainable from ALANFOWLER@compuserve.com.

Franz, Wendy E. *Changing the Climate? Non-State Actors in International Environmental Politics.* Doctoral dissertation, Harvard University, Cambridge, MA.

Geneva Call. *Engaging Nonstate Actors in a Landmine Ban.* Full conference proceedings, International Conference Centre of Geneva, Geneva, March 24–25, 2000.

George, Susan. "A Short History of Neoliberalism." Paper presented at the conference on Economic Sovereignty in a Globalising World, March 24–26, 1999. Also available at www.globalpolicy.org/globaliz/econ/histneol.htm.

Gleditsch, Nils Petter, Harard Strand, Mikael Erikkson, Margareta Sollenberg, and Peter Wallensteen. "Armed Conflict 1946–99: A New Dataset." Paper presented at the 42nd Annual Convention of the International Studies Association, Chicago, IL, February 20–24, 2001.

Hall, Peter Dobkin. "Globalization: A Chapter in the Sociology of Knowledge." Paper presented to the panel on Discerning Globalization: Language, Identity, and Emergent Transnational Collectivities, Social Science History Association, St. Louis, MO, October 25, 2002.

International Council of Scientific Unions, United Nations Environment Programme, and World Meteorological Organization. *Report of the International Conference on the Assessment of the Role of Carbon Dioxide and of Other Greenhouse Gases in Climate Variations and Associated Impacts.* WMO document no. 661. Geneva: WMO, 1986.

Khagram, Sanjeev, and Peggy Levitt. "Towards a Sociology of Transnationalism and a Transnational Sociology." Working paper no. 24, Hauser Center for Nonprofit Organizations Working Paper Series, Harvard University, Cambridge, MA, April 2004.

Roncerel, A., and Navroz Dubash. "Needs, Challenges and Opportunities for Environmental Action: The Case of Climate Action Network." Paper presented at a workshop on *The New Europe Conference: Opportunities for Foundations,* Paris, July 9, 1992.

Sen, Amartya. "Global Doubts." Commencement address, Harvard University, Cambridge, MA, June 8, 2000.

Legal Documents and Surveys

GATT Dispute Settlement Panel Report on United States' Restrictions on Imports of Tuna. 33 ILM 839 (1994) [Tuna/Dolphin II].

United States Restrictions on Imports of Tuna. August 16, 1991, GATT BISD (39th Supp.) at 1SS (1993), 30 ILM 1594 (1991) [Tuna/Dolphin I].

US Department of Education. National Center for Education Statistics. Higher Education General Information Survey. "Degrees and Other Formal Awards Conferred."

————. National Center for Education Statistics. Integrated Postsecondary Education Data System. "Completions." 2001.

Contributing Authors

Sarah Alvord is a Senior Program Officer at the Hauser Center for Nonprofit Organizations at Harvard University. She currently manages several domestic and international projects at the Center including the *Transnational Studies Initiative* with Peggy Levitt, the *Civil Society Legitimacy, Accountability and Transparency* project with Dave Brown, and the *International Advocacy NGO Workshops* with Dave Brown and Srilatha Batliwala. Until Spring 2005, she also coordinated the Center's Doctoral Fellowship program with Peter Dobkin Hall. She was the lead author of "Social Entrepreneurship and Societal Transformation: An Exploratory Study," with Dave Brown and Christine Letts, which was published in the September 2004 issue of the *Journal of Applied Behavioral Science*. She has spent fourteen years working in the nonprofit and social service sectors, with specific experience in philanthropy, education, and mental health. She is a Chair of the Board of the Family Institute of Cambridge. Sarah has a MA in Counseling Psychology from Boston College and a BA from Wesleyan University.

Peggy Antrobus is a women's rights activist and scholar. Her current work focuses on feminist approaches to Sustainable Livelihoods and the Millennium Development Goals (MDGs). Her doctoral work focused on the impact of government policies on women, and the ways in which these policies reflect global trends. Her book, *The Global Women's Movement: Issues, Strategies and Challenges,* was recently published by Zed Books. In 1969 she launched the Community Development Programme for the Government of St.Vincent and in 1974/5 she headed Jamaica's national machinery for the "integration of women in development" (the Women's Bureau). In 1978 she established the Women and Development Unit (WAND) at the University of the West Indies. Beginning in the 1980s she has been more involved in civil society organizations: she was a founding member of CAFRA (the Caribbean Association for Feminist Research and Action) and of

the network of Third World women promoting Development Alternatives with Women for a New Era (DAWN), of which she was General
Coordinator from 1991–1996. In the 1990s she was a founding member of the International and Caribbean Gender & Trade Networks
(IGTN and CGTN) and serves on the Steering Committee of both networks.

Arjun Appadurai serves as Provost and Senior Vice President for Academic Affairs at New School University in New York City, where he also
holds a Distinguished Professorship as the John Dewey Professor in
the Social Sciences. His current research has three foci: ethnic violence in the context of globalization, the cultural dimensions of social
crisis in Mumbai, India, and a comparative ethnographic project on
grassroots globalization, exploring emergent transnational organizational forms and new practices of sovereignty. His most recent book is
Modernity at Large: Cultural Dimensions of Globalization (1996, University
of Minnesota Press; 1997, Oxford University Press, Delhi). He is one
of the founding editors of the journal *Public Culture* and was the
founding Director of the Chicago Humanities Institute at the University of Chicago (1992–1998). He is one of the founders of the Interdisciplinary Network on Globalization, a consortium of institutions in
various parts of the world devoted to the study of global politics and
culture, and is the founder and now the President of PUKAR (Partners for Urban Knowledge Action and Research), a non-profit group
of practically-oriented researchers concerned with urban global
issues, centered in the city of Mumbai (India). Prior to his current
position at New School, he was the William K. Lanman Jr. Professor of
International Studies, a Professor of Anthropology, and Director of
the Center on Cities and Globalization at Yale University.

Srilatha Batliwala is a feminist scholar-practitioner who has combined
grassroots activism and research throughout her career. She is currently Civil Society Research Fellow at the Hauser Center for Nonprofit Organizations at Harvard University, where her work focuses on
transnational civil society, particularly on transnational grassroots
movements, and on bridging the divide between practitioners and
scholars. She is also Chair of the Board of the Women's Environment
and Development Organization, New York, member of the Board of
PLAN International, member of the Board of the International Society for Third Sector Research, and a Research Associate of Gender at
Work, an international learning network on gender and institutional
change. Prior to coming to Harvard, Srilatha was Civil Society Program Officer at the Ford Foundation in New York from 1997–2000.

Before going to work in the United States in 1997, Srilatha lived and worked in India, where she had over 25 years' experience as a grassroots activist, gender equality advocate, and women's studies teacher and researcher. She is well known in South Asia for her leadership of movements that organized, mobilized and empowered thousands of poor women and communities in both urban and rural areas in India. Srilatha has published extensively on women's issues, empowerment, and grassroots movements, including the landmark *"Women's Empowerment in South Asia: Concepts and Practices."* She is currently working on a book *"Grassroots Movements as Global Actors"* containing case studies of five major transnational grassroots movements.

L. David Brown is Director of International Programs at the Hauser Center for Nonprofit Organizations and Lecturer in Public Policy at the Kennedy School of Government. Prior to coming to Harvard he was President of the Institute for Development Research, a not-for-profit center for research and consultation on institution-building for development, and Professor of Organizational Behavior at the Boston University School of Management. His research and consulting has focused on strategies for handling change and conflict in organizations and institutions concerned with social change and development. He has worked for the last twenty years especially with civil society organizations and networks to foster social transformation in national and international contexts, and with cross-sectoral coalitions that bring together civil society, government, and business actors to solve problems of sustainable development. He serves on the Boards of PRIA International, Oxfam America, World Education and the Consensus Building Institute. He authored or co-authored *Practice-Research Engagement for Civil Society in a Globalizing World, The Struggle for Accountability: NGOs, Social Movements and the World Bank* (with Jonathan Fox); *Managing Conflict at Organizational Interfaces*; and *Learning from Changing: Organizational Diagnosis and Development* (with Clayton Alderfer) and a variety of articles in professional and practitioner journals. He has been a Fulbright Lecturer in India, a Peace Corps community organizer in Ethiopia, and more recently, a proud grandfather.

Alison Brysk is Professor of Political Science at the University of California, Irvine. Her current research focuses on global promotion of human rights by principled states. Her publications include *The Politics of Human Rights in Argentina* (Stanford, 1994), *From Tribal Village to Global Village: Indian Rights and International Relations in Latin America* (Stanford, 2000), and *Human Rights and Private Wrongs* (Routledge,

2004). In addition, she has edited *Globalization and Human Rights* (University of California, 2002) and co-edited *People Out of Place* (Routledge, 2004). Professor Brysk teaches courses on thematic regional human rights, international relations, democratization, and the political role of civil society.

John Clark is currently Lead Social Development Specialist for the East Asia Region of the World Bank, where he also worked from 1992–2000 on the Bank's strategy for collaboration and dialogue with civil society globally. His career has focused on poverty reduction, participation, and bridging the gap between grassroots organizations and official agencies, and he has worked with development NGOs, the World Bank, United Nations, universities, and as an advisor to governments on development and civil society issues. He is the author of the books *Democratizing Development: The Role of Voluntary Organizations* (1991) and *Worlds Apart: Civil Society and the Battle for Ethical Globalization,* published by Kumarian in the USA and Earthscan in the UK in 2003. He recently completed a stint as project director for the high-level panel on UN-civil society relations in UN General Secretary Kofi Annan's office. He was also Visiting Fellow at the London School of Economics, and served on a task force advising the British Prime Minister about Africa. Prior to joining the Bank in 1992, he worked for 18 years in NGOs, mostly with Oxfam UK, where he was head of campaigns and policy.

Marsha J. Tyson Darling is Professor of History and Interdisciplinary Studies and Director of African American & Ethnic Studies at Adelphi University, where she teaches African American history and culture, the history of conscience and social justice movements, women and international development, and significant issues in globalization. She does research on the impact of the Voting Rights Act of 1965, and the impact of globalization on distributive justice, including the emergence of biomedical technologies and their impact on privacy and human rights. Prof. Darling is a member of the Committee on Women, Population and the Environment, and formerly served on the board of the Association for Women's Rights in International Development (AWID). She is the author of "Eugenics Unbound: Race, Gender and Genetics" in *Women's Health, Women's Rights: Perspectives on Global Health Issues* (Ed. Vijay Agnew, York University Press, 2003) and is the editor of the three-volume collection of legal documents and essays on *Race, Redistricting and the Constitution: Sources and Explorations on the Fifteenth Amendment* (Taylor and Francis, 2001). She has also written numerous articles on ethnic history and women's human rights, eugenics, and most recently, the impact of genetics technologies on agriculture, animals, plants, and humans.

Dan Gallin is Chair of the Global Labour Institute (GLI), a foundation established in 1997 that investigates the consequences of the globalization of the world economy for workers and trade unions, develops and proposes counterstrategies, and promotes international thinking and action in the labor movement. Gallin worked from August 1960 until April 1997 for the International Union of Food, Agricultural, Hotel, Restaurant and Catering, Tobacco and Allied Workers' Associations (IUF), since 1968 as General Secretary. He has served as President of the International Federation of Workers' Education Associations (IFWEA) from 1992 to 2003 and has been Director of the Organization and Representation Program of WIEGO (Women in Informal Employment Globalizing and Organizing), and continues to serve on the WIEGO Steering Committee.

Peter Dobkin Hall is Hauser Lecturer on Nonprofit Organizations at the John F. Kennedy School of Government of Harvard University. His current research interests include the development of the modern welfare state and social welfare policy, the role of educational institutions in creating leadership and civic engagement, and the emergence of transnational institutions, communities, and identities. His publications include *Inventing the Nonprofit Sector: Essays on Philanthropy, Voluntarism, and Nonprofit Organizations* (1992); *Lives in Trust: The Fortunes of Dynastic Families in Late Twentieth Century America* (1992). He co-edited *Sacred Companies: Organizational Aspects of Religion and Religious Aspects of Organizations* (1998) and wrote a chapter on nonprofits for the forthcoming *Millennial Edition of Historical Statistics of the United States*. Before coming to the Kennedy School, Hall served as director of Yale's Program on Nonprofit Organizations (PONPO) and held teaching appointments in Yale's Department of History, School of Management, Divinity School, and Ethics, Politics, and Economics Program.

Céline A. Jacquemin is Director of Undergraduate International Relations and Assistant Professor of Political Science at St. Mary's University. Her current research projects include looking at how major international actors understand and frame instances of human rights violations which in turn affects how they respond, and contends that international actors' descriptions of violations and their institutional context constrain and enable the range of solutions and responses considered. She is also conducting research that examines Female

Genital Mutilation as a human rights violation committed mostly by women. She received her Ph.D. in Political Science with an emphasis in International Relations from the University of California, Irvine.

Sanjeev Khagram is currently Director, Marc Lindenburg Center for Humanitarian Action, International Development and Global Citizenship, and Associate Professor, Daniel J. Evans School of Public Affairs and Jackson School of International Studies, University of Washington. His book, *Dams and Development: Transnational Struggles for Water and Power*, was published by Cornell and Oxford Presses in 2004 and his co-edited volume, *Restructuring World Politics: Transnational Social Movements, Networks and Norms,* was published by Minnesota Press in 2002. He is the co-leader of the Transnational Studies Initiative, International Advocacy NGOs Leaders Session, and Program on Social Movements in the Tropics. He was Senior Policy Advisor to the World Commission on Dams and lead author of its final report from 1998–2000.

Motoko Mekata is a Professor of the Faculty of Policy Studies at Chuo University, Tokyo, Japan. She is also a board member of the Japan NPO Research Association since 2003, and a steering committee member of the Japan Campaign to Ban Landmines since 1997. Her current research works focus on the role of NGOs in negotiating with Non-State Actors and in building peace, especially in Asian countries. Her publications include: *Forefront of the Global Civil Society* (in Japanese, Iwanami Shoten, 2004), *Transnational Civil Society* (in Japanese, Toyo-keizai Shimposha, 2003), *Towards a Landmine Free World* (in Japanese, Iwanami Shoten, 1998), "Building Partnerships toward a Common Goal: Experiences of the International Campaign to Ban Landmines," in Ann Florini ed., *The Third Force: The Rise of Transnational Civil Society,* Carnegie Endowment for International Peace, 2000, "Japan," in Helmut Anheier and Regina List, eds., *"Cross-border Philanthropy, An Exploratory Study of International Giving in the United Kingdom, United States, Germany and Japan,"* Center for Civil Society, Johns Hopkins University, 2000, and others. Before joining Chuo University, she held a variety of teaching and policy advisory positions in the universities of Tokyo, Tsukuba, and Waseda, and various ministries of the Japanese Government.

Kumi Naidoo is the Secretary General and CEO of CIVICUS: World Alliance for Citizen Participation, an international alliance of civil society organizations dedicated to strengthening citizen participation and civil society worldwide. After having living in exile from South

Africa for several years, in 1990 he returned to South Africa to work (on a voluntary basis) on the legalization of the African National Congress (ANC) as a political party. During the democratic elections in 1994, Kumi was the official spokesperson of the Independent Electoral Commission and directed the training of all electoral staff in the country. He then went on to serve as Executive Director of the National Literacy Cooperation of South Africa, as well as a director of the Independent Electoral Commission and the South African Committee for Higher Education Trust. Kumi has a long history of involvement in the nongovernmental sector and was previously the founding Executive Director of the South African NGO Coalition (SANGOCO), an umbrella agency for the South African NGO community. Kumi was appointed by U.N. Secretary-General Kofi Annan to the Panel of Eminent Persons on UN Civil Society Relations. He holds a Ph.D. in Politics from Magdalen College, Oxford and has published and spoken widely on issues relating to civil society, education and resistance to apartheid.

Gita Sen is Sir Ratan Tata Chair Professor at the Indian Institute of Management in Bangalore, India, and Adjunct Professor of Population and International Health at the Faculty of Public Health, Harvard University. She is a development economist whose research focuses especially on gender and development. Her recent work includes research and policy advocacy on the gender implications of globalization and economic liberalization, the gender dimensions of population policies, and the equity dimensions of health. She is the author of *Gender Mainstreaming in Finance: a reference manual for governments and other stakeholders* (London, Commonwealth Secretariat, 1999), coeditor of *Engendering International Health: the Challenge of Equity* (with Asha George and Piroska Ostlin; The MIT Press, 2002), *Women's Empowerment and Demographic Processes — Moving Beyond Cairo,* (with Harriet Presser; Oxford University Press/IUSSP, 2000), *Population Policies Reconsidered: Health, Empowerment and Rights* (with Adrienne Germain and Lincoln Chen; Harvard Center for Population and Development Studies, 1994), and several other publications. She is a founding member of DAWN (Development Alternatives with Women for a New Era), a network of Third World researchers, activists and policy makers committed to alternative development and gender justice, and is currently DAWN's research coordinator on the Political Economy of Globalization. She is also a member of the WHO Global Advisory Committee on Health Research, and a member of the CSO Advisory Committee of UNDP. Previously, she has been on the Board of the UN Research Institute for Social Development (UNRISD), chairperson of the International Advisory Group on Population of the MacArthur Foundation (USA), and chairperson of the External Gender Consultative Group of the World Bank.

Wendy E. F. Torrance is currently in transition but served as Lecturer on Social Studies and Assistant Dean of Freshmen at Harvard University till mid-2005. She also directed Undergraduate Student Programs at the Weatherhead Center for International Affairs at Harvard. Her teaching and research interests concern the international politics of the environment, international institutions and cooperation, and the role of nongovernmental organizations in international affairs. She received her Ph.D. in Political Science from Harvard University, where her dissertation concerned the role of nongovernmental organizations in the international politics of climate change. In addition to her contribution to this book, she has written "Global Environmental Assessments: Information, Institutions, and Influence. (Ed. Ronald B. Mitchell et al., under review at MIT Press).

Andrew W. Torrance is Associate Professor of Law, School of Law, University of Kansas. Till mid-2005, he was a scholar based at Harvard University, where he earned his Ph.D. in Biology and his J.D. At Harvard, Dr. Torrance was also the Hardy Fellow in Conservation Biology and a member of the faculty in Environmental Science and Public Policy (2003), and taught the course Biodiversity: Science, Policy and Law since 1999. He also served as chair of the Scientific and Creative Board for the Darwin Project, a new biodiversity institution being established in Boston. His research interests include the intersections between science, policy, and law as they relate to environmental issues, particularly biodiversity and biotechnology.

INDEX

accountability, globalization and, 134
action networks, 77
activism. *See also* transnational peace activism
  transnational, 60, 62, 170, 172
  Web-based, 129, 130
Afghanistan, 76, 187
Africa
  campaign against racial apartheid, 168–69
  democracy deficits in, 128
  human rights issues, 162–63, 168–69, 172
  labor movement in, 93, 94
African National Congress (ANC), 169
Aga Khan, 70, 76
Agenda 21, 106, 107
Agreement on Agriculture (AOA), 45
Agreement on Textiles and Clothing (ATC), 45
Agreement on Trade Related Aspects of Intellectual Property Rights (TRIPS), 45
Agreement on Trade Related Investment Measures (TRIMS), 45
agriculture, genetically modified foods, 43
Al Jazeera, 73
Al-Qaeda, 76
Alien Torts Act, 176
All India Trade Union Congress, 92
alliances
  balancing influence of members of, 221
  with environmental organizations, 111
Amazon Alliance, 172
American Enterprise Institute, 219
American Federation of Labor (AFofL), 91, 92, 93, 183
American Friends Service Committee, 172
American Railway Union, 91
Amnesty International, 66, 126, 170, 172
Annan, Kofi, 136, 195
Anti-Ballistic Missile Systems (ABM) Treaty, 187, 189
Anti-Slavery Society, 172
Anti-Terrorism Ordinance, Pakistan's, 219
antiglobalization movement, 124, 129
antipersonnel land mines (AP mines), 194, 198
apartheid, 168–69
Apollo 8 space flight, 1968, 18

Asia
  Asian governments as transnational actors, 75
  East Asian economic crisis, 132
  human rights issues, 164, 170–71, 175–76
  labor movement in, 93, 94, 95
  Track II diplomacy, 196–97
  transnational environmentalism in, 111
Asian-American college students, 25–27
Association for the Taxation of Financial Transactions for the Aid of Citizens, 131
Association of Southeast Asian Nations (ASEAN), 44
associations
  civil society, 2, 3
  professional, 73
  transnational, 208–10, 220, 221
Atlantic Monthly, 22
Atomic Development Authority, 183
Axworthy, Lloyd, 194

Babyfood Campaign, 1–2, 3, 5, 6, 7, 8
Beatles, the (music group), 17
Berlin Wall, 76, 190
bilateral trade agreements, 36–37
biodiversity, 110, 111
biopiracy, 43
biotechnology, 43
Black Block group, 131
British Conservative Party, 128
British Petroleum (BP), 75, 117
Brundtland Commission, 106
Bruyn, Severyn T., 33
Bulletin of Atomic Scientists, 187
Bush, George W., 199

Campaign for Nuclear Disarmament (CND), 184, 188, 189
capitalism. *See* world capitalism
carbon dioxide emissions, 112, 115, 116, 117
Cardoso, Fernando Henrique, 135, 136
CARE, 7, 126
care economy, 145
Carnegie Endowment for International Peace, 51
Carson, Rachel, 104
Catholic Church, 73, 91

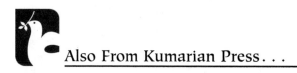

Also From Kumarian Press...

New and Forthcoming:

Non-State Actors in the Human Rights Universe
Edited by George Andreopoulos, Zehra F. Kabasakal Arat, and Peter Juviler

Development Brokers and Translators: The Ethnography of Aid and Agencies
Edited by David Lewis and David Mosse

Cinderella or Cyberella? Empowering Women in the Knowledge Society
Edited by Nancy Hafkin and Sophia Huyer

Development and the Private Sector
Edited by Deborah Eade and John Sayer

Of Related Interest:

Global Civil Society: Dimensions of the Nonprofit Sector, Volume Two
Lester M. Salamon, S. Wojciech Sokolowski, and Associates.

Advocacy for Social Justice: A Global Action and Reflection Guide
David Cohen, Rosa de la Vega, and Gabrielle Watson

Worlds Apart: Civil Society and the Battle for Ethical Globalization
John Clark

Creating a Better World: Interpreting Global Civil Society
Edited by Rupert Taylor

Visit Kumarian Press at **www.kpbooks.com** or
call **toll-free 800.289.2664** for a complete catalog.

Kumarian Press, located in Bloomfield, Connecticut, is a forward-looking, scholarly press that promotes active international engagement and an awareness of global connectedness.